THE MARGINAL MAN

The Marginal Man

A STUDY IN PERSONALITY
AND CULTURE CONFLICT

By

Everett V. Stonequist

Professor of Sociology
Skidmore College

NEW YORK

RUSSELL & RUSSELL · INC

TO
ROBERT E. PARK

ACKNOWLEDGMENTS

Grateful acknowledgment is made to the following authors and publishers for permission to use selections from their copyrighted publications: Carnegie Corporation for selections from *Old World Traits Transplanted* by R. E. Park and H. A. Miller, and for a selection from *The Immigrant Press and Its Control* by R. E. Park; Coward-McCann for a selection from *Understanding India* by G. M. Williams; Doubleday, Doran & Co., for selections from *What the Negro Thinks* by R. R. Moton, for a selection from *Up From Slavery* by Booker T. Washington, and for a selection from *Following the Color Line* by Ray Stannard Baker; E. P. Dutton & Co., Inc., for a selection from *New Masters of the Baltic* by Arthur Ruhl; Harcourt, Brace & Co., Inc., for selections from *I, The Jew* by M. Samuel, and for selections from *A History of Nationalism in the East* by Hans Kohn; Harper & Brothers for a selection from *Africa View* by J. Huxley, and for a selection from *An American in the Making* by M. E. Ravage; J. B. Lippincott Company for a selection from *Criminology* by E. H. Sutherland; Little, Brown & Co. for a selection from *An American Saga* by C. J. Jensen; Liveright Publishing Corporation for selections from *Up Stream* by Ludwig Lewisohn; The Macmillan Company for selections from *My Mother and I* by E. G. Stern, and for a selection from *That Man Heine* by Lewis Browne; A. C. McClurg & Co. and the author for selections from *The Souls of Black Folk* by W. E. B. DuBois; Oxford University Press for a selection from *A Study of History* by A. J. Toynbee; Simon & Schuster for a selection from *Transition* by Will Durant; Silvio Villa for a selection from his *The Unbidden Guest;* The Viking Press for a selection from *Awakening Japan* by Erwin Baelz; Yale University Press for a selection from *Theory of History* by F. J. Teggart.

*   *

Preface

MY INTEREST in this subject began with a lecture given by
Lord Lugard at the Geneva School of International Studies in
1925 describing the effects of European ideas and practices
upon native life in Africa. His comments upon detribalized,
Europeanized Africans seemed to me to have some close parallels with the problem of personal denationalization in Europe,
a subject previously brought to my attention by the stimulating
teachings of Sir Alfred Zimmern of Oxford University. I
found the French term, *déraciné*, a convenient label to use in
this connection.

In 1928 I met Professor Robert E. Park of the University
of Chicago and learned of his concept of the "marginal man,"
a conception which enlarged my understanding of this general
problem and placed it more definitely in what may be called a
sociological frame of reference. With Professor Park's encour-
agement and counsel, and the useful suggestions of other members of the University of Chicago Department of Sociology, I
undertook to analyze further the validity of this hypothesis,
presenting the preliminary results of the study in 1930. Since
then I have pursued the subject by travel in Europe, in Hawaii,
and in the Caribbean. In so doing I have accumulated other
debts.

I am grateful to Presidents Henry T. Moore of Skidmore
College and David L. Crawford of the University of Hawaii
for arranging a year's exchange professorship at the latter university during 1934–35. While in Hawaii I was aided by

Professors Romanzo Adams, Andrew W. Lind, and Edgar T. Thompson, and by Miss Margaret Lam. In Jamaica I found Mr. and Mrs. Frank Chapman, Manager and Editor, respectively, of *The West Indian Review,* both hospitable and helpful in directing me to sources of information. Mr. Lewis Mumford of New York City, Professor Robert C. Angell of the University of Michigan, Professor L. Lévy-Bruhl of the University of Paris, as well as several of the friends mentioned above, have kindly read and commented upon this study in manuscript form. Lastly, the many persons—friends, acquaintances and strangers—who as "marginal men" have contributed to my understanding of this subject deserve the fullest measure of my thanks.   EVERETT V. STONEQUIST.

Contents

Introduction

WILLIAM GRAHAM SUMNER, in what is probably the most frequently quoted passage in the *Folkways,* tells us that we should conceive primitive society as a congeries of small ethnocentric groups scattered over a territory. In such a society each group thinks of itself in the first person and regards itself as "the center of everything." It is a "we-group." Others are outsiders. They are part of the landscape.

The size of such a group is determined "by the conditions of the struggle for existence, and its internal organization corresponds to its size but is further conditioned by its relations with all the others. This is because order and discipline in each 'we-group' or 'in-group' depends upon the exigences of war and peace with the 'others-groups' or 'out-groups.' " Thus society, primitive society at least, turns out to be "a group of groups," in which the normal relation of each to every other is "one of war and plunder, except so far as agreements have modified it." Under these circumstances "the relation of comradeship and peace in the we-group and that of hostility and war towards others-groups are correlative to each other." The loyalties that bind together the members of the little world—the world of the family, the clan and the tribe—are in direct proportion to the intensity of the fears and hatreds with which they view their enemies and rivals in the larger intertribal and international world outside.

In the course of the long historical process from which the modern world has emerged this picture of primitive society has been progressively altered. Now that the aeroplane has wellnigh abolished the distances that once separated the nations and peoples and the radio has converted the world into one vast whispering gallery, the great world—intertribal, interracial, and international—the world of business and politics—has grown at the expense of the little world, the world of intimate, personal loyalties in which men were bound together by tradition, custom, and natural piety.

Nevertheless the general patterns of primitive society still persist and human nature is, on the whole, what it has been. It is still in the family and under the influence of the tribe, the sect or the local community, as Cooley insisted, that the individual acquires those habits, sentiments, attitudes and other personality traits that characterize him as human.

On the other hand, it was and is in the market place where men from distant places come together to chaffer and bargain, that men first learn the subtleties of commerce and exchange; the necessity for cool calculation, even in human affairs, and the freedom to act, as individuals, in accordance with interests rather than sentiments. It is with the expansion of the market, as a matter of fact, that intellectual life has prospered and local tribal cultures have been progressively integrated into that wider and more rational social order we call civilization.

Thus the vast expansion of Europe during the last four hundred years has brought about changes more devastating than in any earlier period in the world's history. Europeans have invaded every part of the world, and no part of the earth has escaped the disturbing, even if vivifying, contacts of European commerce and culture. The movements and migrations incident to this expansion have brought about everywhere an interpenetration of peoples and a fusion of cultures. Incidentally it has produced, at certain times and under certain conditions, a personality type, a type which if not wholly new is at any rate peculiarly characteristic of the modern world. It is a type to which some of us, including the author of this volume, have given the title "The Marginal Man."

The marginal man, as here conceived, is one whom fate has condemned to live in two societies and in two, not merely different but antagonistic, cultures. Thus, the individual whose mother is a Jew and whose father is a Gentile is fatally condemned to grow up under the influence of two traditions. In that case, his mind is the crucible in which two different and refractory cultures may be said to melt and, either wholly or in part, fuse. One runs across individuals who are caught in this conflict of cultures in the most unlikely places.

Readers of George Santayana's *The Last Puritan* will hardly fail to discover—even if the subtitle, "A Memoir in the Form of a Novel," did not advertise the fact—that the story it tells, if not an autobiography, is nevertheless, in some subtle and symbolic way, autobiographical. Obviously the two leading characters, Oliver and Mario, are the symbols of the two cultures, which the author united in his own person, and the almost mystical friendship which, in spite of differences of temperament and tradition, unites them indicates how intimately the traditions they represent were related in the mind of the author.

In the epilogue the author refers to this novel as a "fable," and Mario, with whom he represents himself as discussing the import of the fable, adds, that "perhaps there is a better philosophy in it than in your other books."

Perhaps the best philosophy is one that achieves, as in the case of Plato, its fullest and happiest expression in fables. In any case a man's philosophy is always an aspect, if not an integral part, of his personality, and Santayana's philosophy reflects the effect, upon a mind conscious of a conflict in its natural loyalties, of an effort to achieve an inner harmony and consistency; such a harmony and consistency as is essential to that "life of reason" which he has so persuasively set forth in the volumes he has written under that title.

Santayana was born in Spain of Spanish parents, but fate ordained that he should get his education and live most of his life in America and England. It is evident from his account of life in Boston, that he lived there with his mother, as he did in fact in Spain with his father, more or less as an alien, always conscious of a different tradition and of intimate and indissoluble connections with another and a different world. In fact his life in both Spain and America seems to have been that of the typical "stranger," as described by Simmel in his *Sociology;* that is, one who lives in intimate association with the world about him but never so completely identified with it that he is unable to look at it with a certain critical detachment. In Santayana's case this detachment has become, as Edman expresses it, an intimate but "compassionate understanding" of his world.[1]

In an article, contributed to a symposium on the subject of contemporary American philosophy, Santayana[2] has described "the mixed associations" under which his "opinions" came into existence, subjected as they were to the strain of his "complex allegiances." He says: "My philosophy may be regarded as a synthesis of these various traditions, or an attempt to view them from a level from which their several deliverances may be justly understood."

Of himself a little later, he adds: "I felt like a foreigner in Spain, more acutely so than in America, although for more trivial reasons. . . . English had become my only possible instrument, and I deliberately put away everything that might confuse me in that medium. English, and the whole Anglo-

[1]See Irwin Edman's Introductory Essay to his volume of Selections from Santayana's Works, *The Philosophy of Santayana,* Introduction, p. lvi.
[2]Irwin Edman, *op. cit.,* pp. 1–20.

Saxon tradition in literature and philosophy, have always been a medium to me rather than a scholarship, and learning of any sort seemed to me a means, not an end. . . . Thus in renouncing everything else for the sake of English letters I might be said to have been guilty, quite unintentionally, of a little stratagem, as if I had set out to say plausibly in English as many un-English things as possible."[3]

The Last Puritan, whether it be an "indirect memoir" of the author, as Edman assumes, or a philosophy in the form of a fable, as Santayana himself suggests, is in any case for the student of human nature a human document in which the conflict and fusion of cultures, as it actually takes place under certain circumstances and in certain minds, is clearly reflected.

The fundamental notion upon which this present study of the so-called marginal man is based is, I should say, the conviction that the individual's personality, while based on instincts, temperament and the endocrine balance, achieves its final form under the influence of the individual's conception of himself. The conception which each individual inevitably forms of himself is determined by the rôle which fate assigns to him in some society, and upon the opinion and attitude which persons in that society form of him—depends, in short, upon his social status. The individual's conception of himself is, in this sense, not an individual but a social product.

The marginal man is a personality type that arises at a time and a place where, out of the conflict of races and cultures, new societies, new peoples and cultures are coming into existence. The fate which condemns him to live, at the same time, in two worlds is the same which compels him to assume, in relation to the worlds in which he lives, the rôle of a cosmopolitan and a stranger. Inevitably he becomes, relatively to his cultural milieu, the individual with the wider horizon, the

[3]*Philosophy of Santayana,* Selections from the Complete Works of George Santayana, pp. 4–5.

keener intelligence, the more detached and rational viewpoint. The marginal man is always relatively the more civilized human being. He occupies the position which has been, historically, that of the Jew in the Diaspora. The Jew, particularly the Jew who has emerged from the provincialism of the ghetto, has everywhere and always been the most civilized of human creatures.

From what has been said one may infer that the marginal man is an incidental product of a process of acculturation, such as inevitably ensues when peoples of different cultures and different races come together to carry on a common life. He is, as I have suggested, an effect of imperialism, economic, political and cultural; an incident of the process by which civilization, as Spengler has said, grows up at the expense of earlier and simpler cultures.[4]

The Marginal Man is concerned finally and fundamentally less, as the title might suggest, with a personality type, than with a social process, the process of acculturation. The distinction is that, in the latter case, the author has chosen to investigate the process less from the point of view of the person than of the society of which he is a part; less from the point of view of custom and culture than from habit and personality.

ROBERT E. PARK.

[4]See Oswald Spengler's *The Decline of the West* (translated) (1926).

THE MARGINAL MAN

CHAPTER I

The Marginal Man

INTRODUCTION

FROM THE MOMENT of his birth the human being is the responding subject of a stream of social influences. Before he has learned to speak a single word, or experienced the first glimmer of self-consciousness, he has felt the impress of those activities, standards, and objects which make up that complex whole termed *culture*. With the acquisition of language his mental, social, and physical development expand into new dimensions and he gradually learns consciously to adjust himself to the expectations of his social group. Through unconscious as well as conscious interaction with other persons he gradually comes to have a recognized place in his particular social world, to plan a career, and to live up to those standards which are evolved out of his experience and doubly rooted in his own self-respect and in the established codes of his social group. If well adjusted to himself and his social world he becomes a mature and harmonized personality.

Such an evolution of personality takes place most easily and spontaneously when the individual is born with normal human capacities and lives in a reasonably stable and organized society. Tradition and custom then chart the course of his career. The definite limits thus set may to the modern mind seem narrow and imprisoning, but to the individual concerned they are quite natural and desirable, since he has no other standard by which to make a comparison. He has but one tribal or national tradition to acquire, one language to learn, one political loyalty to develop, one moral code to which to conform, one religion to follow. The unity and harmony of the social system are reflected in the unity and harmony of his personality: in his sentiments, his conception of himself, his aspirations, and his style of life.

Thus his personal sentiments will mirror the sentiments of his society, and will be well integrated with the other aspects of his personality. His conception of himself will have a core of certainty paralleling the certainty of his group membership; there will be a minimum of uneasy self-consciousness and sensitiveness. The stability of his sentiments and conception of self will prevent that chronic restlessness which deflects normal ambition into avenues of escape rather than towards realistic goals which have a possibility of achievement. The manner and method of meeting crises and reaching goals—the "style of life"—will therefore be attuned to adjustment.

Such stable societies as exist today will be found only among relatively isolated or protected peoples, classes, and other groups. The modern world of economic competition and shifting social relations places the individual in a situation where change and uncertainty are the keynotes. Fixed or permanent adjustments become impossible. The world moves and the individual must continually readjust himself. The possibility that he will not do this with complete success is greater than ever before. Social maladjustment, whether slight or great, then becomes characteristic of modern man.

One sees this social dislocation clearly and sharply in the case of those individuals who fall between two major racial or cultural groups, but it is also apparent in the relations of minor groups such as social classes, religious sects, and communities. The individual who through migration, education, marriage, or some other influence leaves one social group or culture without making a satisfactory adjustment to another finds himself on the margin of each but a member of neither. He is a "marginal man."

The marginal personality is most clearly portrayed in those individuals who are unwittingly initiated into two or more historic traditions, languages, political loyalties, moral codes, or religions. This occurs for instance as a result of migration. Migration is so common in the modern world that nearly every land and city is something of a melting-pot of races and nationalities. New countries like the United States are only the conspicuous examples of a world-wide condition.

Consequently we need not search far in order to find acute instances of the marginal man. He may be our next-door neighbour: the economically successful but socially unadjusted immigrant who as a young man left his peasant environment in some distant country to make his fortune in newer and richer lands; perhaps also the native-born son of this immigrant whose career is affected by an unanalyzed hangover of the ancestral heritage; the Jew whose emancipation from the physical walls of the ghetto has not yet freed his consciousness from the subtle but resistant barriers imposed by historic group attitudes. Farther away perhaps lives the man of Negro, Mongolian, or mixed blood who carries in his face the tell-tale evidence of an alien background, but whose inner personality may be indistinguishable from that of our closest neighbour.

Wherever there are cultural transitions and cultural conflicts there are marginal personalities. If the cultural differences are of major importance, if they include sharp contrasts in race, and if the social attitudes are hostile, the problem of the individual whose sentiments and career are bound up with both societies may well be acute. His dual social connections will then be reflected in the type of life he leads, the nature of his achievements or failures, his conception of himself, and many of his social attitudes and aspirations. He will, in fact, be a kind of dual personality.

This dualism does not always constitute a personal problem. Man is a plastic or teachable being. He comes into the world with a flexible nature and with multiple potentialities which enable him to fit into the most varied of culture patterns and social organizations. Each group in which he participates requires a special type of adjustment and conformity. As William James once observed, the individual "has as many different social selves as there are distinct groups of persons about whose opinions he cares. He generally shows a different side of himself to each of these different groups."[1] Even the normal individual, therefore, is in a mild degree a kind of multiple personality.

When the standards of two or more social groups come into active contrast or conflict, the individual who is identified with both groups experiences the conflict as an acute personal difficulty or mental tension. He may be compelled to choose between two national loyalities, or only between two minor groups: in either case the situation is the same: the external conflict of the groups finds an echo in the mind of the individual concerned.

Varieties of Culture Conflict

Many types of culture conflict are to be found in the present-day world. One thinks of the struggles between religions and sects; between science and theology; between social classes; between country and city; between one community and another; and even between the sexes. These divisions indicate the complexity of modern culture as well as its unsettled, changing condition.

A volume like Will Durant's *Transition* admirably depicts

[1]*Psychology*, Briefer Course (New York, 1920), Chap. XII, p. 179.

one form of such a culture conflict. "John Lemaire" found his conventional religious beliefs disintegrating under the acids of modern inquiry and doubt and, in reflecting back, writes:

> ... I felt like a man adventuring into a dangerous wilderness alone. The thought that other young men everywhere were going through the same slow change from belief to unbelief was too vague to comfort me. I was marked off from my fellows as one darkly unlike the rest, a Byronic hero of the intellect, and I bore my solitude in majestic silence. I could say nothing of my theological puberty to any of my family; they would not have understood me, and would have looked upon me as a leper. I could say nothing to my teachers, for excepting Father Collins they knew too little of science to be able to discuss the matter fruitfully. For months I carried the demon of unbelief in my breast like the Spartan boy with his stolen fox.[2]

Another example of culture conflict is the *parvenu*. In a society where social classes are sharply outlined and almost fixed, the "bourgeois gentilhomme" or *parvenu* finds himself exposed to severe social tension. William Graham Sumner writes of him: "If a man passes from one class to another, his acts show the contrast between the *mores* in which he was bred and those in which he finds himself. The satirists have made much fun of the *parvenu* for centuries. His mistakes and misfortunes reveal the nature of the *mores,* their power over the individual, their pertinacity against later influences, the confusion in character produced by changing them, and the grip of habit which appears both in the persistence of old *mores* and the weakness of new ones."[3]

What is true of the *parvenu* is equally true of the *déclassé.* He is forced through a period of acute maladjustment, from

[2]Will Durant, *Transition: A Sentimental Story of One Mind and One Era* (New York, 1927), p. 65.
[3]*Folkways* (Boston, 1906), pp. 107–8.

which he may never recover his peace of mind. But in a society of relatively open classes, where ancestors count less heavily in the balance sheet of the individual's present status, the *parvenu* is the rule instead of the exception. Instead of being regarded with suspicion, as in an old country like England, in America he becomes glorified in the doctrine of the "self-made man" and immortalized in the epic "from log-cabin to White House." In such a situation there are strictly speaking no *parvenus*.

The migrant from the country into the city likewise finds his customary ways of conduct inadequate to his new environment. He quickly discovers that he is the object of the city dweller's attitude of amused superiority, and while possibly amazed and thrilled at the stupendous sights, he is often painfully self-conscious and bewildered for a time. He, too, like the *parvenu,* is something of a *déraciné*—a man without roots, who is in danger of being blown about by every gust of circumstance. Maurice Barrès has pictured one type in his famous novel *Les Déracinés*—though he preaches a moral from it which need not be wholly accepted. The important point is that the *déraciné* has lost something of his former self and has not yet acquired a new and stable self. For the individual's self is an integral part of his social rôle, and when this social rôle is fundamentally changed the individual's self is forced through a similar transformation.

The modern transformation in the traditional rôle of women has produced like dilemmas in ambition and conduct. The declining functions of the home and the growing opportunities in industry, government and the professions have lured, if they have not compelled, many women to seek careers in the "man-made world" outside the home. But public opinion and moral codes have been slow to sanction the new departures, and the pioneers thus find themselves between two fires: men who resist their encroachment, and women who are outraged by their free and seemingly adventurous conduct. The successfully married stay-at-homes may find time heavy on their hands and look upon the "modern woman" with mingled feelings of envy and dissatisfaction; the successful career-woman in turn may regret the sacrifices in marriage and family life which her ambitions have entailed.[4]

Important as such problems of transition are they are neither so profound nor so acute as the conflicts which center about race and nationality. For the individual's racial and nationality membership is relatively fixed and permanent, and related to a definite group organization having political significance. His race he can never change, though some mixed bloods do "pass." His nationality forms the widest social environment in which his personality develops and unless he separates himself from it when young, it prints an indelible mark. Thus the sense of racial or nationality identity is one of the very deeply lodged elements in an individual's self.

In external relations also, nationality and what is termed "race"[5] exercise a powerful influence. In many modern countries society is based directly or indirectly upon the principle of nationality. Other types of groups are subordinated to the nationally organized state. Consequently, if an individual is

[4]For a penetrating analysis in terms of Alfred Adler's psychology see Olga Knopf, *The Art of Being a Woman* (Boston, 1932).

[5]The term "race" is a difficult one. In the following pages I have tried to use it to refer to those inherited physical differences which characterize groups of men (such as colour, hair structure, head form, stature, etc.) even when there is much variability of traits within a given social group. This conforms to more scientific usage. However, in common speech and in less scientific writing the term is also employed to include culture groups, especially nationalities. Since popular usage is important in social and political relations, the sociologist must take account of it even when he rejects it from the standpoint of physical science. Thus, for example, the racial ideology of the Nazis has no scientific basis, yet it is of great practical importance. Again, most Japanese can be distinguished physically from most Englishmen, yet there is no "Japanese race." When as a matter of convenience the wider meaning is given to the term in this volume, it is hoped that the context will make the meaning clear to the reader. Sometimes quotation marks will be used to put him on guard.

ostracized because of his "race" or nationality, he is automatically excluded from numerous spheres of social activity—from a *system* of group relationships. This is all the more galling because it is based upon birth or ancestry and not upon personal choice, for the solution is then automatically removed beyond the individual's control.

An additional source of difficulty is to be found in modern theories of race superiority. These often constitute vital parts of the social situation of the marginal man. Cultural differences among national groups are popularly explained in terms of biological causation. Since Western culture is at the pinnacle of power, the assumption of white racial superiority is common and natural. The so-called "Nordic" nations are the leaders of the leaders, and have evolved the doctrine of inherent Nordic superiority. This doctrine is supported by social prestige and enforced by economic and political power. But it is slowly cracking as the non-white peoples of the world make the adjustment between their own and Western civilization.

So the marginal man as conceived in this study is one who is poised in psychological uncertainty between two (or more) social worlds; reflecting in his soul the discords and harmonies, repulsions and attractions of these worlds, one of which is often "dominant" over the other; within which membership is implicitly if not explicitly based upon birth or ancestry (race or nationality); and where exclusion removes the individual from a system of group relations. Since each concrete situation varies in the degree of its conflicts as well as in its trend of adjustment, the marginal person also has a varying character. At one end of the scale are the acute and prolonged conflicts of many mixed bloods and such historic minorities as the Jews; at the other end are those groups whose degree of exclusion is small and transitory, such as northwest European immigrants and their descendants in the United States. Finally there are differences according to the phase of the life-cycle of the individual.

In the following pages we shall consider some of the more representative types of marginal men and their social backgrounds. Because of the limitations of space this will often be done in a summary manner. We shall begin with persons of mixed race, and then pass to those who are not of mixed blood. Parallels and contrasts will be drawn from a wide range of situations so that the theme and variations will both become apparent. Beginning with the fifth chapter attention will shift more strongly from the situation to the personality. Emphasis will be given to the typical evolution of the marginal man, his traits of personality, and the main forms of his adjustment and maladjustment. For it is only by keeping in mind the interrelations of the specific social environment and the evolving personality that an accurate understanding of the marginal man is possible. The final chapter will outline some of the more theoretical implications and connections of the study.

CHAPTER II

The Racial Hybrid

THE MOST OBVIOUS type of marginal man is the person of mixed racial ancestry. His very biological origin places him between the two races. Generally he has distinctive physical traits which mark him off from both parent races. He also frequently possesses some characteristics of manner, thought and speech which are derived from both lines of his ancestry. Because of these peculiarities the mixed blood presents a special problem for the community: what is to be his place in the social organization? As he matures he too will become aware of his problematic and anomalous social position. He will become the target of whatever hostile sentiments exist between the parent races. Thus his problem of adjustment will be made more acute. Since the contact of races in the modern age has rarely been smooth and harmonious, there is something universal in the problem of racial hybrids. While emphasizing this fact it would be misleading, nevertheless, not to recognize the important differences which occur between one situation and another.

It should be pointed out in this connection that race mixture is not a new phenomenon. Indeed, from a strictly scientific point of view pure races do not exist, for the whole history of man has been characterized by the crossing and recrossing of races. In the early phases of intermixture the mixed-blood children are conspicuous merely because they differ from the parents. Theirs is a problem of incomplete social assimilation as well as of incomplete biological amalgamation. As the processes of assimilation and amalgamation continue the status of the mixed bloods changes. They gradually become the preponderant or "normal" type and then are no longer considered hybrids but a new "race." In this way complete racial intermixture in any given region solves the problem which arises from partial intermixture.

It is apparent, therefore, that the social and psychological traits of mixed bloods depend upon many factors. Among these should be mentioned the manner in which the hybrids have arisen, whether as the result of sanctioned marriages or irregular unions; the extent to which they are a numerical and social minority; their cultural rôle; and the general social attitudes which they have encountered from one or both of the parent races. During the course of Western expansion Southern European nations have developed relatively mild race prejudices and have intermarried freely with coloured peoples, whereas Anglo-Saxon and Teutonic nations have been noteworthy for their racial aloofness. Probably this contrast is not rooted in biological nature but is a product of divergent historical conditions. In any case it greatly influences the social position and character of racial hybrids.

To bring out what is typical and what is variable in the social psychology of the mixed blood, we shall now consider some concrete examples. In view of the limitations of space such an analysis must be confined to a relatively few cases. These cases have been selected because they illustrate a very wide range of condition, location, history and race. They consist of the following mixed-blood groups: the Eurasians or Anglo-Indians of India, the Cape Coloured of South Africa, the Mulattoes of the United States, the Coloured people of Jamaica, the Indo-Europeans of Java, the Part Hawaiians, and the *Métis* of Brazil.

The Eurasians (Anglo-Indians) of India

The racial situation of India is unique. It contains over one-sixth of the population of the world, is ruled by a little island located off the west coast of Europe, has a history of repeated invasion and conquest by foreign races, and exhibits an unequalled variety and complexity of races, religions, languages and cultures. The coming of Europeans to India during the past few centuries has added another chapter to the racial diversity of the land: a population of mixed-blood Eurasians, now often termed "Anglo-Indians."

The mixed bloods of India are socially ostracized by both Indians and Englishmen. The caste system of India logically means a strong disapproval of mixed marriages and their children, while the ruling position of the British and the necessity for maintaining prestige have also resulted in severe condemnation of interracial unions. Consequently the mixed bloods today are in a doubly outcast situation.

During the Portuguese and early English periods of colonization the Eurasians had a relatively high position. They were of great value as trade and cultural intermediaries, and also as soldiers—so useful indeed that both the Portuguese government and the East India Company actively encouraged interracial marriages. Many Eurasians achieved high places in the service of the Company; Eurasian women married into the British nobility. But with the consolidation of British rule, the growth of the English community in India, and the tightening of ties with the home land through improved transportation, interracial marriages were increasingly disapproved of until finally they were stigmatized as a disgrace. Illicit relations likewise were denounced, and opportunities for the Eurasians proportionately restricted. No doubt the Indian caste system on its side favoured the growth of the English caste system.

The cumulative effects of these and other events had a disheartening and somewhat demoralizing effect upon the Eurasian community. Those who could afford to do so did what many had done before—went to England; others gradually merged into the Indian population; but a third group of perhaps 150,000[1] exists today as a self-conscious but poorly organized racial group. A recent traveller has described them in the following general terms:

The most pathetic of India's minority groups are the mixed bloods. They were formerly called Eurasians; but they coveted the name Anglo-Indian. . . . Call them what you will, there is little chance of mistaking the mixed blood for the pure. Some of the women are almost blonde and very pretty. Most of them have an anæmic look. They speak in a metallic falsetto with a curious singsong accent. They always wear European clothes. . . . They are ostracized by both English and Indians. They in turn look down on the Indian with a scorn that is acid with hatred, for it is their Indian blood that is their curse. They fawn upon the English and make pitiful advances to them. They always speak of England as "home," though they may never have been there, and they are forever vainly trying to include themselves with the British.[2]

The psychological traits of the Anglo-Indian reflect his social position: he is placed between two societies with each of which he has ties of kinship but neither of which accepts him. In accordance with his English culture and the general human tendency to aspire toward the group with the greater power and prestige, the Anglo-Indian would like to be accepted as an Englishman. His actual subservience—economic, political and social

[1]The census of 1921 recorded 113,000; that of 1931, 138,396. These figures are not precise, "for some who might have been included get classed as Europeans, while there is a tendency for some Indian Christians who have adopted British names to seek inclusion in the Anglo-Indian category." The great majority live in the cities of British India. *Report of the Indian Statutory Commission* (London, 1930), Vol. I, p. 42.
[2]Gertrude Marvin Williams, *Understanding India* (New York, 1928), pp. 167–68.

—gives him an attitude of subservience and inferiority, even of timidity, as the following verses by a Eurasian poet, H. L. V. Derozio, indicate:

> And wilt thou tremble so, my heart,
> When the mighty breathe on thee?
> And shall thy light like this depart?
> Away! It cannot be![3]

A volume by another Anglo-Indian, Herbert Alick Stark, reveals in its very title, *Hostages to India*,[4] the psychology of the situation. "In truth we are England's Hostages to India, and they who give and they who receive hostages are bound to regard them as a trust" (p. 146). He concludes his interesting book with these words:

We cannot give up our Christian Faith, our British ideals, our Western culture. Ask the devout Hindu to exchange his ancestral caste for secular advantage. Ask the pious Musalman to abandon his holy creed for temporal gain. Ask us to sell our British heritage for a mess of political pottage. In every case the answer is instant and clear. Ours speaks in the heart of each of us. It throbs in the blood that mingles with our breath. It leaps to our lips in the soul-stirring appeal—"O England! who are these if not thy sons?"

This attitude of dependence is severely criticized by the author of *Cimmerii*. Referring to the desire of the mixed blood to substitute the term "Anglo-Indian" for Eurasian he writes, "The psychologist will understand the tendency to get away from the term Eurasian and its attendant stigma of contempti-

---

[3] Quoted by another Eurasian, Cedric Dover, in *Cimmerii? or Eurasians and Their Future* (Calcutta, 1929). This writer urges Eurasians to develop more of the aggressive spirit found among American Negroes. He uses the following lines of E. A. Robinson to suggest the desirable attitude:

> Let us, the Children of the Night,
> Put off the cloak that hides the scar!
> Let us be Children of the Light,
> And tell the ages what we are!

[4] The full title is *Hostages to India, or The Life-Story of the Anglo-Indian Race* (Calcutta, 1926).

bility, but the Eurasian must be taught that the only way to conquer an evil is to fight it, not to run away from it."[5] To those who cry "Britishers we are and Britishers we ever must and shall be. Once relinquish this name and permit ourselves to be styled 'Eurasians' or 'statutory natives of India,' and we become estranged from our proud heritage as Britishers," he replies caustically, "A stirring appeal to the multitude, but tripe to the sensitive constitution of the student. The Eurasians must realize that Eurasians they ever shall be, that a Bengalee dressed up in a kilt does not become a Highlander." Farther on he vigorously sounds the note of independence:

Let us teach Colonel Gidney and Mr. Stark that protection weakens a people; that it reduces competition, increases inertia, and produces a false sense of security. Moreover, *the protected are always at the mercy of the protectors;* they get only what they are given; and they live under the constant shadow of a political sword of Damocles. The great truth must be learned that the road to Eurasian emancipation lies not in supplication, nor only in righteous demands for fair and just treatment, but in developing themselves to be at least as good as the other fellow.

Associated with the feelings of inferiority and subservience are such traits as exaggerated self-consciousness, sensitiveness, psychological over-compensation, etc. Colour prejudices exist within the group, the lighter individuals scorning the darker and striving for inclusion in the white race. Passing as Englishmen may occur for those light enough in colour, but this "is bitterly resented by those left behind. It leaves the Anglo-Indians a rabble without leaders."[6] In short, the struggle for

[5]Cedric Dover, *op. cit.,* pp. 50–51.
[6]*The New York Times,* Sept. 10, 1932. See also Julius Smith, *Ten Years in Burma,* Chap. VI. There is an excellent discussion of mental conflicts among the Eurasians of Malaysia by Linden B. Jenkins, "Mental Conflicts of Eurasian Adolescents." *The Journal of Social Psychology,* August, 1934, pp. 402–7.

status dominates the minds and the behaviour of members of the community—a struggle carried on by individuals without much effective support from one another, and therefore rather hopeless in character. It produces a deep-lying emotional conflict which has been formulated in these words by one of the ablest of recent Eurasian writers: "There is, therefore, on the one hand a tendency to hate the Indian, and on the other a turmoil between dependence on, and resentment against, the European."[7]

Economically the status of the Anglo-Indian is low. There is much poverty, and in the cities where most of them live, considerable population congestion. Occupationally they belong to the lower white-collar class, many being employed by the government in clerical positions and in the telegraph and railway services. Anglo-Indian women are employed largely as nurses and teachers.[8] The community has not developed an independent basis of livelihood.

The Indian Eurasians have been the subject of much comment concerning the adverse consequences of race mixture. Morally, mentally, and physically they have been cited to prove the contention that mixed bloods inherit the vices of both parent races. Such statements fail to account for the historical change of status in this group of people. Besides, it seems gratuitous to make biological assumptions without first considering the social situation in which the Anglo-Indians live. When this is understood, it is not surprising that the Eurasians today have not accomplished more. Neither the caste system of the Hindus nor the caste attitudes of the English are easy matters for such a small group to overcome. To be confronted by them both at

[7]Kenneth E. Wallace, *The Eurasian Problem Constructively Approached* (Calcutta, 1930). See also his *Brave New Anglo-India* (Calcutta, 1935). These volumes have been sent me through the courtesy of Mr. Cedric Dover.

[8]Report of the Indian Statutory Commission, I, pp. 43–44. See also Elmer L. Hedin, "The Anglo-Indian Community," *The American Journal of Sociology*, September, 1934, pp. 170 ff.

the same time may indeed be overwhelming. May not this be the key to the understanding of the Anglo-Indians?

What is the future of the Anglo-Indian community? In the face of a rising Indian nationalism their position is growing more and more precarious. They have been identified so long with British civilization that national-minded Indians may not have any more sympathy for them in the future than caste-minded Indians have had in the past; indeed their claims to racial superiority are now resented far more than similar claims of Englishmen.[9] It is the racial factor which prevents them from functioning satisfactorily as intermediaries between the two races.[10] Indian politicians have promised them fair treatment if they will "acknowledge themselves to be sons of the soil, children of Mother India." Perhaps this, together with British moves toward further self-government, has created a more conciliatory attitude among Anglo-Indians.[11]

From the economic standpoint, the Anglo-Indians face the prospect of a reduction in standard of living along two fronts: (1) the progressive Indianization of the services; (2) the increasing number of educated Indians willing to work for lower wages. These influences will continue to undermine their position in private industry also.

The achievement of Indian self-government, therefore, seems likely to reduce their status. It is possible, on the other hand, that the successive shocks which lie ahead during the transition

[9]Sir Valentine Chirol, *India* (London, 1926), p. 78. Some conclude, therefore, that their best safeguard lies in the continuance of British rule. See, for example, Sir Reginald Craddock, *The Dilemma of India* (London, 1929), p. 108.

[10]". . . many managers have the idea that Eurasian foremen are the best intermediaries between the Indian workman and the European manager. But the fact is that the Eurasian is the worst possible intermediary, because he stands to lose far more than the pure-bred European from the abandonment of the old dominant race idea." J. T. Gwynn, *Indian Politics: A Survey* (London), pp. 315–16. Indian labour also resents the willingness of Anglo-Indians to act as strikebreakers.

[11]Hedin, *op. cit.*, pp. 174–75.

period may spur them on and develop a new attitude of self-reliance and independence. What requires to be changed, if they are to survive, is the group's conception of itself so that it will be impossible to speak as one of them has done, "To the European we are half-caste, among ourselves we are no caste, and to the Indian we are outcaste."[12]

THE CAPE COLOURED OF SOUTH AFRICA

The mixed bloods of South Africa, particularly the Cape Coloured, occupy a somewhat different position from that of the Eurasians of India. They number about 600,000, a considerable population in comparison with the 2,000,000 whites, 5,000,000 natives (largely Bantu), and 200,000 Indians. They are concentrated in the Cape Province and so are separated in space as well as in history and origin from the bulk of the Bantu people. According to one South African writer they "form an embarrassment as acute as Ishmael once was to Isaac. They speak the white man's languages—Afrikaans or English—and they have lost all tribal organization. Socially, politically, and economically there is little to differentiate them from the lower strata of white South Africa, and those able to 'pass' as white are constantly crossing the colour line. Yet the majority of white South Africans are afraid to break down the accepted social conventions which make colour—at any rate, obvious colour—a bar to social relationship."[13]

In origin the Cape Coloured go back to early intermixture between the Portuguese and Hottentots, a process favoured by the excess of white men as well as by the slave and serf sys-

[12]Quoted in Mary H. Lee, *The Eurasian: A Social Problem*, p. 10 (Thesis in the University of Chicago Library). Ultimately the Anglo-Indians will probably fuse into the Indian population. This, of course, assumes that Britain will hand over the government to Indians and that the growing nationalism will break down the caste system. Separate political representation may help to prolong their communal identity.

[13]Edgar H. Brookes, "The Color Bar in South Africa," *Current History*, July, 1932, p. 429.

tems. In addition to the Portuguese, the Hottentots, and the Dutch, slaves brought in from West Africa, Mozambique and Madagascar, Malays imported from the East, and the Bantu peoples advancing from the northeast, contributed to the mixture. After slavery was abolished in 1833, and as self-government was extended to the Cape, the mixed people were placed upon a plane of legal equality with the white population. Today, in contrast with the other provinces, they may vote, hold office, and legally intermarry with the whites.

Although the Cape policy and attitude have been more tolerant than the policy and attitude of the Boer provinces, there has been no disposition to accept the mixed population as social equals. Occasional individuals white in appearance and of superior achievement are accepted as white; many others pass as white.[14] The rest form a distinct social group in the population, clinging to their white background, seeking to merge with the white population, having little or no contact with the unmixed natives, and in turn being socially avoided by the Europeans. They lack group pride and the incentives which flow from *esprit de corps.* "With no home base of their own, they have no social standing in the European life around them, but are helplessly suspended between white and black, and can only think white."[15]

The majority are low-grade urban workers. Some do skilled

[14]George Findlay in *Miscegenation* (Pretoria, 1936), p. 44, estimates that more than 700,000 "Europeans" have coloured ancestry.

Sarah Gertrude Millin in her powerful novel depicting the South African half-castes, *God's Step-Children* (New York, 1924), writes as follows: "In spite of talk and talk and talk, if a man looked white, and had success enough, he was, in the fullest sense, accepted. That was the truth, and much of the shuddering and crawling was conventional hypocrisy. Heaven knows through what generations of sorrow; through what daily bitterness of self-distrust; through what oceans of ostracism, the man with that fading, but never dying, darkness in him arrived at havens of social grace; but once arrived his life was distinguished in no noticeable sense from the lives of those around him, and, as far as all outward appearances might indicate, the world held him to be as white as he looked," p. 254. This subject is also interestingly discussed by Findlay.

[15]W. M. Macmillan, *The Cape Colour Question: A Historical Survey* (London, 1927), p. 287.

work, and in the rural areas many are agricultural labourers or farmers. Although the group as a whole has made considerable progress since the beginning of the nineteenth century, only a few individuals have achieved distinction.

The Cape Coloured consciously identify themselves with the white race both in culture and in sentiment. However, the strong race prejudices of the white people toward natives also apply to those of mixed ancestry, perhaps even in a heightened and more complex manner, for "the careless aversion the pure white man has for the native is, in the case of the half-caste, intensified by secret, subconscious fear, and the nearness to danger."[16] In turn the mixed bloods hold aloof from and abhor the natives, and the latter—who possess much race pride —reciprocate and despise the mixed bloods for being mixed. Concerning the mixed blood's attitude toward the white man, Millin writes: "It is not the author of the calamity that the Cape man abhors. . . . Of his white blood he is terribly proud. It is the black man that calls up the bitterness in his heart, the reflections of the shamed, betrayed, and desolate half within himself."[17]

The distinguished South African author, Olive Schreiner, has written some very understanding pages concerning the psychology of the South African mixed blood, from which we quote the following:

The true key to the Half-caste's position lay in the past, as it still lies today, in the fact that he is *not at harmony within himself*. He alone of all living creatures despises his own blood.

[16]Millin, *The South Africans* (New York, 1927), p. 206. The prejudice against the blacks is derived primarily from economic and political fear; that against the coloured is social in the sense of intermarriage, etc. It is less open and public.
[17]*Ibid.*, p. 206. Upon visiting South Africa, the West African Negro, Doctor Aggrey, wrote to his wife: "The prejudice against the Natives by the Coloured is as bad, if not worse than the prejudice of the unchanged Southerner toward the Negro. A Coloured person would not marry, would not be

"I could bite my own arm," a coloured girl once said in our presence, "when I see how black it is. My father was a white man!" The Half-caste alone of all created things is at war within his own individuality. The white man loves the white man incarnate in him, and the black man loves the black. We are each of us our own ideal. The black may envy the white his power or his knowledge, but he admires himself most. "You say the devil is black. But I picture him a white man with blue eyes and yellow hair," said to us a Bantu once. "I have a great sorrow," said an intelligent native preacher, "I know that the Lord Jesus Christ was a white man, yet I could not pray to Him and love Him as I do if I did not picture Him as black and with wool like myself."

Of that divine contentment with his own inalienable personality which lies at the root of all the heroic and half the social virtues, the Half-caste can know little. If it were possible for him with red-hot pincers to draw out every ounce of flesh that was black man's, and leave only the white, in most cases he would do it. That race which would accept him he despises; and the race he aspires to refuses him.

So the first Half-caste arose: a creature without a family, without a nationality, without a stable kind, with which it might feel itself allied, and whose ideals it might accept.

As time has passed in South Africa the slave has been set free, the Half-caste has multiplied, and now forms a more or less distinct section of society, and so, to a certain extent, his position has improved on that of his first progenitor. He may now marry legally with one of his own more or less uncertain type; he may have his home; and his children are his own. Nevertheless, socially his position remains much what it was. Without nationality, traditions, or racial ideals, his position is even today not analogous in South Africa with that of any folk of pure-bred race. For even the Bantu, till we have utterly broken him under the wheels of our civilization, grows up with a solid social matrix about him, which inevitably results in a social training from which the Half-caste is excluded. . . . His

seen in the street walking with a Native; they (would) rather not have any Native in the Coloured Y. M. C. A. . . ." Edwin W. Smith, *Aggrey of Africa: A Study in Black and White* (New York, 1929), p. 167.

tribe may be broken up, but he still feels himself an integral part of a great people, up to whose standard he is bound to live, and in whose eyes, as in his own, he is one of the goodliest and completest creatures of God's earth. Until we have robbed him entirely of this sense of racial unity and of racial self-respect he is not morally on the same footing as the Half-caste.[18]

It appears that the social isolation of the Cape Coloured is the most significant factor in his present condition. He cannot now find a place in Bantu society—even if he wished it; he is blocked socially from the side of the white man. Compared to the unmixed natives his status is sufficiently superior to give him some feelings of satisfaction; on the other hand he cannot hope for acceptance as the white man's equal. "And if he cannot hope, he does not hope."[19]

As a whole the mixed bloods of the Cape have the rôle of a "buffer" group, separating the whites from the natives. (In the Boer provinces they are small in number and in influence, being either isolated or outcasts.) Their future rôle in South Africa will be determined largely by the social evolution of the Bantu. As the latter become further detribalized and assimilate more of white civilization, the opportunity for leadership by the mixed bloods may increase. "History has still to record whether the coloured man will be the rear guard of the white or ad-

[18]*Thoughts on South Africa* (London, 1896 and 1923), pp. 126–27. Sarah Gertrude Millin has made some penetrating analyses of mixed blood personality conflicts. It must suffice here to recall her character, Barry. He is light enough to "pass," but, in so doing, becomes an apprehensive conformist, ". . . . it was not only the fear of discovery and contumely that burdened his heart, it was, with advancing years, the fear that, being what he was, he could not maintain accepted white standards. He sometimes wondered whether he had the same instincts and feelings as the other boys. . . . He tried, in a panic-stricken way, to have the same point of view, to voice the same opinions, to act in the same manner as all the other fellows; and yet even when, as far as appearances went, there was no noticeable distinction between him and anybody else, he could not help worrying lest some essential, intangible difference might still not be *felt*. He was always expecting slights, always self-conscious, never at peace." *God's Step-Children*, p. 255.

[19]Millin, *The South Africans*, p. 215. Those who successfully pass as white, however, "shine in the professions, in science, in the political world and in society generally. Findlay, *op. cit.*, p. 47.

vanced guard of the black," writes one South African.[20] Some white leaders clearly recognize the latter possibility. Thus General Hertzog, the Prime Minister and Nationalist leader, in proposing a policy of native segregation, was careful to exclude the Cape Coloured. He said:

We have to remember that we have to do with a section of the community closely allied to the white population, and one that is fundamentally different from the natives. He owes his origin to us and knows no other civilization than that of the European (although he is sometimes lacking in appreciation of it), and even speaks the language of the European as his mother tongue. There can thus be no talk of segregation. That is the reason why, during the last seven years, the Nationalists in Parliament have held the view that Cape Coloured people must be treated on an equality with Europeans—economically, industrially and politically.

The result of this policy has been that an alliance between them and the native population has been stopped. Luckily they felt that their interests were more closely allied to those of the European than to that of the native. It is their wish just as much as it is ours that they should stand by themselves with regard to the franchise.[21]

The political influence of the Cape Coloured voters is stated to have had a significant part in causing the Europeans to class them on their side.[22] If this policy continues one may expect an increase in racial intermixture between the whites and the mixed bloods.[23] On the other hand, if the policy is reversed the

[20]Brookes, op. cit., p. 429.

[21]Quoted in Raymond L. Buell, The Native Problem in Africa (New York, 1928), I, p. 142. Chapter 9 contains an excellent discussion of the Hertzog native policy and its effects upon the mixed bloods, as it had developed up to that time.

[22]Macmillan, op. cit., p. 288. There are more than 14,000 mixed or native voters in the Cape; i.e. 10 per cent of the total. Buell, op. cit., p. 132.

[23]This seems to have been the trend for some time. See W. H. Dawson, South Africa (1925), footnote p. 28. Also W. C. Cotton, The Race Problem in South Africa (London, 1926), p. 18. In the Transvaal and Orange Free State, in spite of legal penalties and social pressure, "illicit unions of white men and black women are common." E. W. Smith, The Golden Stool (London, 1926), p. 61.

mixed bloods may eventually be driven over to associate themselves with and assume the leadership of the increasing mass of detribalized and race-conscious blacks. Whatever policy is pursued it is almost certain that in the growing racial dilemmas of South Africa the Cape Coloured and other mixed bloods, unlike the Anglo-Indians in India, will have an increasingly important, and possibly determining, part.

THE MULATTOES OF THE UNITED STATES

In the United States the mixed bloods have yet another position and rôle. The significant feature of the American problem is the unwillingness of the white man to make any distinction between mixed bloods and full bloods. They are all classed as "Negroes." Even the man who cannot be distinguished from the purest Nordic is a "Negro" if it is known that he has a Negro ancestor or one drop of "Negro blood." "In South Africa a drop of black blood is, if possible—and despite all talk to the contrary—ignored. In America it is hunted out."[24] To a realist it appears that America can afford to practice this extreme racial policy, since the whites constitute nine-tenths of the total poulation, whereas in South Africa the Europeans are in the minority and the support of every white or part-white man is needed. The American mulatto group, therefore, does not function as a buffer group as in South Africa. Neither is it an outcast group like that of the Eurasians of India. Instead, it is merged into the Negro people and contributes very largely to its leadership.[25]

This fact is of fundamental significance in understanding the general characteristics of the American mixed blood. He is not

24Millin, *The South Africans,* p. 210.

25This is not to assert that there are no full-blood Negro leaders. The fact is, however, that the mulattoes contribute very much more than their proportionate share to Negro leadership. See E. B. Reuter, *The Mulatto in the United States* for the evidence on this point. Its significance will be discussed further in Chap. IV.

the dejected, spiritless outcast; neither is he the inhibited conformist. He is more likely to be restless and race-conscious, aggressive and radical, ambitious and creative. The lower status to which he is assigned naturally creates discontented and rebellious feelings. From an earlier, spontaneous identification with the white man, he has, under the rebuffs of a categorical race prejudice, turned about and identified himself with the Negro race. In the process of so doing, he suffers a profound inner conflict. After all, does not the blood of the white man flow in his veins? Does he not share the higher culture in common with the white American? Is he not legally and morally an American citizen? And yet he finds himself condemned to a lower caste in the American system! So the mulatto is likely to think to himself. Living in two such social worlds, between which there is antagonism and prejudice, he experiences in himself the same conflict. In his own consciousness the play and the strife of the two group attitudes take place, and the manner in which he responds forms one of the most interesting chapters in the history of the Negro.

Perhaps no one has voiced this inner conflict with more dramatic self-analysis than W. E. B. Du Bois, in *The Souls of Black Folk*. When he writes:

The history of the American Negro is the history of this strife—this longing to attain self-conscious manhood, to merge his double self into a better and truer self. In this merging he wishes neither of the older selves to be lost. He would not Africanize America, for America has too much to teach the world and Africa. He would not bleach his Negro soul in a flood of white Americanism, for he knows that Negro blood has a message for the world. He simply wishes to make it possible for a man to be both a Negro and an American, without being cursed and spit upon by his fellows, without having the doors of Opportunity closed roughly in his face[26]—

[26]P. 4 (Chicago, 1903). See also *Darkwater: Voices from Within the Veil* (New York, 1920).

he is not, however, portraying "the spiritual world in which ten thousand thousand Americans live and strive,"[27] so much as he is expressing the experiences and sentiments of that smaller group of mulattoes and educated black Negroes who have moved in a wider social framework than the accommodated plantation Negro in the South. But it is the expression, nevertheless, of an ever-increasing proportion of the American Negro race, and particularly of the mulatto group. It is, perhaps, the prophetic utterance of the poet rather than the descriptive statement of the historian.

The American Negro problem, it must be emphasized, is characterized by the fact that in the process of enslavement and adjustment to the plantation system the Negroes lost practically all of their African culture. They were forced through an abrupt Americanization experience. American cultural values in modified form were substituted for African, and this fact, together with the memories of slavery, has proved to be a distinguishing mark of the whole race question. Since the mulatto has tended to occupy a higher cultural level and to possess more of white social and physical traits than the average black man, he has generally been looked up to by the latter. This attitude has facilitated the leadership rôle of the mulatto. In India and South Africa, however, the unmixed natives have a distinctive culture and social organization of their own—in India this is being strengthened in some respects by a growing nationalist movement[28]—which creates a cultural as well as psychological gulf between natives and both Eurasians and Eurafricans. Consequently, while these Eurasians and Eurafricans face ostracism or at least indifference and social isolation from both whites and natives, the American mulatto experiences this from only the white race. As the black man progresses it becomes easier for the mulatto to identify himself with his lot, and the black

[27] *Ibid.* Preface.   [28] See Chap. VII for a brief analysis.

man in turn profits from the stimulus of the mulatto's leadership and association. Thus a nationalistic movement of the racial type is set in motion: its unique psychological dilemma is that it must express itself in terms of the white American culture, instead of reviving an indigenous culture like the usual nationalist movement. This movement has not only a growing political and economic significance: it also means an intellectual, artistic, and general spiritual awakening.

The Coloured People of Jamaica

Where the competition and conflict of the races is less severe, the mixed group may have a position closer to the dominant race. In certain colonial areas where white men come to live temporarily, or else live as a capitalistic—not a working—class, the mixed-blood group approximates a middle class in status. The white group is small in number, it occupies the leading positions, and it may find a middle class of mixed bloods useful both from an economic standpoint and because it acts as a buffer group separating the two unmixed races. In this case, where accommodation rather than conflict prevails, the mixed blood develops the traits of the conformist anxious to preserve his superior status. The British West Indian Island of Jamaica is an example.

The chief racial elements in Jamaica (aside from some Asiatics) resemble those of the Southern United States: Anglo-Saxons (2 per cent of the total population), Negroes (77 per cent), and the "Coloured" or mixed bloods (18 per cent). Since the freeing of the slaves following 1834, the darker peoples have made much progress and today they are intensely loyal to the British crown. In contrast with the United States, the outstanding facts in the Jamaican racial situation are the code of racial equality, the importance of the coloured and black groups, and the separate position of the coloured people. These features are inter-related: the code of equality reflects British colonial policy and the minority position of the local white population; in turn the rôles of the Negro and Negroid are a consequence of all these influences; while the separate status of the coloured reflects both the code and their special historical experience.

The small proportion[29] of white persons is important in reducing economic competition and, consequently, racial friction. The mixed bloods and blacks thus have freedom to rise in the economic scale. There is no political or legal discrimination between the races, and the fact that ultimate political control lies with London reduces the possibility of any local racial group exploiting the others.

Jamaican society has a complex form of semi-stratification in which English class traditions, significantly modified by racial considerations, are the determining forces. In a rough manner, and allowing for class overlapping as well as wider individual exceptions, the white population forms a kind of social aristocracy; the coloured people are largely of middle class; while the blacks are peasants and labourers. Within each of these broad classes are numerous subdivisions and social sets where economic status, family lineage, education, and personal qualities interact with traits of race to determine the individual's status. The physical (racial) traits of the individual are always important; but the handicap of a dark skin or kinky

[29]The white population has decreased. In 1800 it was estimated at 30,000; in 1911 it was 16,000. The total population is estimated to have increased from about 300,000 in 1800 to 828,000 in 1911, 858,000 in 1921, and over 1,000,000 in 1931. The mixed bloods numbered about 10,000 or 3.4 per cent of the total population in 1791; 40,000 or 10.8 per cent in 1834; and 110,000 or 18.9 per cent in 1881. The birth-rate for 1931 was given as 34.8 per 1,000 and the death-rate as 18.6 per 1,000. See Frank Cundall, *Handbook of Jamaica* for 1920 and 1935. The mixed bloods are probably underestimated, the darker ones being enumerated as black, and the fairer sometimes being designated as white. In 1913 H. G. De Lisser stated that at least one-third of the population was mixed. *Twentieth Century Jamaica* (Kingston, 1913), p. 44.

hair can be partially overcome by other qualities. To this extent race relations are "humanized."

This suggests the subtle manner in which race feeling operates. There is no open colour line—no public segregation or discrimination—but in the sphere of intimate social relationships and personal intercourse the colour factor intrudes with disconcerting pervasiveness. This is not merely a matter between whites on the one hand, and coloured or blacks on the other : it also exists within the coloured class and between the coloured and black. Indeed, the coloured group—particularly those individuals with an imperceptible amount of Negro blood, sometimes called "Jamaica whites" because they consider themselves to be white—are generally thought to possess the largest share of race prejudice. Psychologically this is not difficult to explain. They are anxious to receive recognition as white people, yet know that they are not quite pure white. Consequently they feel a greater need for protecting their precarious status, and do so by drawing a sharp line between themselves and those who are obviously coloured or black. The latter in turn resent this attitude of the "Jamaica whites" and so take a certain pleasure in pointing out that they are "not really white."

Some of the black people also resent the assumptions of superiority of the coloured. Thus an intelligent black servant woman stated that she preferred to marry a black man rather than a brown man since the latter would feel himself superior and probably treat her with less consideration. Such facts, taken in conjunction with the undoubted prestige of the white race, lead some black persons to prefer employment by white people rather than by coloured people. Yet, as Lord Olivier has observed, there is also some "latent jealousy and hostility toward the 'buckra' (white) in the mind of the coloured"[30] so

[30]*White Capital and Coloured Labour* (London, 1924, Revised Edition), pp. 64–66. See also H. G. De Lisser, *op. cit.*, Chapters II and III.

that each racial group in Jamaica is in some degree prejudiced.[31]

These conflicting feelings are held in check and accommodated through traditional bonds of common interest and by a
powerful sentiment of pride in being British subjects. A large
degree of self-government, together with the code of equality
and the possibility of personal advancement, prevents the development of any widespread discontent with the system. The
trend of change is in the direction of British standards, and the
operation of the social ladder induces the coloured and an increasing number of the blacks eagerly to imitate and assimilate English culture. This is aided by a lack of pride in Negro
ancestry; or perhaps one should say that is is partly propelled
by the stigma of black blood. There is a strong desire to be
white in colour as well as English in culture.

The mental conflicts of the Jamaican coloured become understandable in this context. He feels acutely the underlying attitude of superiority of the white man—whether this attitude is
one of kindly patronage or one of cold contempt. Yet he also
admires the Englishman, accepts his superiority as inherent,
and anxiously conforms to English social ritual and ideals. Indeed there is no other alternative for him since he has no pride
in his black ancestry. He implicitly despises his own share of
blackness—or more consciously despises those who are blacker

[31] The psychology of race relations in Jamaica has been interestingly portrayed by Esther Hyman (Mrs. Frank Chapman) in her *Study in Bronze*
(London, 1928). For instance, Lucea, the chief character, is the child of a
white father and a black mother but, even from her black servants, she feels
a "lack of deference for her, because of her mixed blood. It was very subtly
indicated, and had her perceptions been less sensitive might have escaped
her; but she knew well enough that the full-blooded blacks had the usual contempt of nearly all races for the individual who belongs to two races and to
neither. For her father, she knew, they felt and showed the respect due to a
higher race: for in their hearts they admitted inferiority, even if their speech
frequently denied it. Even she, in her secret thoughts, admitted that she
considered a white skin a sign of superiority, though her mind rebelled
against the knowledge. She felt a strong individual superiority to such numbers of white people; yet she felt, all the same, that there was something in
being white that set people apart. Apart and above." Pp. 47–48.

than he is. The very fact that colour does not become a public question, yet strongly affects intimate social life, leads to its psychological accentuation. As one coloured girl wrote in a letter: "Colour prejudice in Jamaica drives us in upon ourselves so much that we shut ourselves in from ourselves." Thus below the surface of Jamaican life broods an uneasy, sensitive, even obsessive spirit of race consciousness which, because it is inhibited, produces a conformist type of behaviour and diverts ambition into social and economic success rather than into artistic expression or political innovation.

In such a situation the "Back to Africa" movement of Marcus Garvey, its Jamaican black leader, could enlist but weak support. Garvey, although not too well trusted personally, blamed the attitude of the coloured people. One of his characteristic utterances follows:

But nobody wanted to be a Negro. "Garvey is crazy; he has lost his head." "Is that the use he is going to make of his experience and intelligence?"—such were the criticisms passed upon me. Men and women as black as I, and even more so, had believed themselves white under the West Indian order of society. I was simply an impossible man to use openly the term "Negro"; yet every one beneath his breath was calling the black man a nigger.[32]

It is evident that the rôle of the mixed bloods of Jamaica is that of a buffer group between blacks and whites. They absorb shocks from both sides and at the same time bind the two races

[32]*Philosophy and Opinions of Marcus Garvey or Africa for the Africans,* compiled by Amy Jacques-Garvey, Vol. II (New York, 1926), p. 127. W. P. Livingstone, in *The Race Conflict* (London, 1911), p. 41, states that "it is curious that even among the pure Negroes of the West Indies the word 'Negro' is not in favor; they prefer 'black man' and 'black person.' "
Garvey's movement is now nearly dead. The American Negro has no real desire to go back to Africa, but the movement did have a great psychological appeal for those who felt down-trodden. E. Franklin Frazier writes that the religious, other-worldly attitudes of the Southern Negro were a decisive obstacle to Garvey's success. See "The Garvey Movement," *Opportunity,* November, 1926, p. 346.

together. Except for that due to illicit relations, a small amount of white blood enters the mixed classes by marriage, and from them is introduced into the black group. Culture proceeds in the same manner. By giving the mixed bloods a middle class status, the British have developed a safety-valve for ambitious and discontented individuals. A restless black man may rise into the middle class, marry a mulatto, and so become effectively incorporated into the existing social structure. It is no wonder, therefore, that a former Governor of Jamaica, Lord Olivier, should view the existence of a mixed-blood class as an asset rather than as a liability:

Whatever it may be possible to argue in justification of a prejudice against interbreeding, it is unquestionable that the coloured people of blended race as they at present exist form a valuable and quite indispensable part of any West Indian community, and that a colony of black, coloured, and white people has far more organic efficiency and far more promise in it than a colony of white and black alone. A community of white and black alone is in far greater danger of remaining, as is conspicuously to be observed in South Africa, a community of employers and serfs, concessionnaires and tributaries, with, at best, a bureaucracy to keep the peace between them. The graded element of mixed race in Jamaica and in other Western Indian colonies contributes very valuably and very wholesomely to making an organic whole of the community and preserves it from this distinct cleavage.[33]

THE INDO-EUROPEANS OF JAVA

Another variety of mixed-blood condition exists in Java, the most populous island in the Dutch East Indies. Until recent years, race relations in Java presented a picture of stratified harmony not unlike that of Jamaica. Holland was pointed out as a model colonizing power; the Dutch East Indies seemed a

[33] *Op. cit.*, pp. 65–66.

quiet zone in an agitated Asia. That picture is now changing, and changing at a rapid pace, as if to make up for lost time.

Java is one of the most densely inhabited areas in the world. Its population of 41,718,000 native Indonesians, 582,000 Chinese and part Chinese, and some 52,000 Arabs is ruled by only 193,000 Europeans, of whom about two-thirds or 128,000 are Indo-European mixed bloods. The Dutch entered the East Indies as traders at the close of the sixteenth century, but they soon found it necessary to govern if they were to trade. The dearth of European women led to much intermarriage or concubinage. Little if any stigma was attached to such unions and even today it is assumed that "the concubine *always exists.*"[34] The resulting "half-castes" proved of value to the government, and they have been, and are today, legally considered Europeans. Those of more wealthy parentage have been educated in the Netherlands. Many others also have assimilated European culture, but economically they constitute a lower middle class.[35]

The extent of this assimilation cannot be measured by the fact of their legal status as Europeans. Those who are legally recognized by their European fathers are ranked as Europeans. The others have a special status under the protection of the Governor-General, except that they may apply for, and perhaps receive, the status of a European. Their cultural assimilation actually depends upon the social conditions in which they live. Many unions occur between Dutch soldiers and native women,[36] for the latter are proud to bear mixed-blood children. If these unions are of the casual or unstable type—as when the fathers

[34]H. J. Scheuer, quoted in S. H. Roberts, *Population Problems of the Pacific* (London, 1927), p. 377.
[35]Amry Vandenbosh, *The Dutch East Indies: Its Government, Problems, and Politics.* (Grand Rapids, Michigan, 1933), p. 30.
[36]One Dutch plantation owner is said to have had fourteen hundred mixed blood descendants in thirty years. See Robert E. Park, "Race Relations and Certain Frontiers," in E. B. Reuter, *Race and Culture Contacts* (New York, 1934), p. 75.

return to Holland—the children may have an ambiguous and inferior social status resembling that of the "beach comber or the indigent whites in other tropical lands. Too idle for manual labor and clinging tenaciously to their status as Europeans, they live useless discontented lives, and are likely to become a source of danger to the community. It was from this class that Pieter Eberveld sprang, the traitor of 'accursed memory.'[37] Even those who are more fortunate in their family life and cultural opportunities find some social barriers in their path, for while the Dutch do not have the caste-like prejudices of the British in India, they do tend to look down upon those who are not pure Europeans.[38]

Although outnumbering the Europeans of pure Dutch blood (the *totoks*) two or three times, the Indo-Europeans as a whole occupy an inferior position in government and industry. The Dutch hold the major posts, the Indos the medium and minor ones. Some of the administrative branches, such as the postal, water and forest services, are practically Indo monopolies. Most of the Indos are poorly paid, the average income being only one-half or one-third that of the Dutch, although many times higher than the income of the average native.[39] Their chief aim is to become officials. They despise manual labour and so are not found in agriculture, except in supervising positions.

Rapid changes now taking place in Java among natives and Dutch are profoundly affecting the position and attitudes of the

[37]Horace Bleackley, *A Tour of Southern Asia* (London, 1928), p. 231. G. Angoulvant states that if abandoned by the father the mixed blood will fall socially and hate the Europeans; then he has the vices of both races. *Les Indes Néerlandaises* (Paris, 1926), p. 103.

[38]Vandenbosh, *op. cit.*, p. 358. Also Sir Hesketh Bell, *Foreign Colonial Administration in the Far East* (London, 1928), p. 94. Frank G. Carpenter, *Java and the East Indies* (New York, 1925), p. 61.

[39]Meyer J. S. Ranneft, "The Economic Structure of Java," in Doctor B. Schrieke, *The Effect of Western Influence on Native Civilizations in the Malay Archipelago* (Batavia, 1929), p. 83.

Indo-Europeans. They are being subjected to increased pressure and competition from above and below. On the one hand, improvements in communication and transportation connect the Dutch more closely with Holland and so increase the cultural and psychological distance with the Javanese-born population. Incoming Dutchmen are taking over the better positions. On the other hand, the Indonesian population has burst the shell of its cultural isolation and is gaining education along Western lines. This enables them to compete more and more successfully with the Indos. One consequence of this has been the formation of a powerful organization, the Indo-European Union, to defend their interests.

A parallel change in the personality traits of the Indo is taking place. Hitherto his assimilation to the Dutch population led him to feel identified with European culture. His dependence produced a conformist mentality, the average Indo type having been postulated as "usually temperate, civil to the point of sycophancy, hospitable, and essentially devoted to his family."[40] The increased competition to which he is now subjected is arousing fear and uneasiness. The growing social distance of the Dutch, together with the rising tide of nationalistic sentiment among the native or Indonesian population, is creating painful dilemmas in the mind of the Indo: shall he continue to be loyal to the Dutch, or shall he ally himself with the Indonesian? "There is for him something tragic in this state of things, as he is fully aware of the fact that complete assimilation to the one group or the other is an impossibility for him."[41] Race feeling is becoming a significant feature. One Dutchman complains, "Life is sombre here, we always live in the shadow of racial sentiment"; while a highly intelligent Indonesian trained in the Netherlands declares at a mixed pub-

[40]H. J. Scheuer (Roberts, *op. cit.*, p. 378).
[41]J. C. Kielstra, "The 'Indo-European' Problem in the Dutch East Indies," *The Asiatic Review*, October, 1929, p. 589.

lic meeting, "We suffer from an inferiority complex and you Europeans from a superiority complex. Co-operation would be easier and matters would be better if we both moved toward the centre in this respect."[42] Because of his European status the Indo is denied the right of land ownership, a question which he now views as of paramount interest. As a consequence of these changes, the Indos are threatening to join the nationalist cause if their demands are not granted.[43]

In addition to the Dutch, the Indos, and the Indonesians, there are the Chinese and Chinese mixed bloods to consider. The Chinese were in the East Indies long before the Dutch and they have always outnumbered them. Economically they perform the rôle of middlemen or traders, and some are very wealthy. Socially they form a separate group with tendencies in three directions: Dutch, Indonesian, and Chinese. The majority are loyal Dutch subjects and have only a sentimental interest in China. The mixed bloods (Indo-Chinese), however, tend to align themselves with the Indonesian nationalists.[44]

It seems evident that the mixed bloods of Java, both European and Chinese, are destined to have a large part in the future of the Dutch East Indies. At present they are shifting their focus of identification and assuming an intermediary rôle in which they hold the balance of power. Unlike most of the Dutch population, they regard the Indies as their native land. One may expect, therefore, that their future attitudes and conduct will hinge upon the course of Indonesian nationalism. And the latter, in turn, is but one phase of the larger struggle in progress between the emerging East and the contracting West.

[42]Quotations from Vandenbosch, *The Dutch East Indies*, p. 57.
[43]For a discussion of the nationalist movement see Amry Vandenbosch, "East Indian Nationalism," *Pacific Affairs*, December, 1931; also the volume of Vandenbosch already cited.
[44]See Amry Vandenbosch, "A Problem in Java," *Pacific Affairs*, November, 1930, pp. 1001 ff.

THE PART HAWAIIANS

The several small islands in mid-Pacific which make up the territory of Hawaii have an exceedingly complex racial composition. Largely because of their location on the "Crossroads of the Pacific" and the labour requirements of the sugar plantations, a variety of races and nationalities have settled on the islands and gradually intermarried. Out of this intermixture have come a great many types of racial hybrids but chiefly Caucasian-Hawaiians, Chinese-Hawaiians and Caucasian-Chinese-Hawaiians, or "three-way" mixtures. The part Hawaiians outnumber the pure Hawaiians,[45] and the trend of intermarriage indicates that they will constitute a majority of the population by the end of this century.

Several influences have been important in shaping the peculiar[46] racial pattern of Hawaii. The early trade relationship resulting from her location, together with the survival of the native Hawaiian monarchy, were effective in creating interracial *mores* of equality. The white trader found it necessary to conciliate the natives, while the white man who settled in the islands likewise had to respect the government which gave him protection. The absence of white women among the settlers encouraged intermarriage, and this strengthened the equalitarian relationship. Annexation to the United States in 1898 established more firmly the principle of democratic government. The fact that today no race is in a majority position compels each to conciliate and co-operate with the others. All these influences serve to create a pattern of racial equality in Hawaii.

[45]The census of 1930 listed the following "racial" or nationality groups: Hawaiian 22,636; Caucasian-Hawaiian 15,632; Asiatic-Hawaiian 12,592; Puerto-Rican 6,671; Portuguese 27,588; Spanish 1,219; Other Caucasian 44,-895; Chinese 27,179; Japanese 139,631; Korean 6,461; Filipino 63,052; Total 368,336.

[46]See Romanzo Adams, "The Unorthodox Race Doctrine of Hawaii," in E. B. Reuter, Editor, *Race and Culture Contacts* (New York, 1934).

But there is also a pattern of inequality. The weakening of the Hawaiian people through population decline and cultural disorganization, together with the growing strength of invading "races," particularly of American and British origin, caused actual power to shift away from the Hawaiians. New England missionaries and their descendants residing in the islands became the most powerful group. The rise of prosperous sugar plantations from about 1850 created a wealthy capitalist white class, and this class was chiefly responsible for the overthrow of the native ruler, Queen Liliuokalani, and the annexation of the islands as a Territory of the United States. With annexation and the making of Hawaii into a vital naval base, an additional complicating factor has entered: the attitude of soldiers and sailors. Their necessary preoccupation with problems of strategy lead them to view the large Oriental population of the islands with considerable suspicion and distrust. Thus in spite of the doctrine and system of racial equality, the racial and nationality groups in Hawaii are not equal in terms of cultural status, social prestige, eeconomic power, or political influence. There is in fact a dual pattern of race relations.

This dual system has psychological repercussions in each of the resident groups. Here we shall consider only the effects upon the mixed bloods. The oldest and most advanced of these are the Caucasian-Hawaiians. Their social position is relatively high, for they are in many cases the descendants of important white and Hawaiian ancestors. Those of good family, education, and means may be accepted in the highest American circles. But like part Hawaiians generally they seem to be quite sensitive to privately expressed condemnation of interracial marriage, as well as to other manifestations of race prejudice. At its minimum the prejudice against mixed persons is likely to be a subtle matter—a matter of elusive reserves, of *arrière-pensées*, and concealed social distances. There are, to be sure, congenial social groups available where the mixed person is fully acceptable and feels at home. Many find a satisfactory adjustment in such groups. Again, race mixture is so well established in the islands that apparently unmixed individuals often state their racial mixture and express pride in their Hawaiian ancestry. But frequently they also feel impelled to explain or "rationalize" about it, thereby indicating an awareness that condemnation exists. Those who secure acceptance in the circles they desire have a sense of satisfaction; those who fail may become embittered—"*Haole*[47] haters," in the current phraseology of the Territory.

Since the overthrow of the Hawaiian kingdom and the rise of a more stable *Haole* society having strong social connections with the United States, the ratio of *Haole* intermarriages with Hawaiians has declined. In fact, among the upper-class *Haoles* it now involves a definite loss of social status. The American attitude toward coloured races tends to diffuse into the islands, but it is not made into a public doctrine. Thus more and more Caucasian-Hawaiians of education and refinement, who really are equal to the *Haoles* in culture, find this social attitude a very real barrier. Some of them marry white Americans and go to the Pacific Coast where they may be socially accepted or perhaps become the object of a romantic sentiment. In Hawaii their position among the *Haole* social élite is at best equivocal. They are accepted by some, but not by others. For instance, an educated young woman who is three-sixteenths Hawaiian and

---

[47]*Haoles* are persons of supposed Nordic descent, largely of upper-class status. The older residents among them are termed *kamaainas* while the newcomers are called *malihinis*. The *kamaainas* accept the racial system but do not personally favour interracial marriage or anything which might endanger their leading position. The *malihinis* have the more obvious racial prejudices of mainland Americans, but if alone they are also more apt eventually to marry into other races.

thirteen-sixteenths Anglo-Saxon in ancestry and who associates chiefly with white persons states:

. . . On the surface, I am regarded by my white friends as White. When I am in their company they are as cordial and friendly as they can be; but there is always this doubt in my mind—"If they speak of a man or woman of my acquaintance who is part Hawaiian in a critical or slurring manner, I wonder if they speak of me in the same way when I am not in their company." They always seem sincere and show me in many ways that they mean what they do say; but still the doubt remains. It is either that they are marvellous actors or I am needlessly suspicious.

Those who are closer to their Hawaiian parentage in race, in culture, or in sentiment may find themselves rejected by the white side of their family, and so identify themselves with other part Hawaiians, thus forming a mixed blood social group. The following account illustrates the emotional ambivalence of some of these part Hawaiians.

. . . My mother's people (Hawaiians) accept me gladly into their society—they look up to me. This makes me proud to be a Hawaiian, but I do not wish to accept their culture wholly because they have not greatly progressed and I'm not especially fond of the life they lead. The whites look upon me as a person with Hawaiian blood and although I hold the same position as many of the whites do (teaching) I am never accepted socially. I accept their culture more than I do the Hawaiians. I live like the whites and yet I frankly do not care to be accepted by the whites. Maybe this is because I know it is useless to try to belong to the white group. . . . On the whole I'm glad I'm not a pure white for I do not like pure whites, but I'm glad I'm half white for it enables me to get along easier in this world. My white skin has gotten me a long way in this world. . . . I like to belong to a second class of people—the mixed bloods. However, I accept the whites as the superior race (not so much now after a trip to the mainland) and I have an inferiority complex because of this acceptance, I guess.[48]

The Chinese-Hawaiians live in a more complex social position. They must adjust themselves to the two parent groups as well as to the *Haoles*. Since the Chinese in Hawaii are regarded as culturally superior to the Hawaiians, many Chinese-Hawaiians prefer acceptance by the Chinese. This is seldom possible in a complete sense because the Chinese-Hawaiians differ from the Chinese both in cultural traits and in physical appearance. Their social situation parallels that of the Caucasian-Hawaiians relative to the *Haoles,* except that the Chinese are not yet so conscious of the purely physical differences. The influence of the cultural factor is indicated by the remarks of a Chinese-Hawaiian ($\frac{3}{4}$ Chinese and $\frac{1}{4}$ Hawaiian), "I prefer the Chinese to the Hawaiians and I associate with them more. In fact, I don't care to go with Hawaiians; I don't like their ways. Yet, I don't feel comfortable with the older Chinese. They are surprised that I don't know any Chinese; and their formal ways of behaviour make me feel uncomfortable in their presence."

In some instances of interracial marriage the Chinese husband lived among Hawaiians so that the family life and personality traits of the children reflected more of the Hawaiian influence. Although the Chinese husband—often chosen by a Hawaiian woman because he was more industrious and considerate than the Hawaiian men she knew—was able to modify the family life to a considerable degree, yet it was not enough to make the children Chinese. The children were most Hawaiian in character when they were adopted and reared by

[48]It may be of interest to record the extent of intermixture of her family, a not unusual condition. A brother married a Korean; one sister married a white man; another a Japanese; a third a Chinese-Hawaiian; a fourth a Chinese-Hawaiian-Caucasian; and she herself plans to marry one who is English-Hawaiian-Filipino.

Hawaiian relatives. Thus, depending upon the particular situation, including the degree of intermixture and the personalities of the two parents, a range of variation arose extending from Hawaiian to Chinese, and always including a portion of Western culture traits.[49]

Identification with the white group is apt to be strengthened when white blood is added to that of the Chinese and Hawaiian. But the complexity of the Hawaiian situation is evidenced by the fact that many Caucasian-Chinese-Hawaiians move fairly freely in any direction. For intimate association, however, other mixed persons seem to be the most congenial. The perplexities of some "three-way" mixtures can be illustrated by the following statements made by a school teacher:

I have often been in a dilemma when it came to identifying myself with a group. It is never clear to me just where I belong. I have to occupy an intermediary position. . . . Though there has been no personal rebuff from the white group I have a phobia for it. It must be self-consciousness. . . . As for the Chinese and the Hawaiian groups, I have no feeling of prejudice towards them yet I maintain a suitable remoteness from either. It is my intention not to marry any one of pure stock, either Chinese, Hawaiian or any other. . . . Perhaps one factor that has drawn me away from the Chinese side is that I do not speak that language. My father when asked why he did not teach us the language said that he thought we would be ashamed and not use it when we grew up. . . . I have met in the last month some Chinese people whom I find very agreeable and not too "Chinese." I often plan to be with them. . . . I am glad that I am half Chinese. As to Hawaiian culture, I have adopted their music, dances, a little of their language as well as food. I don't know whether I should say that I am proud of my fourth Hawaiian blood, nevertheless I'm glad for having it.

You are wondering what is left to my liking. I stand for

[49]Unpublished materials of Margaret Lam of the University of Hawaii have been of great assistance to me. See also Doris M. Lorden, "The Chinese-Hawaiian Family," *The American Journal of Sociology*, January, 1935.

American ways sandwiched with Chinese and Hawaiian "this and that." From all indications I may seem aloof but I assimilate fairly well. Perhaps I do because I have been fortunate enough to know how to play the piano. That alone has enabled me to enter various groups and be accepted by them. With it all, my mind is still confused and not at rest.[50]

Some part Hawaiians react to their situation in terms of nativism or nationalism, but this is not a widespread or organized response. It exists more as a sentiment than as a plan of action.[51] Too many recognize its hopelessness; others find sufficient equality and opportunity in the present situation. Thus the mixed bloods of Hawaii are not in the doubly outcast position of the Anglo-Indians, nor are they socially as isolated as the South African Cape Coloured. Their status also differs greatly from that of the American mulattoes. Of the situations described in this chapter they probably fall between that of Jamaica and that of Brazil. The former possesses some economic, social and political resemblances with Hawaii;[52] but the extensive intermarriage in Hawaii brings it closer to Brazil in that respect. The relative freedom of the Hawaiian situation reacts upon the personalities of the part Hawaiians: their sensitiveness, while quick, seems on the average to be less deeply rooted; they are less introverted and more expansive; the spirit of gaiety and optimism tends more often to override

[50]It may be important to note that the Chinese-Caucasian-Hawaiian mixture (where the Caucasians are northwest European in origin) has been found to rank higher in psychological tests than other Hawaiian mixtures, or most of the pure "races" in Hawaii. One group of sixty-five had an average I.Q. of 108. See S. D. Porteus, *Human Studies in Hawaii*, for a summary of the results. A possible explanation for their superiority may be found in the fact that a three-way mixture necessarily involves at least two generations of racial amalgamation, with corresponding opportunities for the breakup of old culture patterns and the assimilation of new ones. In practice this means relatively greater Americanization.

[51]See the historical analysis by Andrew W. Lind, "Modifications of Hawaiian Character," in E. B. Reuter, *op. cit.*, Chap. XIV.

[52]I have made a more detailed comparison of Hawaii and Jamaica in an article entitled "From Mid-Pacific to Mid-Caribbean," appearing in *The West Indian Review* for September, 1935.

that of moodiness and melancholy. Their individual traits of inheritance and experience find greater opportunity for expression, and social adjustment becomes easier. If the present pace of intermixture continues the part-Hawaiian population will soon become the dominant type and so will gradually cease to have a marginal character, except perhaps as it is affected by incoming currents of opinion from mainland America, or if in the future it is caught in conflicting tides of sentiment arising in and sweeping over the whole Pacific area.

THE MÉTIS OF BRAZIL

In each of the mixed-blood situations described above the hybrids are not effectively incorporated into the dominant race. When we turn to Latin America, and notably to Brazil, this degree of fusion is most nearly realized. Here the mixed blood is not designated as "coloured."[53] He "counts as a white. His half-Indian blood is no disparagement to his social standing, no obstacle to his reaching any public position."[54] Not only is every person who is not pure Indian classed as white; intermarriage also goes on freely between the Brazilian lower class and the black people, between the Brazilian middle class and the mulattoes and quadroons. No less an authority than Lord Bryce affirms that "Brazil is the one country in the world, besides the Portuguese colonies on the east and west coasts of Africa, in which a fusion of the European and African races is proceeding unchecked by law or custom. The doctrine of human equality and human solidarity have here their perfect

[53]Both the mixed blood and the Negro are "'Homen Brazileiro' and the word Negro, even when applied to one of pure Negro race, has come to be used only as a term of abuse, which may be made still further offensive by supplementing it with the words 'de Africa.' This has come to be one of the most offensive terms one can apply to a Brazilian citizen, even though he may be of unmixed Negro descent. If you must discriminate as to colour in conversation, you speak of a 'preto' (preto in Portuguese is black)." H. H. Johnston, *The Negro in the New World*, p. 100.
[54]James Bryce, *South America* (New York, 1912), pp. 472–73.

work. The result is so far satisfactory that there is little or no class friction."[55]

Racial amalgamation has gone far in Brazil. The Portuguese have experienced some 400 years of blending with the Indians, and up to 200 years with imported Negroes. The scarcity of white women, and the policies of assimilation of Church and State, led to rapid mixture with the agricultural Indian tribes. Portuguese racial attitudes interposed no resistance to this process, for centuries of mixture with the darker but culturally superior Moors had accustomed them to swarthy colour; indeed, they were themselves rather dusky and racially mixed. Furthermore, the small population of Portugal, weakened by colonial expansion, was an incentive to regard the mixed bloods as necessary allies.[56]

Early mixture with the Indians facilitated later mixture with the Negro slaves, so that today there are few old Portuguese families in Brazil who do not have some traces of Indian or African blood.[57] This has given rise to a practice sharply in contrast to that of the United States whereby individuals with any mixture of white blood are considered as white. No doubt this is a reason why no attempt has been made since 1890 to ascertain the number of mixed bloods. In that census 32.4 per cent of the population was recorded as of mixed race; 44 per cent as white; 14.6 per cent as Negro; and 9 per cent as Indian.

[55]*Ibid.*, pp. 479–80. See also pp. 566–67, and de Lacerda in G. Spiller: *Inter-Racial Problems* (London, 1911), pp. 377 ff.

[56]This influence apparently helped to make Brazil less racially divided than the Spanish-American countries were in their early history. The Spanish countries developed a class system based upon or connected with race differences. Only individuals with one-sixth or less of Negro or Indian blood could rank as white: "que se tenga per blanco. Each caste was full of envy for those above and of disdain for those below. Mulattoes, Negroes, and Indians detested each other as much as did the *métis* and creoles." Paul Leroy-Beaulieu, *De la Colonisation chez les Peuples Modernes* (Paris, fifth edition, 1902), I, p. 11.

[57]Edward Tomlinson, "Brazil: A Land of Contrasts," *Current History*, December, 1930, p. 373.

Many of these "white" persons were slightly mixed,[58] so that one can readily understand why it is impossible to draw a colour line in Brazil today.

The various races are not evenly distributed throughout Brazil. The Negroes predominate in the tropical and coastal lowlands of rivers; the Indians, in the interior jungles; the whites, in the temperate plateau regions of the South; and the mixed bloods, in the Atlantic Coast zone between the Amazon estuary and Rio de Janeiro.[59] The white race is least mixed in the southern, temperate areas, especially where immigrants from northern European countries are located. Here also are to be found whatever strong race prejudices Brazil possesses.

There is no legal or political discrimination of race in Brazil. Race prejudice in that sense is absent. Nevertheless, there is no doubt that the white race and its culture represent the highest social values and prestige toward which the non-white groups aspire. Bryce recognized this when he noted that the "mestizo deems himself a white, wishes to be a white, tries to live and think as a white, and is practically recognized by others as a white. . . . In Brazil, when the Negro is able to take his stand, so far as education and property go, beside the white, he too thinks and acts like a white man and is so treated."[60] The Brazilian scholar, De Lacerda, noted a preference on the part of the mixed blood for marriages which will "bring back his descendants to the pure white type."[61] But the chief distinctions

[58]Upon the basis of some documentary evidence, A. H. Keane made a calculation for the year 1907, concluding that of the total population 14.1 per cent were pure white; 15.0 per cent were "reputed whites, with slight Negro or Indian strain"; 51.8 per cent were "other half-castes of all shades"; 13.5 per cent were Negroes; and 4.7 per cent were Indians. *Central and South America* (London, 1909), pp. 492–93.

[59]*Ibid.*   [60]*Op. cit.*, p. 566.

[61]*Op. cit.*, p. 382. See also L. L. and J. S. Bernard, "The Negro in Relation to Other Races in Latin America." *Annals of the American Academy of Political and Social Science*, November, 1928, p. 314.

appear to be cultural rather than racial. An individual's status depends primarily upon his education and economic condition. Since there is generally a wide class gulf between the whites and pure Indians or Negroes it rarely happens that they intermarry. Members of each race, however, are likely to marry with persons of mixed race who have a similar class position.[62]

The *métis* (largely Negro-white mixtures) have taken an important and varied part in Brazilian history. As slaves they were well cared for and generally set free, thereupon assuming a place with the more advanced section of the population. Today they are found in many walks of life. They are not so interested or successful in agricultural, commercial or industrial activities as in public affairs, the professions and the arts. According to De Lacerda they are often intellectually superior to both parents: "Some unknown force gives rise in them to an intelligence that is capable of developing to a pitch that neither of the parents could reach." Temperamentally and emotionally, he suggests, they are somewhat less stable:

. . . As a rule, they squander what they have, are irresistibly fond of ostentation, are unpractical in their affairs, versatile, and intemperate in their enterprises. No one, however, can dispute that they are keenly intelligent, and have a disposition for letters and science, and a fair political capacity. The *métis* of Brazil have given birth down to our own time to poets of no mean inspiration, painters, sculptors, distinguished musicians, magistrates, lawyers, eloquent orators, remarkable writers, medical men, and engineers, who have been unrivalled in their technical skill and professional ability. As politicians they are clever, insinuating, and very acute in profiting by any favourable opportunity to secure a position; they are usually energetic and courageous in the struggle, in which they use every weapon with equal zest.[63]

[62]Bryce, *op. cit.,* pp. 470–71.
[63]De Lacerda, *op. cit.,* p. 379. See also Johnston, *op. cit.,* p. vi.

Johnston[64] found the Negroid in America generally to be "A thousand times more touchy, more acutely self-conscious" than the black man.

Such characteristics are not surprising, considering the race relations of Brazil. There seems to be no race prejudice strong enough to restrain the advance of the mixed bloods. But the prestige of the white race and its culture exerts an influence upon those whose minds move in a wider orbit, producing racial consciousness and racial preferences of a not insignificant sort. It is possible that this has the effect of producing some emotional conflict and of inducing the *métis* to aim for those occupations with the highest social status.

Consciously, however, the race doctrines of Brazil rationalize and justify the fact of race mixture. A mixed people is viewed by some as an ideal. Brazilians pride themselves upon their lack of race prejudice. At the same time they have a strong belief in the possibilities of progressive "Arianization": namely, that the mixture of races will gradually make the Brazilian people as a whole more and more Aryan or white. De Lacerda even goes so far as to state that "it is logical to expect that in the course of another century the *métis* will have disappeared from Brazil. This will coincide with the parallel extinction of the black race in our midst."[65] Thus doctrines arise which sanction domestic conditions and at the same time meet the criticisms of outsiders. Perhaps even more significant is the belief that Brazil's experience is an object-lesson for the rest of the world; "Many of the most highly cultured Brazilians will tell you that this country will reveal one day to all the world the one and only method of racial interpenetration, the only one that will prevent racial wars and bloodshed."[66]

[64]*Op. cit.*, p. viii.   [65]*Op. cit.*, p. 382.
[66]Clayton S. Cooper, *The Brazilians and Their Country* (New York, 1917), p. 24.

Concluding Summary and Analysis

Each of the seven mixed-blood situations discussed in this chapter has its distinctive characteristics. The Anglo-Indians (Eurasians) are virtually in an outcast position, being ostracized by both English and Indians. The Cape Coloured are socially almost as isolated but receive legal equality and political recognition from the whites. The mulattoes of the United States are rejected by the whites but accepted as leaders by the blacks. The Jamaican coloured have a relatively independent position as a middle-class group and are accommodated but not assimilated to both whites and blacks. The Indo-Europeans of Java, more nearly assimilated by the Dutch in the past, are now becoming increasingly restive, group conscious and uncertain of their future. The part Hawaiians, although identified with a dual system of racial equality and racial inequality, are becoming the nucleus of a new and mixed race of "Hawaiians" whose culture will be largely American. The *métis* of Brazil are so far assimilated that they with the whites constitute the controlling class.

Each of these situations has its special influence upon the character and personality of the mixed bloods. Some of these effects have been indicated above. Here it may be sufficient to add that in those situations where race feeling is most intense (such as India, South Africa and the United States) one is likely to hear that the mixed blood is an undesirable type, having (usually thought to "inherit") the weaknesses of both parent races. In the other four situations, more favourable, even laudatory, statements are common, the mixed blood occasionally being viewed as superior to both parent races. Is it possible that the theories about the character of mixed bloods are merely "rationalizations" of the existing practices and prejudices of the particular situation?

There are important resemblances among the various mixed bloods. All of these cases represent some cultural mixture as well as racial mixture. The tendency, however, is powerfully in the direction of the dominant culture, and away from the subordinate culture. The mixed blood's first impulse is to identify himself with the race which is considered superior. Failing this he may develop a negative or ambivalent attitude, perhaps a desire for differentiation in some form. This is evident in the case of the United States, and a beginning is visible in Java. Because of his anomalous position—not fully belonging to either parent race—he becomes more than ordinarily conscious of himself and conscious of his ancestry. There is an increase in sensitiveness. This may be an advantage or a disadvantage, depending upon the existing social definitions and opportunities. His uncertain social position intensifies his concern about status. His anxiety to solve his personal problem forces him to take an interest in the racial problem as a whole. Consequently he has an important part in defining and eventually changing the general pattern of race relations. As his numbers increase he may become allied with one of the parent races, or form a new racial type. Whatever fusion of culture occurs is likely to centre about the mixed-blood group, especially in the early stages of racial contact. Thus the status and rôle of a particular mixed-blood group can be taken as an index of the larger race problem; and in turn the development of the mixed-blood class reacts back upon the general racial situation modifying it to a significant, sometimes determining, extent.

In general, mixed bloods are considered to be intermediate in physical and cultural traits and to have intermediary rôles. This generalization requires some qualification. As regards physical and cultural traits there is a tendency to move toward the dominant group. If not too strongly opposed this tendency may in time and under certain conditions create a gulf between the mixed bloods and the subordinate race. This is evident in India, South Africa, and to a degree in Brazil. Pertinent in this respect is the fact that as regards India and the Cape Coloured, intermixture with the darker race has greatly decreased. In these as well as in other cases the culture of the dominant race continues to spread without the necessity of blood intermixture. Where slavery and enforced migration occur, the culture of the dominant group is imposed upon the subject group. This may go so far as to destroy the culture of the enslaved group.

The rôle of intermediary is not uniform or consistent. The Anglo-Indian once had this rôle but has lost it. It is not now greatly in evidence in the case of the Cape Coloured, but this may change in the future. Furthermore, the intermediary rôle varies: it may be by one which favours complete assimilation to the dominant culture, or it may result in a process of differentiation and the cutural revival of the subordinate race. In the latter case there is only limited assimilation. The phenomenon of nascent nationalism must be reckoned with in extensive areas of the world.

The processes of racial amalgamation and cultural assimilation are favoured or hindered by the following important conditions: (1) a deficiency of women in the dominant race encourages intermixture. The mixed bloods are then apt to be included in the paternal group. (2) Economic relations which imply reciprocity and equality—*i.e.,* trade relations—are conducive to intermarriage. Where there is severe economic competition between divergent races, however, intense hatreds occur. Such antagonisms may lead to the segregation, the expulsion, or even the extermination of the weaker group. They reduce racial fusion. Sometimes conditions of extreme racial inequality favour interbreeding. This is true of plantations that employ slave labour. When in addition there is an excess of men in the slave-holding group, the hybrids are also assimilated more rapidly. (3) Religious organizations may encourage conversion and assimilation. This is true of the Catholic and Mohammedan religions. Hinduism, on the other hand, forbids intermarriage. (4) The relative size of each race in contact influences the rate of intermixture and assimilation. If the subordinate group is small it may be viewed with equanimity or even with pathos. On the other hand, if it is relatively large, as in Jamaica, expediency may compel a policy of tolerance and good will on the part of the dominant but smaller group. (5) Political relations which have been based upon conflict and conquest are apt to leave a heritage of hate and fear, thus slowing down the process of fusion; while peaceful co-operation, alliances, etc., work in the contrary direction. (6) The degree of racial and cultural difference is important. Other things being equal, large differences retard the growth of sympathy and understanding. (7) Relatively free sex and marriage *mores* speed up the process of assimilation. Thus it is easier for continental Europeans than for Anglo-Saxons to adopt the practice of open concubinage with native women. (8) Attitudes conditioned in one situation are carried over into another situation. The Portuguese illustrate favourable conditioning; the English and Americans unfavourable conditioning. (9) Where several races are involved, codes of segregation are difficult to establish so that assimilation is facilitated (Brazil, Hawaii). (10) The stage of race contact is important. The first contacts, especially of the frontier and slave type, speed up the process of mixture.[67] If this does not end the problem, the process may slow down as a more settled and stable society is organized. At this point acculturation may proceed rapidly without racial amalgamation. Ultimately it is to be expected that cultural assimilation will result in racial amalgamation, unless persistent conflict re-

[67]See Robert E. Park in Reuter, *op. cit.*

organizes the racial groups upon another basis. However, the modern period of race mixture has hardly proceeded far enough for conclusions to be drawn about this latest stage in the interaction of races.

CHAPTER III

The Cultural Hybrid

THE RISE of a mixed-blood population is necessarily conditioned by the migration and contact of different racial stocks. The migrating group may be the dominant class, as in modern Western expansion; or it may be the subordinate class, as in the migration of slave, contract or other immigrant labour. In both of these types of migration there is a problem of contact of different cultures in addition to the racial difference. The mixed blood is therefore also of mixed culture—a "cultural hybrid" as well as a racial hybrid.

Persons having a mixed culture may and do emerge aside from the process of race mixture. In other words, an individual may be a "cultural hybrid" but not a racial hybrid. Some cultural hybrids are a consequence of culture diffusion; or, more exactly, of a certain type of culture diffusion: that where a whole culture system moves, not merely some fragmentary traits. Others are a product of migration, especially the migration of persons or groups into a strange land where they must make a new cultural adjustment.

THE DIFFUSION OF EUROPEAN CULTURE

Culture traits have been transmitted from one group to another since the beginning of human history. No group invents more than a small part of the culture it possesses. Most of it is borrowed from others. As the range of human contacts increases, the range and speed of cultural interchange are likewise increased. It is in the regions of extended contacts and cultural interchange that the main civilizations of the world have developed. During the past few centuries these semi-separated civilizations have themselves come closely together so that the whole world now forms a single arena of cultural contact and diffusion, permitting the development of what may some day become a world civilization.

The chief influence in developing this world phase of acculturation has been the diffusion of European civilization over the surface of the globe. A series of favourable circumstances in Western Europe gave birth to an age of science, invention, and power production which have revolutionized its mode of living. As this system emerged in the Western countries it quickly began to spread along the main routes of travel and then into the minor, finally embracing the most isolated of peoples. Its power and prestige gave the Western peoples a place of dominance in the world. Because Western diffusion has been so rapid and so overwhelming, gradual adjustment and assimilation have been impossible. Consequently, problems of culture conflict have arisen. These culture conflicts are so widespread and so acute that they merit special attention.

The Europeanization of the globe has involved changes in thought as well as changes in modes of living. The first contacts of culture often result in a simple exchange of material objects such as guns, steel knives and cloth in return for food, precious stones, and metals. Further contacts lead to deeper changes, particularly in the native culture: in language and government, morals and religion. In the course of time the weaker group falls under the influence or control of the stronger group. As this occurs its ethnocentric pattern of mind is challenged or undermined: "Ethnocentrism is the technical name for this view of things in which one's own group is the center of everything, and all others are scaled and rated with reference to it."[1] Social and cultural disorganization begins and continues until the period of transition has been surmounted. Then there is a rebirth of ethnocentrism—but this rebirth arises in quite a new social and cultural framework.

Primitive people often succumb rapidly to the pressure of a powerful Western people. Sometimes force is ruthlessly employed in their subjugation, but the same result may be achieved in more peaceful and indirect ways. Missionary efforts may secure support from the government; the attempt to repress "cruel and inhuman practices" may result in the destruction of important native customs; the desire to increase trade or production may eventually transform the native economic and social system from a collectivistic to an individualistic one—with disturbing consequences; the need for establishing order and safety for traders and missionaries may lead to political control. All such influences lead directly or indirectly to a modification of fundamental native institutions. The breakdown or weakening of one institution—such as the authority of the chief, the polygamous family, or even such a custom as head-hunting[2] reacts upon other parts of the social organization. The result is uncertainty, restlessness, confusion, and conflict—perhaps complete social disorganization.

Such social disorganization may go so far as to lead to the extinction of the native people. This has occurred in the past and is happening today. Wherever the disparity between the

[1]William G. Sumner, *Folkways* (Boston, 1906), p. 13. The borrowing of non-material culture traits does not necessarily destroy ethnocentrism. It may persist underneath the new observances, as with the Eskimos described by V. Stefansson: "Fundamentally, the Eskimo consider themselves better men than we are. In the matter of Christianity they concede that we introduced it; but they do not concede that we know more about it than they do." *My Life with the Eskimos* (New York, 1926), p. 429.

[2]Head-hunting among the Melanesians was deeply rooted in the religious and ceremonial life of the people. . . . It also had practical significance, for "The chief stimulus to the making of canoes in Eddystone Island came out of the practice of head-hunting." W. H. R. Rivers, "The Psychological Factor," in *Essays on the Depopulation of Melanesia* (Edited by Rivers), p. 108.

two groups and cultures is great, there is danger that the native peoples will be reduced in numbers if not destroyed. The introduction of firearms, alcohol, venereal and other diseases—even the use of unsuitable clothing and the building of unhealthy houses—has greatly increased the native death-rate.

There is sometimes a subtler, more profound consequence, that which W. H. R. Rivers[3] has named the "loss of interest in life." By destroying or devitalizing the essential native institutions—those about which the life of the tribe is organized—the native may lose his interest and vigour, thereby weakening his resistance to illness, and reducing the birth-rate.

While the Western trader, administrator and missionary have been the fundamental agents in foisting Western culture upon the natives, the latter do not always resist. What Wissler[4] calls "spontaneous borrowing" also goes on; that is, the native takes over some of the white man's customs without any pressure being exerted. This sometimes means that the native has come to value European culture as superior or more desirable than his own, and to look at himself and his culture through the eyes of the white man. The profound social and psychological transformation involved in this change undoubtedly occurs in a variety of ways. It denotes a partial destruction of the indigenous *mores* and the emergence of an inferiority complex. In some cases the native develops a sense of helplessness and hopelessness in the face of this overwhelming power and way of life which he cannot understand, much less appreciate, and which visibly reduces his numbers. Glimpses into the minds of such individuals, although rare, are revealing. As long ago as 1893, a Fijian wrote of the "white chiefs" as follows:

[3]*Op. cit.* Alexander Goldenweiser agrees with this interpretation. See the *Journal of Social Forces,* Vol. III (1924–25), pp. 127 ff. Louis LeFevre in *Liberty and Restraint* (New York, 1931), has developed an impressive thesis in favour of liberty by considering many such instances.
[4]*An Introduction to Social Anthropology* (New York, 1929), p. 359.

... They are great and we are insignificant. A plant cannot grow under the great Ivi tree, for the great Ivi overshadows it, and the grass or plant beneath withers away. It is thus with the chiefs from the great lands who live among us. This is the reason why we Fijians are decreasing. "Let us move more gently: we stand in the glare of the light" (Fijian proverb): Let us practice religion.[5]

And note Robert Louis Stevenson's description of a conversation with Stanislao, a Marquesan educated in South America who, while inwardly torn between his ancestral and Western cultures, yet protected himself by adopting the appraisals of the white man. Although "he had always an eye upon the past," nevertheless,

In all his talk, Stanislao was particular to speak of his country as a land of savages; and when he stated an opinion of his own, it was with some apologetic preface alleging that he was "a savage who had travelled." There was a deal, in this elaborate modesty, of honest pride. Yet there was something in the precaution that saddened me; and I could not but fear he was only forestalling a taunt that he had heard too often.[6]

The inferiority complex has a variety of forms and consequences. It may lead to a withdrawal type of response or loss of interest in life; or it may stimulate the further assimilation of the dominant culture, as noted in the preceding discussion. In this connection it should be emphasized that the native group frequently responds in a varied manner and so develops internal dissensions and schisms corresponding to the "right," "centre," and "left" parties of continental parliaments. The younger generation is more apt to imitate Western customs and to resent the authority of chiefs and elders whose interest is in

[5]Basil Thomson: *The Fijians: A Study in the Decay of Custom* (London, 1908), p. 253.
[6]*In the South Seas* (New York, 1905), pp. 91, 92.

maintaining tribal customs. A moderate or compromise group arises in between.[7] Eventually, if conditions are unfavourable for assimilation—especially if the desire for equality is rebuffed by the whites—resentment arises and the inferiority complex is compensated for by a new feeling of self-appreciation and even of self-exaltation. This feeling arises out of a collective interaction which heralds the birth of a nativistic or nationalistic movement. The essential need for individual and group self-respect thus reasserts itself, social reorganization is undertaken, and if successful, the cycle of ethnocentrism is completed.

EUROPEANIZED AFRICANS

The process of transition from an indigenous to a Westernized culture is now a world-wide phenomenon, moderately advanced along the more accessible areas, but visible in an incipient form even in remote districts. Africa, the last of the continents to be opened by the white man, is changing with breathtaking speed. The trails of the explorer and pioneer missionary have been quickly followed by the administrator, the trader, the planter, and even by the ubiquitous tourist. Bicycles, automobiles, airplanes, radios, motion pictures, and all the paraphernalia of Western civilization, are penetrating and transforming the outer and inner life of the African. No longer is he restricted to the traditional pathways of his ancestors: new opportunities and experiences in conflict with older compulsions function to detribalize and individualize his attitudes and behaviour. The contrast between his former life inside the tribe and his life outside is sometimes startling and revolutionary. Norman Leys has vividly described this contrast, especially with reference to Kenya in British East Africa:

The old rigidity is gone. In his tribe and village home the individual is wedged tight in an unchanging frame of customs.

[7]Thomas Jesse Jones, *Education in East Africa* (New York,), p. 10.

In employment as a wage-earner he suddenly finds himself liberated except for the inexorable demands of the task his master sets him. But he may change his master at the month's end, and travel a couple of hundred miles to work for a new master among a strange tribe. He may live, if he will, without wife or children or home or tribe, and have no obligations that money cannot discharge. Tribal public opinion, once omnipotent, no longer exists for him. Once he never dreamed of doing anything but what every one else he knew always did. Now, unless he has come under mission influence, no law but instinct and appetite is discoverable. For he cannot carry with him to the new life his old convictions of right and wrong.[8]

Detribalization and Europeanization have proceeded farther in some areas than others. Where conditions favour white settlement, as for example in the British East African territory of Kenya, the development of plantations using native labour may have disruptive consequences. The death-rate mounts as native life becomes uprooted and disorganized, while the *déraciné* native makes an unfavourable impression upon the sympathetic observer. Julian Huxley records his impressions in the following words:

. . . there is here the ill-regulated untidiness of the uprooted African, the neither-one-thing-nor-the other-feeling, of human beings truly belonging to no stable order, neither the tribalism they have left nor the white civilization for which they are working. Their clothing has neither idea nor tradition behind it—just scraps of European clothes; untidy, often ragged, whatever they fancy and can afford, or even anything European they can pick up. They live in ramshackle labour lines, which look as if they had been put up only to be taken down again as soon as possible, with no suggestion such as a genuine native village gives, however primitive or dirty it may be, of home. They are kicking off many of the restraints of tribalism without really emancipating themselves from its more pervasive

[8]*Kenya* (London, 1925), p. 301.

idea; their mental life would seem to be as patchy and promiscuous an affair as their clothing.[9]

The product of the missionary's effort, the Christian convert, is one who has been pulled out of the old order of things without necessarily becoming a part of the new order. "Converts often come to despise all their own customs. They throw the baby out with the bath, and abandon respect for tribal elders and tribal traditions. Yet they almost inevitably fail to imbibe our Western traditions properly—how could they in a few short months?—and so usually fall between two stools."[10] Their conversion involves a break with their tribe, which, though not always severe, will include some social ostracism.[11]

The convert is also likely to encounter ostracism, if not worse, from the non-missionary European groups. There appears to be a fundamental clash in viewpoint between missionaries, planters, and administrators, which reacts upon the convert. The planters are interested in cheap labour, which resolves itself into the doctrine of keeping the native in a lowly, subordinate place; the governmental official, like the planter, is secular-minded, but he is more responsive to the Colonial Office in London. Neither finds the missionary's religious idealism,

[9]*Africa View* (New York, 1931), pp. 150–51.
[10]Huxley, *op. cit.*, p. 345.
[11]For an illuminating account of the conflicts and problems involved in becoming a convert see "An African Autobiography. A Fragment by Daniel Nhlane, a Christian Convert." Presented by Rev. Donald Fraser, Nyasaland. *Missionary Review of the World*. New Series, XXXII (1919). The convert has critics as well as defenders. Several decades ago, for instance, Mary H. Kingsley wrote in this vein: "The missionary-made man is the curse of the Coast, and you find him in European clothes and without. . . . The pagans despise him, the whites hate him, still he thinks enough of himself to keep him comfortable. His conceit is marvellous . . ." *Travels in West Africa* (London, 1897), p. 490. The superior convert, however, may give us another view, as is illustrated by Doctor Aggrey: "I was born a pagan and am not ashamed of it. But if the missionaries had not sought and found me I should today have, perhaps, a dozen wives; I should be making a beast of myself with palm wine; I should be a chief, honoured by my people, but I should know neither Shakespeare nor philosophy, nor the Gospel." E. W. Smith, *Aggrey of Africa* (New York, 1929), p. 176.

moral rigidity and often narrow outlook particularly agreeable. Neither is willing to accept the educated native as an equal. Thus the convert, like other detribalized natives, finds himself in an equivocal position. Generally more educated he will also be more sensitive; encouraged by missionary idealism he will be all the more disillusioned by non-missionary materialism. As a consequence, race-consciousness and resentment are developing. Some rebellions have grown out of these conditions.

Such rebellions are probably a prelude to broader collective movements of a nationalistic type. Detribalization breaks down traditional ideas and introduces some of the Western; exploitation sharpens the ensuing restlessness into discontent; missionary education provides leaders and unwittingly furnishes much of the ideology and patterns of expression, for African revolts are frequently a mixture of religious fanaticism and anti-European sentiment.[12] Hymns, such as "Onward Christian Soldiers," "Forward be your Watchword," and stories like that of David and Goliath, become imbued with revolutionary meaning. Prophets and miracle-workers arise and sweep the natives into new movements and organizations inimical to European hegemony. As a consequence, colonial governments have sought more and more to prevent tribal disorganization and to control missionary efforts.

This problem exists everywhere in Africa, but most of all in those regions affected directly by Western industrial penetration. British West Africa, whose tropical lowlands are less inviting to the European, has had less acute problems. Here the method of "indirect administration" was first worked out by Sir Frederick Lugard, now member of the Permanent Man-

12For illustrations consult the Index under "Native Revolts" in R. L. Buell's two-volume work, *The Native Problem in Africa.*

dates Commission of the League of Nations.[13] Instead of governing the natives directly by Europeans, indirect rule aims to recognize, maintain and develop the traditional native institutions as the fundamental form of social organization and control. It does not displace indigenous councils and recognized chiefs, but works through them; it introduces new ideas gradually by means of the chiefs, adjusting them to the special characteristics of each native group. Nevertheless, Western missionary education has produced a class of Europeanized Africans who have been described by Lugard in these words:

The educated African imitates European dress and customs closely, however ill-adapted to his conditions of life, and may be heard to speak of going "home" to England. He has, as a rule, little in common with the indigenous tribes of Africa, and seldom leaves his native town except to travel by sea or railway. The Europeanized African is indeed separated from the rest of the people by a gulf which no racial affinity can bridge. He must be treated—and seems to desire to be treated—as though he were of a different race. Some even appear to resent being called Negroes, the universal race-term in America. The Rev. R. Keable complains in *East and West* that even native priests showed in the war a contempt for and aloofness from the natives in their spiritual charge unknown between white men of unequal social standing.[14]

The marginal African develops under French rule also—even when that rule has the explicit objective of assimilation into

[13]Although this Commission hesitates to take a clear stand between indirect rule and the theory of assimilation (see *Minutes of the Fifth Session, Extraordinary,* Oct. 23 to Nov. 6, 1924, p. 118), it does favour specific policies which maintain basic native customs, land rights and native production; encourage self-government; prevent labour exploitation by Europeans; increase education in the vernacular, etc.

[14]Lugard, *The Dual Mandate in British Tropical Africa* (London, 1923), pp. 80–81. The result is "that the illiterate native, even of the coast cities, is more ready to give his confidence to the white man than to the educated native," p. 88. Lugard does not attempt to distinguish the mixed blood from the educated full-blood African, evidently not finding any great distinction between the two. This corroborates our thesis.

French culture, and even though Frenchmen are less aloof than Englishmen in their social relations with darker peoples. Consequently, although some "Black Frenchmen" are satisfactorily adjusted[15] to French culture, others are incompletely assimilated. A few years of French schooling do not constitute cultural assimilation: the student merely "lives in two separate worlds: the real world from which he has come, and to which he is passionately attached by the language of the country; and an artificial world—a temporary existence where he for the time being comes into contact with the French language. A native does not assimilate this language and give up his former modes of thought."[16] A French scholar and traveller has questioned the theory in the following words:

Does not this teaching of French, which can only be superficial, risk the formation of *déclassés?* As soon as he knows but a few words of our language, the native believes himself to be of a superior race and of a class which has a right to all rights. He feels it below his dignity to go back to the soil. What he wants is a situation as a clerk in some business or, preferably, in the all-powerful administration. But such positions are few and overcrowded, and often badly paid. Then the unfortunate one believes himself to be the victim of a gross injustice, for, having wished to make him half French, we shall have made him "anti-French," an agent of discontent and revolt.[17]

In recent years French colonial policy, like that of Britain, is seeking to control the upheavals produced by European in-

---

[15]Thus Blaise Diagne, the Senegalese Negro deputy in Parliament, wrote to Marcus Garvey, Jamaican leader of the "Back to Africa" movement: "We black Frenchmen wish to remain French, since France has given us every liberty, and since she has unreservedly accepted us upon the same basis as her own European children. None of us aspires to see French Africa delivered exclusively to the Africans as is demanded, though without any authority, by the American Negroes, at the head of whom you have placed yourself." Letter of July 3, 1922, *Revue Indigène*, 1922, p. 275. (Quoted from Buell, *op. cit.*, II, p. 81.)

[16]Buell, II, p. 59.   [17]J. Weulersse, *Noirs et Blancs* (Paris, 1931), p. 16.

fluence. A new theory known as "association"[18] has emerged. This resembles the British method of indirect administration. In practice, however, it differs in at least two ways: (1) the French tendency towards centralization and assimilation remains powerful; (2) the French lack of color prejudice[19] changes the spirit of administration. The test will come as more and more educated Africans, encouraged by the theory of race equality, demand effective political power.

WESTERNIZED ORIENTALS: INDIA

Turning from Africa to Asia we are again confronted with the fact of culture clash. Its conditions and the ensuing problems differ from those of Africa both in scope and variety, for Asia is the population center of the world and her peoples have cultures at least as highly differentiated and developed in some aspects as those of Europe. But the possession of modern science and industrial organization by the European nations have given them a degree of power sufficient to control large populations in Asia. The most amazing instance of this control is the British dominance in India.

Of all the culture contacts that India has had, that with the West has been the most profound. Other migrants into India have fused their interests with the country, but the British have maintained a baffling aloofness while continuing to govern and penetrate the country. The ancient culture of the Indians had already given them a highly conscious and philosophical way of

[18]For an excellent discussion see the *History of French Colonial Policy* (1870–1925), 2 vols. (London, 1929), especially Chap. IV, by Stephen H. Roberts.

[19]In the 1924 election the European opponent of Diagne was reported to have addressed the black voters of Senegal as follows: "In the Cevennes where I was born, there were few men more educated than you, Senegalese, but they enjoy more rights than you. I who speak to you, I am not of a family really white; moreover you can see the colour in my face." This appeal did not save him from defeat. Buell, *op. cit.*, I, p. 956.

life which was in marked contrast to the Occidental *êthos*. Because of this, as well as because of the huge numbers involved, contact with the West has not resulted in a rapid crumbling as in the more primitive cultures. Yet Western civilization of the English variety has entered deeply into the Indian mind, and deeply disturbed the traditional rhythm of India's life. One Indian summarizes these influences in this wise:

. . . Who can deny that western civilization has in the main exercised a disintegrating influence and given a rude shock to the social balance of the people? The communal spirit and sentiment, so deeply ingrained in the hearts of the people, has been invaded by the individualistic tendency of the West as seen in the modern desire of many people to break up the age-long and binding joint-family system. The rigid caste-system, the source of endless irritation and ill-feeling even in former times, has broken to pieces, and the lower classes have been imbued with a new sense of their position, their rights and importance in the social scheme. Even the proverbially docile Indian woman's voice is occasionally heard above the general din crying for her votes and her rights. The village community life, strong and self-contained with its autonomous village panchayats, whose vigorous existence gave stability to the communal life of the people through the vicissitudes of ages, has for varied reasons undergone a disintegrating change and is but a shadow of its former self. Such an unsettled and convulsed social state, without any coherent guiding principles of action, can scarcely contribute to the peace or happiness of the people.[20]

The Western economic system, the British government, and the Christian Church have been obvious forces in this transformation. But even more disturbing, for the educated classes at least, has been the introduction of English education.[21] It is through the English language and English literary education

---

[20]P. K. Narayan, "The Conflict of Cultures in India," *The Hindustan Review*, Vol. XLV, June, 1922, pp. 502–503.
[21]*Ibid.*, p. 498. This has been noted by many students of the subject.

that we may look for the immediate source of much of India's spiritual disruption.[22]

The literary type of education was rooted in both the Hindu and Musalman systems of learning before the coming of the English. When Western education was introduced it naturally became molded in such a way as to emphasize the purely literary to the exclusion of the more practical aspects. Gradually the Western system supplanted the ancient learning.[23] The university degree became more and more important in the career of the middle-class Indian (*the bhadralok*). "The social value of western education was reflected in the fact that a man who had taken his degree, or even only passed the entrance examination of the University, had a definitely improved value in the marriage-market. Western education had made its way into the social system."

Western, and particularly English, ideas of liberty and self-government were bound to unsettle the minds of the young Indian student.

It is through the contact between Indian culture and that of the outer world, and especially the culture of Europe and the West, that painful dilemmas are created in the mind of the thoughtful student of Bengal. He feels the eddying current of western thought, which is forcing its way, in some degree unseen, into the quiet waters of his traditional life. The current brings with it an unfamiliar, but vigorous and agitating literature; a mass of political formulas, charged with feeling and aspiration and sometimes delusively simple in their convenient

[22]Much of the material which follows is taken from the excellent and voluminous report of the *East India Calcutta University Commission,* made up of distinguished British and Indian scholars under the presidency of Sir Michael E. Sadler.

[23]*Ibid.,* p. 29. In the early part of the nineteenth century English schools were established by missionaries. They proved useful to the Government in providing subordinate officials. Because of this, and the advocacy of Lord Macaulay, the Government decided in 1837 to substitute English studies for Oriental studies. *Cf.* Sir J. Bampfylde Fuller, *The Empire of India* (London, 1913), pp. 173 ff.

generalization; fragments of philosophies; some poisonous
weeds of moral scepticism; bright-hued theories of reform; the
flotsam and jetsam of a revolutionary age. The young man's
necessary study of English has given him the power of reading
what the inrushing stream brings with it. His own instinctive
yearnings for social reform, for intellectual enlightenment and
for moral certainty make him eager for fresh truth. And behind this new foreign literature and philosophy, behind the
pressure of those invisible influences for which printed books
and journals are but some of the conduits of communication,
there stands the great authority of colossal Power; Power
evinced in political achievement, in religious conviction, in the
world-wide ramifications of commerce, in stupendous indus-
trialism, in the startling triumphs of applied science, in immeas-
urable resources of wealth; Power, which, even under the strain
of a titanic struggle, puts out new manifestations of energy and
suffers no eclipse.[24]

But the student feels "by instinct" that in these new influences "evil is mixed with good." They are alien to his tradition. Their overwhelming nature confuses him in most instances. He does not perceive clearly that his own *malaise* is
but the psychological echo of a larger, world-wide impact. A
few "are aware of the tension in their thoughts and ideals which
is caused by the twofold appeal of Western influence and of Indian tradition."[25] Their free intellectual and imaginative life
contrasts painfully with the rigid social ritual of daily life.
One Indian writer states the dualism in this manner:

In Bengal, while our mind is highly imaginative and our
intellect peculiarly subtle, our actual social life is wholly circum-
scribed by conventional custom and completely fettered by artificial rules. This divorce of our actual life from the life of our

[24]*Calcutta University Commission Report.*

[25]Pages 122–32 of the *Report* contribute the most significant portion from
the point of view of our study. Hans Kohn in *A History of Nationalism in
the East* (New York, 1929) writes: "These people were unsettled; they
stood in the borderland between two worlds and two eras, akin to both but
nowhere at home." P. 117.

ideas has made us a race of neurasthenics. In addition it is destroying our intellectual power. At present we are too often content merely to imagine and almost never really to achieve.[26]

The conflict of cultures produces an inner mental conflict—a conflict of loyalties. Its peculiarity lies in the fact that the caste system compels an external conformity which does not harmonize with the newly acquired Western sentiments and ideas. The result is that:

The Bengali student, like many a student in other lands, feels upon his mind the pull of two loyalties, the loyalty to the old order and the loyalty to the new. But in his case the difficulty of combining these two loyalties is very great. Each loyalty needs fuller and clearer definition to him. He finds it hard to light upon any real adjustment between them. Therefore, it is often his fate to lead what is in effect a double intellectual life. He is two-minded and lives a parallel life in the atmosphere of two cultures.[27]

This mental tension has a characteristic pattern of development which is dependent upon the evolution of the culture conflict situation as well as upon the life-cycle of the individual.[28] Thus from an earlier tendency to admire and assimilate European ideas there has arisen a counter movement of resentment and differentiation as such assimilation proved impracticable. Indian nationalism has given a new expression and direction to the mental and emotional life of young Indians, and while embittering has also relieved to some extent the psychological tensions of the earlier period.

[26]*The Report*, p. 124. The contrast between thought and overt behaviour is noted by another observer as follows: "For upward of half a century Indian youths have been studying a literature which sets liberty above conventionality, comfort above dignity, and exalts the romantic side of love: they give eager intellectual assent to these ideals, yet live their lives unchanged." Fuller, *op. cit.*, pp. 179–80.

[27]*Calcutta University Commission Report.*

[28]See Chapters V and VII for a fuller discussion.

DENATIONALIZED EUROPEANS

The struggle of submerged nationalities within Europe has also given rise to marginal personalities. Modern nationalities emerged in Europe at the time when Western Europe was reaching out and expanding into the farther corners of the globe. The disintegration of the Medieval structure of Church and State—a supernational structure—left the ground clear for the patterns of nationalism gradually to trace their firm imprint upon the map of Europe. The new forms appeared first in France and England, and last in Central and Eastern Europe. The lag of the latter areas involved an intense struggle of nationalities, largely because of the existence of numerous and overlapping cultural units with inflamed memories of invasion and counter-invasion, domination and subjection. This part of Europe lacked the protection of natural geographical barriers where nationalities could grow and consolidate without being too greatly disturbed from without; it was, on the contrary, the open pathway for the migratory hordes of Asia.

The geographical and historical differences between western and eastern Europe have brought about an important divergence in group sentiment toward the political state and toward nationality.[29]   Western European peoples have developed a sentiment of loyalty to the political state as a distinct institution which embraces lesser loyalties to cultural nationalities. The British government and state, for example, enlist the patriotic devotion of Englishman, Scotchman, and Welshman—although each of these belongs to a distinct cultural nationality. Such a reconciliation of political unity with national diversity is bound up with the development of a spirit of religious toleration, political liberty, and equality of public rights and opportunities.

[29]For a fuller discussion of this distinction consult C. A. Macartney, *National States and National Minorities* (London, 1934), pp. 4 ff. In addition to the influences of geography and migration, he stresses the unifying, assimilating rôle of the Roman legacy in southern and western Europe.

No single nationality is attempting to dominate or denationalize the others. An individual's nationality, therefore, does not become a factor in political struggle. Most Central and Eastern European peoples do not yet make this distinction. Centuries of conflict have produced nationalistic intolerance and oppression. The dominant nationality conceives its mission to be one of ruling the state in its own interests, and thus strives to assimilate, even by forcible measures, the minority nationalities. Patriotism is fused with the sentiment of nationality, the primary loyalty being to the latter. Consequently, in striving to "realize itself" in terms of the Wilsonian doctrine of self-determination, the dominant nationality assumes the right to use the instrumentalities of the state for its own benefit. Naturally in such conditions each self-conscious nationality finds it essential to possess its own government and state: it becomes "nationalistic." In a region so intermingled and patched with nationalities it is impossible for state territorial lines to be drawn without including portions of other nationalities. These portions then become "minorities"— not merely numerical minorities, but also "oppressed" minorities. Their attempts to express themselves culturally are believed to conflict with the aspirations and solidarity of the state, and so are suppressed.

It was in such circumstances that the pre-war empires of Germany, Austria-Hungary, Turkey, and Russia had developed. Each included a number of nationalities which differed in language, customs, and sometimes religion. Each empire was based upon the dominance and control of one nationality: German, Hungarian, Turk, Russian. The subject nationalities were largely Slav in Central Europe, Finnish and Lithuanian in northern Europe, and of varied type in the Balkan region. The problem of nationalism did not arise as a general problem during the feudal period for at that time political sovereignty and the Christian Church were divorced from questions of nationality. The masses of people were illiterate, custom-bound serfs, and the nationality of their feudal lords made little or no difference in their condition.

It is in the modern period of social change that the position of the common people has improved and the spirit of nationality awakened. Economic changes, migration and city-life; the growth of education and literacy; echoes of liberty, equality, and democracy from the French Revolution and from European emigrants in America—such influences set in motion the popular restlessness, discontents, and aspirations which enter into nationalism. The thwartings from the dominant nationalities, their attitudes of contempt and superiority, and their policies of denationalization and forcible assimilation, gradually stung the subject peoples into self-consciousness and common action to defend and raise their status.[30] Such movements arose gradually. The intervening period of transition from inertness to collective action produced difficulties of adjustment for those individuals who were culturally in advance of their peoples. Many were denationalized.

The temptation to become denationalized was very powerful. Self-interest co-operated with class interest and sentiment. Many of the converts made by the Turks to Islam were thus able to preserve their estates and social position. In other countries a young man with ambitions found most of his opportunities for advancement dependent upon acquiring the language, manners, and sentiments of the ruling people. Frequently such individuals succeeded in writing their names in its halls of fame: Kosciusko, the national hero of Poland, was a Lithuanian; Napoleon was a Corsican; Kossuth, the Hungarian patriot, came from the despised Slovaks; Gambetta was of Italian

[30]The feeling of oppression became so intense that H. A. Miller has termed it an "oppression psychosis." See *Races, Nations and Classes* (Philadelphia, 1924).

stock; Cavour of French. Today even dictators may be of foreign origin: Pilsudski of Poland was by birth a Lithuanian, Stalin is a Georgian, and Hitler is a mixture of Austrian and Czech. It is evident that some of the most fervid nationalists of recent history have a background of denationalization. Is there special significance in this fact?

Denationalized nationalists have been conspicuous during the last century and a half of history, a period when nationalism has been in the ascendancy. In their personal lives they seem to have been subjected to two "pulls": that of the dominant nationality and that of the subject nationality.[31] As the nationalism of the former arose in advance of the latter it attracted the middle and upper classes of the subject nationalities. This pull was powerful because it represented cultural superiority and political power. There was pride in belonging to the superior group and in speaking its language; shame in belonging to the inferior group. But the members of the dominant nationality were apt to regard denationalized individuals with some reserve or suspicion. These had to prove their loyalty. This they did by becoming super-nationalists. Meanwhile the subject nationalities increased in group consciousness and regarded the denationalized individuals as renegades. This made it all the more necessary for the latter to prove the genuineness of their conversion.[32]

[31]This produced an ambivalent, and sometimes what Oscar Jaszi terms a "hypocritical loyalty." Writing about Austria-Hungary, he states "Each nation, even the most rebellious, tried to emphasize continually not only its legal fidelity to the dynasty, but even its enthusiastic devotion to it. We witnessed very often real outbursts of loyalty paroxysms and loyalty competitions which undermined both civic consciousness and individual honesty." *The Dissolution of the Habsburg Monarchy* (Chicago, 1929), p. 139.

[32]Some of the most oppressive members of the ruling nationalities were denationalized individuals. An extreme example, Gorgei, is mentioned by R. W. Seton-Watson. "This notorious Serb renegade was filled with such remorseless hatred for his own kith and kin, that, as he assured Count Kolowrat, he would have cursed his own mother in her grave, had he not been certain that he was the offspring of an intrigue with a Magyar officer and thus had inherited nothing save the name from his Serb father." *Racial Problems in Hungary* (London, 1908), p. 104.

The careers of Kossuth, Pilsudski, and Hitler illustrate diverse forms of denationalization. Louis Kossuth, the Magyarized Slovak, did not favor the claims of his native people, the Slovaks. Indeed in spite of his liberal ideas he was an intense Magyarist. Although he learned the Magyar language only after his childhood had passed, he then entered local politics "from which he emerged as a striking combination of demagogue and Magyar Chauvinist."[33] His denationalization earned him the thorough hatred of his close relatives.

Joseph Pilsudski, the dictator of Poland, although an arch-Polish patriot, seems to have had warmer feelings toward his native Lithuanian people. When interviewed on this subject before he became dictator he exclaimed, " 'I am so fond of my native land. It is'—he hesitated, smiled, and opened his hands with a gesture of helplessness—'a weakness of mine. . . . I have such a profound feeling for my own country that it is hard to discuss a problem so difficult and painful. A federation would be the natural solution. But the Lithuanians do not want that.' " Later he added: "I was born in Lithuania. I do not think of myself as Polish in blood. My temperament is different, my very face is different. But in culture, I am Polish." The great Polish poet, Miczkiewicz, the great Kosciusko, were both Lithuanians.[34] Probably the clue to Pilsudski's attitude is to be found in his bitter experiences with Russian attempts to assimilate both Poles and Lithuanians. His hatreds were directed toward Russia, not Poland or tiny Lithuania. Like the Poles generally he believed the Lithuanians would be better off if incorporated into a greater Poland.

Adolf Hitler, dictator of Germany, exemplifies another type. Born in Austria (Bohemia) of an Austrian (German) father and a Czech mother, Hitler grew up in a Czech frontier village

[33]*Ibid.*, p. 49.
[34]Arthur Ruhl, *New Masters of the Baltic* (New York, 1921). Adapted from pp. 238–40.

where the Germans were in the minority. This meant that he was "teased and bullied by Czech boys and humiliated by Czech teachers. It ate into Hitler's soul; it gave him a fanatical devotion to Germanism and pride in being a German."[35] In his own words he states, "I soon became a fanatical German Nationalist."[36]

German nationalism provided an escape from his personality conflicts. He was ashamed of his mother who spoke German with a Czechish accent, and resentful of his authoritarian father, an Austrian official. Shame of his mother facilitated hatred of the Slavs; resentment of his father found release in repudiation of the Austrian state. His half-peasant, half-bourgeois family was looked down on by Germans as well as by Austrians: "These subtle distinctions between in-group and out-group, and his own anomalous position in which he seemed to "belong" nowhere, deeply affected the boy."[37]

At the age of seventeen he went to the Austrian capital, Vienna. Here also he was angered by the presence of numerous Slavs; and when he heard a Czech deputy speaking in Czech in the Reichsrath his disgust was transferred to parliaments generally. His attachment to Germany caused him to develop intense hostility to the Austrian state. "Did not we boys already know that this Austrian State had and could have no love for us Germans?" In Vienna he intended to study painting, but failed in the entrance examinations. He was forced to earn his living by doing odd jobs. As a *déclassé* he had to rub shoulders with socialistic workmen, and so became hostile to social democracy. Experiences with the large and important population of Jews in Vienna then turned him into an anti-Semite, especially when he

[35]Alice Hamilton, "Hitler Speaks, His Book Reveals the Man," *Atlantic Monthly*, October, 1933, p. 399. It has also been asserted that Hitler is partly Jewish in ancestry.
[36]Adolf Hitler, *My Battle* (Boston, 1933), p. 4.
[37]Frederick L. Schuman, *The Nazi Dictatorship* (New York, 1935), p. 7.

learned that they were the leaders of social democracy: "for to my inward satisfaction I knew finally that the Jew was no German." At last he became convinced that Vienna was no place for him: "I hated the motley collection of Czechs, Poles, Hungarians, Ruthenians, Serbs, Croats, and above all that ever-fungoid growth—Jews and again Jews." He fled to Munich, Germany. He himself declares that it was his experiences in Vienna which determined his attitudes toward Judaism and social democracy, and so formed the basis for the post-war Nazi movement.[38]

Not all denationalized or "assimilated" individuals remain in this condition. As their own peoples become more active and group conscious they are likely to return to them in the rôles of leaders. Indeed in the past some of them have had a great deal to do with developing pride and aggressiveness in their people through initiating cultural and linguistic revivals. Others have become political leaders. Their denationalization has been succeeded by a rebirth of national feeling.[39]

The Jews

The Jews deserve special attention as the classic minority group in European history. Unlike other minorities, the Jews do not possess a majority anywhere, not even in present-day Palestine. The German minority in Poland may look to Germany for support, just as the Polish minority in Germany depends upon Poland; but the Jews, until very recently, have lacked a homeland, and mandated Palestine is not in a position to give effective political support. What further distinguishes

[38]All the quotations are from the English translation of Hitler's autobiography mentioned above. Although this volume is expurgated in part it illustrates admirably the political conception of nationality of the Central European peoples mentioned earlier in this section.
[39]See Chap. VII.

the Jews is their dispersed and international character.[40] But in spite of centuries of dispersal, discrimination and forced assimilation, the Jews have tenaciously maintained a group existence.

What is the basis of Jewish unity and persistence? Is it to be found in race? in religion? or in nationality? Although popularly viewed as a "race"—a biologically distinct group—the Jews do not really constitute a well-defined race.[41] Nevertheless the *sense* of kinship and the *belief* in blood relationship are powerful factors in Jewish group solidarity. The religious bond has been historically significant despite the fact that today one notes a multitude of antagonistic sects, a clash of reform with orthodoxy, and an array of skeptics and free-thinkers. Sharing a common history and an intense group consciousness related in some measure to the original homeland, Palestine, the Jews may be reckoned a nationality——the "Chosen People." In the final analysis, considering the present powerful tendency of Jews to assimilate the culture of their surroundings, the one common trait which survives longest is the consciousness of being a Jew. When this vanishes the Jew vanishes. This indeed is the perennial problem of the modern individual Jew: to be, or not to be—a Jew!

Paradoxically, perhaps, it is easiest to be a Jew when the world is hostile and socially distant, when the ghetto exists in fact as well as in law, when no luring contact with the Gentile world has planted the fatal seed of doubt. But in most countries the days of the closed ghetto have passed and have been succeeded by the attractions and repulsions of the open or voluntary ghetto. The Jew has been generally freed to participate in the larger world about him. He has penetrated deeply

---

[40]For outlying Jewish communities see Israel Cohen, *The Journal of a Jewish Traveller* (London, 1925).

[41]Physically there are great variations within the group. The Jewish cast of countenance is not found in the descendants of Jews who have left the ghetto. See Maurice Fishberg, *The Jews* (New York, 1911), Chap. II ff.

into this world, contributed largely to its culture, and yet he
does not feel quite at home in it. Once having entered it he cannot comfortably withdraw again into the ghetto. He is too
much of a Jew to be assimilated; and too little of a Jew to be
isolated. Besides, the intellectual climate of modernism has undermined the religious and racial basis of the ghetto; while the
road of Jewish nationalism leads to an *impasse*.[42]

The modern Jew, the Jew who has emerged from the ghetto,
lives in a duplex culture: Jewish and Gentile. In England he
tends to become an Englishman; in America, an American; in
Germany, a German. The less recent his immigration from
Eastern Europe the more completely is he assimilated. His children desert the "Chedarim"; they mingle with non-Jews; and
many become converted or marry out of the group. The process takes place by stages. These have been classified into four
by Arthur Ruppin in his *Jews of Today:*

(1) Orthodox Jews, of which the Jews in pre-war Russia
and Galicia were typical. Today they are found in less homo-
geneous Jewish communities. They have a low economic status,
a high birth rate, speak Yiddish or Spaniolish and are scarcely
touched by modern culture. They number about six millions,[43]
or one-half of all Jews.

(2) Jews of more liberal religious outlook, of which the
Roumanian Jews and the settlers in England and America are
typical. They have a higher economic status, a moderately high
birth rate, speak the language of the country and perhaps also
Yiddish or Spaniolish, and have been influenced by modern
culture. They number about three millions.

(3) Free-thinking Jews who ignore Jewish ritual and the

[42]That is, it cannot "solve" the Jewish problem. Palestine is not yet too
comfortable a resting place for the small number there. The vast majority
of Jews can not live in Zion. Their permanent adjustment must be made
wherever they happen to reside. In the end, however, Palestine may enable
the Jew to survive if and after he has been assimilated elsewhere.
[43]These and other figures given by Ruppin are for pre-war conditions.

Sabbath, of which the bourgeoisie of Western European countries generally are representative. They are well-to-do, have a fairly low birth rate, and speak the language of the country exclusively. Except for marriage within the faith, and occasional attendance at the synagogue, they are assimilated to the surrounding culture. A small per cent (10–30) marry non-Jews, and some (5–15 annually per 10,000 souls) are converted to the Christian faith. They total about two millions.

(4) Agnostic Jews who have broken completely from Judaism, but who hesitate to marry Christians, and who when they remain Jewish, do so because of "conscientiousness or a sense of honour, or out of family and social considerations." The rich Jews of large towns, and the university educated Jews everywhere, belong in this class. Their birth rate is low (15–20 per 1000 population); their rate of out-marriage high (30–50 per cent); and their annual rate of conversion considerable (15–40 per 10,000 souls). They number about one million.

There is a tendency for each class to supply members to the succeeding class: the orthodox contribute to the liberal, the liberal to the free thinking, and the latter to the agnostic. After about four generations assimilation is complete and the Jew has ceased to be a Jew. In some cases it moves more swiftly; in others more slowly.[44]

Such an analysis does not fully indicate the complexity of the process of Jewish assimilation. Probably there is seldom a steady, continuous movement forward, but rather a series of advances and retreats, of waves of assimilation followed by re-

[44]This is a brief summary of Ruppin (London, 1913), p. 11 ff. Arnold J. Toynbee grades the Jews as follows: Ashkenazi, Sephardi, Dönme or converted, "crypto-Jew, and *ci-devant*, Jewish Catholic—in which the Jewish ethos varies in intensity through all the degrees from maximum to vanishing point; and we observe that these variations in the intensity of the Jewish ethos correspond to variations in the severity of the penalization to which Jewry has been subjected by the Gentiles." *A Study of History*, II, p. 248.

births of Jewish consciousness. The individual meets resist-
ances, both from the prejudice of Gentiles and the traditional
teachings of the Jewish community. He may begin life in the
family as a full-fledged Jew, assimilate Gentile culture as a
youth, encounter the barriers of the adult world and then withdraw to Jewish association, perhaps ending his days in an attitude of secret doubt and perplexity, or experiencing a rebirth
of Jewish soul through Zionism. The pattern of the individual
experience will closely reflect the particular type of community
situation he encounters.[45]

The Jew today illustrates many if not all of the problems discussed in this volume. The popular view that the Jews are a
"race" produces concepts of "Jewish blood" and of "mixed
blood" Jews. Whether because of blood or not, the conflict of
social sentiments in the children of mixed marriages is real
enough. ". . . I am half a Jew by blood, but in all that I have
power to be I am not. I admire their strength, their constancy,
their intelligence, but I hate the Jew because of his nature he is
evil, while the Aryan of his nature is good.[46]

The modern Jew is likewise a cultural hybrid: half he is derived from the traditional Hebrew culture, half he is molded
by Western culture in one of its national forms. Always on
the move he appears in each country as an immigrant. His children in turn belong to the new land in a way in which he does
not: in Western lands they are divorced in language, thought
and sentiment from their parents. Yet they are seldom accepted by the Gentiles. In so far as distinctive Jewish physical

[45]See Chap. V below.
[46]Letter quoted by Henry Wickham Steed, *The Hapsburg Monarchy*,
fourth edition (London, 1919), pp. 169–70. Steed comments, "No full-
blooded 'Aryan' could write more incisively, however meagre his sympathies
for the Jews, and none could write so bitterly because none can have experienced the struggle between the two race-natures that goes on in the
minds of half-breeds when they are conscious of their dual mentality." P.
170. See also a French novel by Jacob Lévy, *Les Demi-Juifs* (Paris, 1926).

traits exist, individual Jews feel racially estranged even though they are culturally assimilated.

Therefore the Jew has a peculiarly complex problem of adjustment. Centuries of experience with this problem have left their imprint upon his character. His group life is organized upon a marginal basis, characteristically expressed in his proclivity for living in the cosmopolitan city by means of trade and banking—"business." The flexible and restless nature of his mind enables him swiftly to seize an advantage and to discount the future. He is quick to adjust himself to his environment but slow to sink his roots into it. Thus he is often regarded as a "foreign element"; and this attitude in turn prolongs his estrangement. His lack of provincialism enables him to see the life of the environing nation from the outside as well as from the inside: he becomes intellectual, thinks abstractly, and yet is introverted and subjective. Perhaps the prominent connection of Jews with such movements as capitalism (Rothschild), socialism (Karl Marx), psychoanalysis (Freud), modern science and philosophy (Einstein and Bergson) is more than accidental. These are some of the fields in which the Jew's special position and mentality find congenial expression.

Can the Jews survive as Jews in modern civilization? This much-debated question has no sure answer. The Jews have always been subject to centrifugal tendencies, and today there is probably more "Jewish blood" outside than inside the "race."[47] Yet they afford the amazing example of a nationality over 3000 years old. When anti-Semitism is severe it has a twofold consequence: some Jews, perhaps more ambitious in a worldly sense, are driven over by means of conversion;[48] others through

[47]According to Leroy-Beaulieu, perhaps five or even ten times as much. Ruppin, *op. cit.*, p. 20.

[48]Ruppin gives statistics, see pp. 183 ff. This tendency was increased by the efforts of dominant nationalities to denationalize their minorities. In this process the Jews have been notorious in taking the colour of whatever environment they were in. Seton-Watson, *op. cit.*, gives detailed information

shame, or pride and idealism, come back to their people. When anti-Semitism relaxes, the rate of intermarriage increases, and conversion, being less necessary, declines,[49] No doubt the great crisis of Jewish group survival is now developing, for modern culture not only undermines the religious basis of Judaism, but also facilitates assimilation through accelerated migration and the building up of large cities where Jews are less conspicuous and where economic contacts inevitably lead to social contacts and assimilation. Hostile reactions, like the Nazi movement in Germany, are probably temporary and serve to retard but not permanently to stop the process. Perhaps the Jews will ultimately survive only in those places—such as Palestine and certain Soviet districts[50]—where a community life having a territorial basis can be maintained. In view of the historic vitality of the Jewish people, and the recrudescence of anti-Semitism in civilized states, however, it would be foolish to predict an early end to their group identity.

for Hungary. The Hungarian Parliament of 1906 contained at least 114 Magyarized members out of a total of 375 Magyars. They were largely Jews in origin, see p. 188. The vicious atmosphere of Austria-Hungary apparently poisoned the minds of many who grew up in it. The "renegades" of all nationalities inverted their hatreds. "Conversion will sometimes change a Jew into the most ferocious and implacable Anti-Semite," wrote Virginio Gaydo, *Modern Austria*, p. 156.

[49]Ruppin, *op. cit.*, p. 189. There is also an intermediate condition where the rate of intermarriage is quite high and the rate of conversion very high. Fishberg, *op. cit.*, Chap. XXI.

[50]See Avrahm Yarmolinski, *The Jews and Other Minor Nationalities under the Soviet* (New York, 1928). The Soviet policy is not motivated by any Zionistic sentiment but rests upon the general principle of cultural (nationality) toleration.

CHAPTER IV

The Cultural Hybrid
(*Continued*)

THE PROBLEM of the Jew introduces the broader topic of all migrant peoples who occupy a minority or subordinate status in the new land. Of all the concrete situations which give rise to the cultural hybrid, that of migration seems to be the most obvious. Nevertheless, the specific experience and cultural background of the migrant people need to be considered in evaluating the difficulties of their cultural adjustment. In this chapter particular attention will be given to immigrants in the United States, to their children, and to the American Negro.

THE IMMIGRANT

In America the lot of the immigrant has been comfortable enough to give rise to legends. Enormous natural resources creating unprecedented economic opportunities have beckoned dissatisfied individuals and groups from every corner of the globe. Economic opportunity has facilitated social adjustment and cultural change so that America has been regarded as a land of freedom for the oppressed as well as a land of gold for the poor. Thus the ecstasy of a Mary Antin is understandable:

So at last I was going to America! Really, really going, at last! The boundaries burst. The arch of heaven soared. A million suns shone out for every star. The winds rushed in from outer space, roaring in my ears, "America! America!"[1]

But migration even to America has involved considerable and often painful readjustments. To some degree the individual becomes *dépaysé, déclassé* and *déraciné*—to use the vivid

[1]Mary Antin, *The Promised Land* (Boston, 1912), p. 162.

French terms. The very decision to leave family, friends, and countrymen produces some premonitory pangs of homesickness. Fear of the unknown, perhaps superstitious forebodings, throw a shadow across even the tougher and bolder spirits. Since the average immigrant's social experience and mental horizon have been quite narrow, extending scarcely beyond his local village and its nearest neighbours, the journey to America was a succession of pleasant and unpleasant revelations. The long voyage in steamer steerage seems to have been a particularly difficult ordeal; and the first glimpses of New York were not infrequently disappointing, sometimes profoundly disillusioning.

Arrived in America the immigrant undergoes a more basic. and prolonged transformation. From being simply *dépaysé* he also becomes *déclassé*, and more generally uprooted, or *déraciné*. If he has no relatives or friends to meet and help him over the first difficulties his position is indeed precarious. If ignorant of the language he is virtually isolated from the American scene. His best prospect is to find some of his countrymen with whom he can at least communicate his difficulties, and perhaps obtain assistance. So he makes his way into the immigrant colony. If he has relatives and friends from the old country he is likely to get there in any case.

At first the immigrant is a "greenhorn," as he soon discovers, sometimes to his intense chagrin. His foreign clothes and foreign manners, his name and his speech—even the expression of his countenance—mark him out as a newcomer and an alien. His countrymen who are more Americanized feel more or less good-naturedly superior to him, and advise him what to do. Some prey upon his ignorance and fears. As he changes the more external characteristics of his appearance and conduct he reduces the chances of arousing ridicule and resentment, and increases his opportunities of finding work. This makes him feel less inferior and out of place.

Being a "greenhorn" symbolizes the immigrant's initial status relative to other immigrants in the community. It does not necessarily indicate his occupational and class status. If he possesses a skill which is valued, and if he can find work, he may earn high wages and immediately rise in the esteem of his group. This does not generally occur, even among those who are skilled workers.[2] In order to subsist, or support his family, an individual may have to take whatever job he can find. The personal satisfaction and social prestige which his work in the old country gave him are lost. He becomes a *déclassé,* and thus undergoes an experience which may be the most significant phase of his immigrant experience.

The immigrant colony in America is a bridge of transition from the old world into the new; a half-way house on the road of assimilation. It looks more American than it really is: indeed the very houses may once have been the residences of the native "Four Hundred." The physical or external aspects are the most American; within this material shell, except for a certain hodge-podge mixture, breathes the weakened spirit of the old world: family life, religious activities, the daily flow of social intercourse—in short, all the intimate life of the people springs from across the water. The language used, and the manner in which it is used, become an index of the degree of assimilation. Some immigrants, particularly women who have not ventured into the American industrial world, live their lives through without learning more than a few words of the English tongue. In contrast to the immigrant in small towns, the city immigrant has little chance to meet socially the best Americans. Lacking this opportunity he may conclude that Americans are largely made up of crooked politicians, hard-boiled "cops," grasping shop-keepers, tough criminals and street bums.

[2]Louis Bloch, "Occupations of Immigrants Before and After Coming to the United States," *Quarterly Publication of the American Statistical Association,* 1920–21, Vol. XVII, p. 760.

With many, America comes to stand merely for material success—the "Almighty Dollar"—because business relations are the immigrant's chief form of contact with Americans. The ordinary American in turn, when he thinks about the subject, views the "foreigner" as so much cheap labour. Perhaps he has visions of "radicals," labour agitators, criminals, etc., connected with this stereotype; and he freely condemns the foreigner's low standard of living as well as his proclivity for sending money to his relatives in the old country. No wonder then if the immigrant is often American in terms of "interest" rather than of "sentiment." As long as he prospers he may boast to his people in the old world how well he is doing; when he fails, his attitudes toward America and his native land are inverted, though pride may keep him from writing home about it. Something of the superficiality of much Americanization as well as of the character of these ambivalent attitudes is indicated by M. E. Ravage:

My Americanized compatriots were not happy, by their own confession. As long as they kept at work or prospered at peddling, they affected a hollow gaiety and delighted in producing a roll of paper dollars (which they always carried loose in their pockets, instead of keeping them securely in purses as at home) on the least provocation, and frequented the coffeehouses, and indulged in high talk about their abilities and their prosperity, and patronizingly inquired of the greenhorn how he liked America, and smiled in a knowing way when the greenhorn replied by cursing Columbus. But no sooner did he lose his job or fail in the business of peddling than he changed his tune and sighed for the fleshpots of his native home, and hung his head when asked how he was getting on, and anathemized America and became interested in socialism. At such times it was quite apparent that America's hold on his affections was very precarious—a thing that needed constant reinforcing by means of very definite, material adhesives, to keep it from ignominious collapse.

How feeble his attachment to his adopted land was, and how easily his sentiments shifted from adoration to indifference or contempt, was strikingly illustrated by the various and contrasting names he had for America. Now it was gratefully termed the home of freedom and then with a shade of irony in the tone, he referred to it as the land of gold. If he brought home a satisfactory bargain from the pushcart merchant he beamed and sang the praises of the "all-right country," and the next moment if the article turned out to be discoloured or rotten or otherwise defective he fussed and fumed and swore that there never had been such a stronghold of fakes in all the world as this same America. His fondest hope was to become a "citisnik" of the Republic, but the merest scratching of the surface showed beyond a doubt that his desire for naturalization did not have its roots in any conversion to the principles of democratic self-government, but rather in certain eminently human motives.[3]

Nevertheless, the immigrant community gradually changes in the direction of Americanization. The pace of change is retarded by transplanted old-world customs and habits of thought. But assimilation is favoured both by the disposition to begin life anew and by the enlarged opportunities of the American environment. In the pre-war period of mass migration and urban growth the more Americanized immigrants moved out of the slums into better neighbourhoods, forming a less concentrated community of "second settlement." As the immigrant pressure from the old world decreased some communities at least have done less shifting. Much of the Americanization of immigrants has taken the form of a gradual change of the whole group.[4] To the extent that this has been true the im-

[3]*An American in the Making* (New York, 1917), pp. 83–84.
[4]It may be worth noting that the ranking of the foreign-born in the Army Tests during the war showed a regular increase according to the number of years of residence in the United States, as follows:

Years in the U. S.	0–5	6–10	11–15	16–20	Over 20 years
Median score, combined tests:	11.29	11.70	12.53	13.50	13.74

From Yerkes and Yoakum, *Psychological Examinations in the United States Army* (New York, 1920), Table 223, p. 704.

migrant experiences much less culture conflict, and becomes less of a cultural hybrid. For it is not the mere mixing of cultures which creates the marginal man, but rather the experience of the conflict of group attitudes flowing from the cultural differences.

It is when the immigrant does not settle in the immigrant community, or when he leaves this community and has closer contacts with native Americans, that the problem of his adjustment is most complex and delicate. He is then an individual on his own, or nearly on his own. If he really wishes to enter American society he must make more than the external changes and accommodations typical of the immigrant community: he must also understand and feel himself into the American spirit and its characteristics of thought and sentiment. It may be fortunate for him that the "American culture" should still be in the first stages of evolution and, with the exception of certain smaller social circles, should have a broad, democratic hospitality which counterbalances its naïve egoism. But the transition is difficult enough for even the immigrants with a European background and of Caucasian race.

The individual who has emigrated from the higher classes of a nationality with a proud and self-conscious history finds it especially difficult to identify himself with the new country. His mind is filled with vivid memories of the old life which, moreover, become idealized with distance and time. The difficulties and rebuffs of the new conditions tend to throw him back in imagination toward the land he has left. He rebels against the thought of giving up tastes and characteristics which he has formed in youth—formed in an artistic culture which seems to him superior to the "crude" and "mechanical" one he has entered.

I considered the days ahead of me. They would be sad. It would not take me long to learn the language, perhaps—but then I had to learn the ways, to know the people, to make my-self known and acknowledged by them. In the meantime I had to endure their aloofness or accept the gift of their indulgence. I had to take my place at the tail end of the line and work my way up slowly, asking and accepting help—I, so proud, who carried in my veins the best blood of my land and in my mind more knowledge than most of them, the wisdom of the race that had given civilization its stamp! A sentiment of revolt was aroused in me. I pronounced aloud absurd words of angry pride. I invoked the day when, breaking the fetters that held me bound, I should make myself recognized for what I was worth by the new people; and I meant to be worth more than they! But, then, for the first time, the thought occurred to me: "Are you so sure of this? Do you know anything about these people you expect to surpass? What have you done thus far in your life to justify your claim? What can you show? Isn't there perhaps something that this country can teach you?"

Then the words of my brother Benjamin came back to my mind: "Be patient. This country is quite different from Europe, but it has something to teach you, all its own. It has beauties that one cannot detect at first sight, it has ideals back of the facts and of the actions of men. There is little that can be seen at a glance, but you will feel it after a long, intimate contact. Some day you will love it."

For a moment I was more unhappy than I had ever been in my life. I felt that, to love this country, I had to tear from my heart what had been most dear to me; I would have to change my tastes, change my life, change my will. What I had loved and dreamed and desired was far away and every day would take it farther from me. Everybody and everything would be leading me into the new life—and I clung with all my force to the memories of the old world over there![5]

Compare the above anticipations with the reflections of one who did not become assimilated:

[5]Silvio Villa, *The Unbidden Guest,* pp. 141–42. Another type of isolation and hardship was encountered on the frontier. This led one educated German to exclaim, "Whoever wants to adapt himself quickly in America and be-come altogether happy must come here as a child." See Edith Abbott, *Historical Aspects of the Immigration Problem: Select Documents* (Chicago, 1926), p. 309.

. . . Two reasons prevented my "Americanization" in the deeper sense of the term: the divergencies which I began to discover after a longer stay in this country between most of the aspirations actually predominant in American society and certain ideals which, in my cosmopolitan training, I have learned to revere as the best part of the general human civilization, independent of national differences; and—more particularly—the attitude of American society towards foreigners and foreign values. . . .

Among other things there is the lack of social freedom, the oppression of the individual by all kinds of traditional or recently created social norms. I have not seen in Europe anything comparable to it except, perhaps, in small and very isolated provincial towns. . . .

No European society I know acts as if it possessed and knew everything worth while and had nothing to learn, whereas this is precisely the way American society acts toward a foreigner as soon as he ceases to play the rôle of a passing "curiosity" and wants to take an active part in American life. I do not think most Americans realize how revolting to a more or less educated emigrant is their naive attitude of superiority, their astonishing self-satisfaction, their inability and unwillingness to look on anything foreign as worth being understood and assimilated. This may work with the peasant who is used in the old country to attitudes of superiority on the part of the higher class, is desirous of imitating them, and finds in this country exactly the same atmosphere, only connected with an unknown language and unknown institutions which make real imitation more difficult. . . .

In the same line, and perhaps even more revolting for the reflecting foreigner who comes with the idea of working and settling in this country, is the current tendency of American society to interpret the relation between the immigrant and America as that of one-sided benefit and one-sided obligation. This is again an attitude which I have never met in Europe, though European countries are incomparably more crowded than America. . . .[6]

[6]These are portions of a larger document to be found in R. E. Park and H. A. Miller, *Old World Traits Transplanted*, Document No. 84, pp. 107 ff.

Commenting upon the preceding document, Eugene S. Bagger,[7] a Magyar intellectual, analyzes the sources of discontent of the European intellectual in America in terms of loss of status, both social and economic; the lack of the richer European cultural atmosphere including the continental café; and the intellectual isolation which "results in a sickly overestimation of his importance, a hypertrophied sensitiveness and that notion of omnipotence which comes from the absence of tests. . . . Just as the lack of academic standards favours an individualism that frequently is mere crankiness, the lack of intellectual give-and-take may result in an elephantiasis of self-consciousness." The result often is a tendency to blame America for the individual's own failure in adjustment. The cultural differences are too great to be easily bridged.

It is impossible to know how many immigrants have returned to Europe[8] because of such psychological maladjustments. How many remain in America in spite of them—because of economic necessity, the bond of children, etc.—is again a matter of speculation. Nor is it accurate to assume that only educated immigrants experience such maladjustments, although one would expect them to have a higher proportion.[9]

Those immigrants who become Americanized by way of the immigrant community go through the fires of two melting-pots: that of the partly Americanized immigrant community, and that of the native American life outside the community. M. E. Ravage, after becoming adjusted to the New York ghetto, felt impelled to learn what the "real" America was like. So he went alone to the University of Missouri. Here he underwent

[7]*Ibid.*, Document No. 85, pp. 113 ff.

[8]For an interesting account of an Englishman who compromised by settling in Canada see Frederick P. Grove, *A Search for America: The Odyssey of an Immigrant* (New York, 1928).

[9]That rough clothes and a pick and shovel often conceal a talented mind is apparent enough from the life-histories of several published autobiographies. For one which is particularly impressive see Pascal d'Angelo: *Son of Italy* (New York, 1924).

a second and more thorough Americanization—although not without a series of difficulties and throwbacks. Finally he felt he could affirm, "I was not a man without a country. I was an American."[10]

The conflict of cultures working in the immigrant's mind is more intricate and profound than that expressed by the concept of the *déclassé*. The idea of the uprooted, of the *déraciné,* comes nearer to the heart of the problem. The individual undergoes transformation in the social, mental and emotional aspects of his personality, each reacting upon the other. Some immigrants speak of these changes as constituting a second birth and childhood:

. . . My first birth was distant and dim and unreal, for I was almost three years old when I awoke, and most of the shock had disappeared. The old world and I grew up together. We just grew in blissful ignorance of one another's growing pains. And my first childhood stole upon me softly.

Not so my second childhood. I was born full-grown, so to speak, and, therefore, was aware of my new birth. I regressed to the greed of infancy. My curiosity was that of a child. My manners lacked poise of adulthood. My angers, fears, and joys were fleeting and childish, and divided the new world into absolute categories—into good and evil. The new world cut into my clay and chronicled something which was not there before— another code of thoughts and feelings.[11]

No doubt the tougher temperaments find the process of transition easier than the sensitive. Possibly those individuals

[10]*An American in the Making,* p. 265.
[11]Carl Christian Jensen, *An American Saga* (Boston, 1927), pp. 64–65. Lewis Mumford, in *The Golden Day: A Study in American Experience and Culture* (New York, 1926), refers to the immigrant in these words, "Unfortunately, a man without a background is not more truly a man: he has merely lost the scenes and institutions which gave him his proper shape. If one studies him closely, one will find that he has secretly arranged another background, made up of shadows that linger in the memory, or he is uneasy and restless, settles down, moves on, comes home again, lives on hopeless tomorrows, or sinks back into mournful yesterdays. Pp. 38–39.

thought of as primarily *extrovert* get on in the pragmatic American world more readily than do the *introverts*. In addition, it may be that in the process of adjustment, introverted peoples become extroverted, particularly when, like the Irish, they make a successful group adjustment. However that may be, the very sensitive person, inclined to analyze feelings, sometimes undergoes shock pervading the entire mental and emotional life. The following example indicates what deep and prolonged disturbance such immigrants experience:

The first period was characterized by a loss in emotional life. There was: (1) a fading of emotional tones [*Gefühlsbetonung*] and a gradual reappearance. I forgot for some years that birds sing, flowers have odour, stars shine. I lost interest in theatre, concert, fiction; (2) a replacement of emotional standards by opportunistic notions. I did not think of what I liked or disliked, but of what was advantageous or disadvantageous. There was a decided shifting from emotional to rational motives. I found it very difficult to adopt a new code of conduct because of an entirely foreign emotional basis. . . .

After some years of life in America a reconstruction of my emotional life took place. I was building up another emotional basis. Some of the means to it were: (1) a groping for new interest (literature, bibliography, history, world politics, science); (2) participation in public interests and activities (*Vereinigung alter Deutscher Studenten in Amerika*, Bibliographical Society, Rifle Club, Military Work); (3) new social contacts (clubs, societies); (4) my family interests.

The transition period caused by my emigration lasted nearly twenty years and was retarded by the Great War. A return to normal emotional life showed itself by the absence of dreams in which I saw myself back at home again. Such dreams were extremely frequent at first. Now all my plans and hopes centered in America and the desire for a permanent return to Europe ceased. Also the fear of isolation in America and a sentiment of coherence with the new country and identification developed and has probably completely established itself. . . .

A very serious handicap in my new life in America was the loss of confidence in my judgment which the shifting from one emotional standard to another one caused. Whenever we must decide quickly we judge subconsciously. The subconscious life was destroyed and badly disorganized. I never knew if my reactions would be in line with the new code of conduct and had to think and reflect. Whenever I decided on the spur of the moment I found myself out of sympathy with my environment. I did not feel as they felt and therefore I felt wrongly according to their standards. To act instinctively in an American fashion and manner was impossible, and I appeared slow and clumsy. The proverbial slowness of foreigners is largely due to this cause.[12]

Those immigrants who have written and published their stories are probably not entirely typical of the average immigrant. Obviously they are more articulate, superior in their gifts of expression. Perhaps they have also been more successful, and so feel themselves examples of the American ideal: the "self-made man." The very process of telling their stories gives them recognition and confirms their identification with America.

A visit to the old country often has an important influence in promoting American adjustment. Back in his native community he may as a successful immigrant play the part of an American. Perhaps he discovers how small and how backward, though charming, his early environment really was. His Americanization, incomplete though it may be, has unfitted him for his former life.[13] He concludes that America is the best place after all. Louis Adamic, after a stirring welcome in his native country, ends his fascinating volume with a stronger sense of belonging to America, "I feel very good, somehow. I'm going home again—to America. I guess that's where I really belong.

[12]R. E. Park and H. A. Miller, *Old World Traits Transplanted*, pp. 54–56.
[13]Others less Americanized settle down in the old country, sometimes because they are under economic compulsion to do so; sometimes because their savings in America enable them to live in ease and superiority for the remainder of their lives.

These ten months in Yugoslavia have made me, among other things, highly appreciative of the United States."[14]

The average immigrant does not become thoroughly assimilated in a cultural sense, but he can and often does become a citizen;[15] and he makes a contribution to the economic development of the country. His membership in the immigrant community helps to give him the self-respect and stability which are essential to a human life. At the same time it insulates him from the higher temperatures of the melting pot, and so makes him less of a marginal man. The lesser number of immigrants who, by participation in the broader American scene, go farther in assimilation experience greater inner change but have a sense of achievement in proportion to their acceptance by Americans. While cultural differences between and within immigrant groups from European countries influence the extent of assimilation, the great barrier—colour prejudice—does not affect them as it does immigrants from non-white countries.[16]

The immigrant who marries and settles down in the United States undergoes further assimilation through his children. They are the means of introducing American ideas and practices into the intimate life of the home. Conflict may arise in this process: conflict which sometimes splits the family and leads the immigrant to feel that he has lost his future as well as his past. In other instances conflict is at a minimum and the immigrant participates vicariously in American life through his children and grandchildren. But this aspect of Americanization

[14]*The Native's Return: An Immigrant Visits Yugoslavia and Discovers His Old Country* (New York, 1934), p. 313. His immigrant experiences were related in a volume entitled *Laughing in the Jungle* (New York, 1932).

[15]In 1930, 58.8 per cent of the foreign-born in the United States were naturalized citizens; 9.3 per cent had taken out first papers; 28.3 per cent were aliens; and 3.5 per cent were unknown. This represented a 10 per cent increase in naturalization over the 1920 figures.

[16]The 1930 census recorded the following non-white immigrant groups in the United States: Mexican 1,422,533; Japanese 138,834; Chinese 74,954; Filipino 45,208; Hindu 3,130; Korean 1,860.

introduces the subject of the next section—the immigrant's children, or the "second generation."

THE SECOND GENERATION

The children of the immigrant are in a distinctive social situation. As native-born residents they are identified with the land of their birth and its institutions; but as children of immigrants they inevitably absorb much of the culture carried over from the "old country." Thus they are the meeting point of two streams of culture. To the extent that the two cultures conflict they experience this conflict as a personal problem.

Usually the first language learned by the second generation will be the mother-tongue of the parents. Within the intimate circle of the family it will be natural for them to acquire standards of morals and religion, food and health habits, which are derived from the ancestral home. The subtler influences of personality—sentiments and patterns of thought—also will be largely of foreign origin. These are the culture traits to which the immigrant clings longest, for, being unconscious of them, he cannot cut them out of his own character.

The greater the difference between the ancestral culture and the American culture, the greater will be the problem of the second generation's adjustment. In general, those whose background is northwest European make the adjustment most easily. Their Protestantism blends readily with the major religious and moral trends of the United States; their industrial and urban experience promotes occupational adjustment in the larger cities; their higher ratios of literacy and their democratic political traditions are important in helping them to understand the American political process; and, in several cases, their family systems and individualistic attitudes toward marriage facilitate assimilation in the deeper realm of the *mores*. On the other hand, those who come from most of the countries in southeastern Europe are faced with a greater problem of adjustment in customs and thought. Their religions (chiefly Roman and Greek Catholic) produce a certain amount of estrangement in that sphere; their rural and peasant experience is a handicap in urban adjustment; their greater illiteracy and ignorance of representative government are obstacles to effective democratic citizenship; while their patriarchal family traditions and kinship form of family organization are incompatible with American ideals of love and marriage. The element of time is also against the latter group of immigrants, for most of them have come to the United States since about 1890.[17] Their children make up the crucial part of the second-generation problem of European origin, but the factors of nationality, social class and individuality are also important.

The most significant fact in the personal histories of the second generation is that they are natives of the country. This automatically makes them American citizens and determines the direction of their careers and major loyalties. Unlike their parents they are neither *dépaysé* nor *déclassé*, and even the concept of *déraciné* cannot be applied to them without qualification.

As native-born citizens, the second generation automatically tend to accept the institutions of the country. This is particularly true when they mingle with children of native descent. When the young child enters school he assimilates its standards and points of view. The Pilgrim Fathers become his ancestors —"our forefathers." He accepts the standards of his school-

[17]In 1930 the foreign-born from northwestern Europe numbered 5,259,607, while those from southeastern Europe totalled 6,483,278. The second generation, including those of mixed (*i.e.*, foreign and native) parentage, totalled 13,506,053 of northwest European descent; 9,429,457 of southeast European descent. These figures do not include those from Canada or any other countries outside Europe. Our *entire* foreign-born population totalled 13,366,407; our *entire* second generation population, 25,361,186. Adding these figures we have 38,727,593 persons not fully assimilated to American life, nearly one-third of our population. If to this total the 11,891,143 Negroes and 332,-397 Indians are added, one secures a crude statistical picture of the race and nationality problems of the United States.

mates in every detail—dress, diet, language, hygiene, play. He refuses to wear the clothing or to eat the food they ridicule. The English language quickly wins his allegiance, and soon he may baffle his parents by answering them in English rather than in the mother-tongue, especially in public. He strives to change his home conditions—particularly from the age of adolescence on—so that he will not be ashamed to bring his schoolmates there. Sometimes the key to the shy and retiring behaviour of the second generation is this sensitiveness about his foreign parents and home life; it may eventually lead him to break home ties completely.

The doubtful social status of the second generation gives rise to a concern for status. This finds expression statistically in two important spheres: marriage and occupation. Delaying or avoiding marriage is one method of raising one's economic and social position. The children of foreign parentage marry less: in 1920, 51.0 per cent of the males and 54.0 per cent of the females fifteen years old and over were married, whereas the figures were 58.9 per cent and 60.4 per cent for males and females, respectively, among the native white of native parentage; and 67.6 per cent and 69.7 per cent for males and females, respectively, among the foreign-born.[18] The second generation who marry also do so at later ages, and they have fewer children. In occupation they seek the white-collar positions, especially clerical and professional.[19]

One of the most powerful factors in assimilation is the Amer-

[18]Niles Carpenter, *Immigrants and Their Children*, Census Monograph VII (Washington, 1927), Table 100, p. 214; discussion on pp. 216 ff. These differences cannot be entirely accounted for by age distribution, sex ratio or urban-rural distribution. See E. Groves and W. F. Ogburn, *Marriage and Family Relationships* (New York, 1928), p. 248.

[19]Carpenter, *op. cit.*, see Table 123, p. 272. In 1920, 12.9 per cent of the second generation gainfully employed workers ten years of age and over were to be found in clerical occupations. For the foreign-born it was 3.4 per cent, and for the native white of native parentage, 8.5 per cent.

ican public school. Here life-long friendships may be formed; here the spirit of a rough democracy rules; here the seeds of patriotism are planted and cultivated; here vocational ideals are first envisaged; here also ideas and sentiments of romantic love and marriage take root and flourish. The school initiates the child into an understanding of the American heritage. Thus the second generation have intimate experiences in the *mores* of America which their parents rarely have. Because of this difference the conflict of parents and children, although not always overt, is fundamental in nature.

The tension in the mind of the second generation is more pervasive and profound than appears on the surface. He is bound to his parents by the usual family sentiments. But his loyalty to them clashes with his loyalty to his friends and to the American culture which they symbolize. The ways of his friends stand for his future; the ways of his parents for his past. "They are so old-fashioned!" is his common complaint. The foreign origin of his parents, their lack of education, their ignorance of American standards all tend to give him an attitude of superiority. This reverses the usual relationship of the generations. In rejecting his parent's advice or authority he has the moral support of the American community. He may even come to despise his parents as "foreigners" and to repudiate the family name.[20]

Such clashes are tragedies for the parents; they are hazardous for the children and the community. The guidance and control which parents must normally assume to socialize their children are weakened or distorted, perhaps entirely frustrated. It

[20]Changes of name illustrate two aspects of the process of assimilation: (1) those changes which are made chiefly in order to facilitate pronunciation and spelling, but which do not necessarily remove the evidence of ancestral origin; (2) those changes of name which completely conceal the nationality origin, and are intended to do so. This is a form of "passing." See Chap. IX.

is then that the children are more likely to become social problems.[21] Their manners and morals suffer because they imitate the grosser phases of American life, especially in industry and business, or merely copy each other. They lack contact with the finer aspects of American life, and often develop an inferiority feeling in a cultural sense. This feeling finds compensation in a superiority feeling toward the parental culture.

The autobiography of E. G. Stern, *My Mother and I,* is an example of the foreign-born child whose cultural situation became that of the second generation. Growing up in an immigrant colony she learned of American ways only through her schooling and reading. The school situation led to assimilation, and this in turn to estrangement and conflict with her parents, particularly her rabbi father:

> My books were doors that gave me entrance into another world. Often I think that I did not grow up in the ghetto but in the books I read as a child in the ghetto. The life in Soho passed me by and did not touch me, once I began to read. My interests, most of my memories and associations, were bound in the covers of books. No longer did our neighbours find occasion to censure for playing: I read incessantly. . . . As I grew older I refused to speak anything but English. In the street I would whisper constantly to mother to speak English. Mother would try, but all she could manage was an occasional "You know" or a "pleesameecha" to introductions. Of course I did not realize that unconsciously I was striving to break down all barriers between America, and me, and my mother. I felt myself intensely a part of America.

The mother sympathized with her daughter's aspirations: "to the standards of the people I was coming to know she altered her standards, her speech, her dress. She even altered the whole plan of her home for me."[22] But with college life there came a time when she felt uncomfortable even with her mother.

[21]See Chap. X.				[22]Page 98.

I was an alien in my mother's home.

I loathed it at home. Oh, it was not the poverty I minded! I have never wanted *money*. But the women who came in their slovenly dresses, content in their stupidity and their sloth, the men who spoke intolerantly and without understanding, of religion and economics, the pale girls who simpered and toiled with the one aim of a dreary married life, the young men who were untidy and dull or overbearing and conceited when they had education—that was what I saw in the ghetto. I could not look into its heart as I since have done.[23]

Such culture conflict does not always end in the snapping of family ties. Differences of opinion may result in a compromise, or may be merely tolerated. They may cease with the gradual Americanization of the parents and the increased understanding brought about by the maturing of the children. Improvement in economic circumstances, or precedents won by older brothers and sisters, may benefit the younger children in a family. Nevertheless, the strain of culture conflict in the immigrant family is a factor which greatly complicates the lives of millions of persons in the United States.

When the second generation are the objects of race prejudice and discrimination their position is particularly difficult. Their tendencies toward assimilation arouse the anxiety and opposition of their parents; their lack of assimilation incurs the antipathy of the native-born. They are between two fires. This condition is more or less true of every second-generation group, but it is most apparent among those who differ considerably from the American type. Southeastern Europeans including Slavs, Jews and Orientals are the outstanding illustrations.

The Slav immigrant is generally of recent peasant origin and occupies a lowly status in America. Often he "is unable to inform his offspring adequately who he is, what his old ancestry is like, what his background (which, *ipso facto*, is his children's

[23]Pages 135-36.

background) consists of. He tells his numerous sons and daughters that he is a Pole, a Croatian, a Slovak, a Slovenian; but that is about all. The children do not know what that really means."[24] This cultural impoverishment, together with names such as Wojciezkowaki and Krmpotick which arouse the ridicule, the contempt or merely the indifference of Americans, produces a devastating sense of inferiority—even a sense of estrangement from America.

The Jews, like other second-generation immigrants, tend to adopt American customs, but they retain their religion, generally in a less orthodox form. Then they discover that some anti-Semitism has also crossed the Atlantic. They encounter this antipathy all the more suddenly because their own advance is so swift. Their background of urban experience, their intense group consciousness, and their developed organizations, enable them to make rapid progress in adjustment to American conditions. Thus they offer keen competition to the older inhabitants and arouse their hostility. When their names and manners do not point them out, some second-generation Jews can be identified by their physical appearance or facial expression, so that anti-Jewish sentiment is more easily focussed upon them. To many young Jews it comes as a distinct shock to discover that they are not fully accepted as Americans.[25]

When the second-generation Oriental is considered, the factor of racial appearance is crucial. The Jew, like the Slav, can, if he will, change his religion and his name, and in our cosmopolitan city life pass as an American. This is seldom possible for the Oriental. His physical traits are too manifest. His soul

---

[24]Louis Adamic, "Thirty Million New Americans," *Harper's Magazine*, November, 1934, p. 686. This contains an interesting account of the Slav second generation. Second-generation Italians often have acute difficulties. See, for example, John Fante, "The Odyssey of a Wop," *The American Mercury*, September, 1933.

[25]For a particularly good example see Ludwig Lewisohn, *Up Stream* (New York, 1922). See below, Chap. VI.

may be American but his face is Oriental.[26] Because of this it seems essential to classify the second generation into two types: those who present no racial (physical) barrier to assimilation, especially in terms of intermarriage; and those who do. The problem of the latter is less transitory—it extends into the third generation, and possibly farther.

As the children of the Oriental immigrant become Americanized, culture conflict arises within the family. There is no essential difference between this type of conflict in the Oriental immigrant family and that of the European immigrant family. The customs differ but the form of the conflict is the same. The divergence between Oriental *mores* which stress family solidarity, patriarchal authority, and respect for ancestors, and the individualistic, equalitarian American standards is particularly great.[27] The young generation complains about the conservatism of its elders, while the latter see the former as lacking in respect, good behaviour, and interest in the ancestral culture.

From the American side the second generation Oriental also feels a certain estrangement. He is considered and treated as an Oriental, not as an American. He meets discrimination, especially in those localities where his racial group has settled in sufficient numbers to create competition with white Americans. Even in Hawaii, where opportunities have been relatively greater and racial tolerance noteworthy, many young Orientals will agree with the statement of a young Japanese:

I feel that the Japanese, second generation as well as first generation, are viewed with suspicion. Unwritten laws favour the whites and keep Orientals down. We are not considered

[26]For some interesting discussions see the Oriental issue of the *Survey*, May, 1926; also the recent story of Aifi Tashiro, "The Rising Son of the Rising Sun," *New Outlook*, September, 1934, pp. 36–40.
[27]For a discussion and illustrative cases see W. C. Smith, "The Second Generation Oriental Americans," *Journal of Applied Sociology*, 10 (1923); also his "Changing Personality Traits of Second Generation Orientals in America," *American Journal of Sociology*, May, 1928.

Americans. We are regarded as aliens and people believe we will always remain Japanese. We of the second generation, on the other hand, are aliens to our parents. That makes us a lost-generation! Our children will feel better—but what good does that do us? Perhaps intermarriage will solve the problem, but, again, what good will that do us of this generation?

Lack of acceptance by Americans is disillusioning and often discouraging. It leads some to return to the Orient. But this is not generally practicable, for the second generation are too Americanized to adjust themselves to their ancestral lands. They do not know the language well, if at all; their manners, customs, and conception of life make them strangers in the land of their fathers. What may happen in such a situation has been graphically described in the following incident:

I recently had the curious experience of talking with a young Japanese woman who was not only born in the United States, but was brought up in an American family, in an American college town, where she had almost no association with members of her own race. I found myself watching her expectantly for some slight accent, some gesture, or intonation that would betray her racial origin. When I was not able, by the slightest expression, to detect the oriental mentality behind the oriental mask, I was still not able to escape the impression that I was listening to an American women in a Japanese disguise.

A few months later I met this same young woman after she had returned from her first, and perhaps her last, visit to Japan. She was unusually reticent about her experiences, but she explained that it was impossible for her to remain longer in Japan, although she had had every intention of doing so. She had found herself at a peculiar disadvantage there, because, though she looked like a Japanese, she was unable to speak the language; and besides, her dress, language, everything about her, in fact, betrayed her American origin. The anomaly struck the Japanese public as something scandalous, almost uncanny. When she appeared on the street, crowds followed her. They resented,

perhaps even more at the time because of the recent passage of
the Alien Land Law, the appearance of a Japanese woman in
the masquerade of an American lady.[28]

So the second generation Oriental becomes a "problem." He
belongs neither to America nor to the Orient. Culturally he is
an American; racially he is of the Orient. He cannot identify
himself completely with either civilization. There is no easy
road for him out of this dilemma.[29]

In the final analysis the adjustment of immigrants and their
descendants is conditioned by the possibility of interracial marriage. Where this is permitted by law and public sentiment,
assimilation proceeds swiftly and with minor difficulties. Where
sentiment is adverse, race problems are prolonged, or even accentuated. The rates of interracial marriage, therefore, are an
index of both racial adjustment and the degree to which particular groups are marginal. In the United States the rates of
interracial marriage are highest for groups of northwest European origin, intermediate for nationalities from central and
southeastern Europe, and lowest for Jews, Orientals and Negroes.[30]

What the issues of contemplated intermarriage may mean to
the individual can be illustrated by the following account:

My real problem centered around the fact that when I entered University, through incidental contacts I discovered I was
in love with a Gentile. There was a complete turmoil. I could
not bring him home, had to lie when I saw him, to listen to my

[28]Robert E. Park, *The Survey*, May 1, 1926, p. 136.
[29]See the discussion of this by Kazuo Kawai, "Three Roads, and None
Easy," *Survey*, May 1, 1926, pp. 164 ff.
[30]For various statistical studies, see Niles Carpenter, *Immigrants and Their
Children*, Census Monograph VII (Washington, 1927); Julius Drachsler,
Intermarriage in New York City (New York, 1921); Edmund de S. Brun-
ner, *Immigrant Farmers and Their Children* (Garden City, New York, 1929);
and T. J. Woofter, *Races and Ethnic Groups in American Life* (New
York, 1933). For Hawaii, see the forthcoming study by Romanzo Adams,
Interracial Marriage in Hawaii.

parents' recriminations and horrible suggestions, and threats to completely disown me. I found myself poisoned and suspicious; I found that I hated the thought of having a child who might be big and blond and blue-eyed and phlegmatic and mechanically minded and slow. I could not have a Gentile child. He admitted he did not want a Jewish baby, although it is probable he could more easily have reconciled himself to that than I. And our romance ended. The problem became of grave concern to me at that time; I read books on intermarriage, on the problem of assimilation, on the Jewish culture heritage; I interviewed people and talked of nothing else—it was the most important problem of my life, and it amazed me beyond all else to find friends of mine, good Jews, who wondered why I got so heated on the subject. And now with the romance quite buried I wonder myself. It is really not of much moment to me. All my intimate social contacts are with Jews; I am, as I have always been, proud of being a Jew, and my child shall be Jewish. I still am objective enough occasionally to be amused at Jewish chauvinism, but justify my attitudes that on this basis I am most contented.[31]

THE AMERICAN NEGRO

Aside from the question of the mixed bloods,[32] Negroes in the United States are a particularly interesting minority group. Unlike most other racial and national minorities they have not a traditional culture of their own making. The immigrants, the Jews, nationality minorities in Europe or elsewhere, have a distinctive cultural background, usually including a distinctive language. When such groups have become racially conscious and have reacted to the attitude of the dominant group by some collective movement, they have turned inward and revived their peculiar customs and speech. By this action they have sought to differentiate themselves from the other group. It has been a means of giving expression to their collective self-respect and pride.

[31]From a life history (manuscript).   [32]See above, Chap. II.

Upon being taken as a slave to the United States the Negro was completely uprooted from his particular African culture. The slave-trade in Africa generally separated the individual from members of his family and tribe. Once he had arrived in this country he was sold to some white man and separated further from relatives and friends. Thus he became an individual without a group and was all the more easily incorporated into the slave system with other *déracinés* like himself. As a slave he became partly Americanized, and subsequently adopted an attitude of superiority toward more recent newcomers:

The attitude of the plantation slave to each fresh arrival seems to have been much like that of the older immigrant toward the greenhorn. Everything that marked him as an alien was regarded as ridiculous and barbaric.[33]

The significance of this estrangement from Africa may be seen today in the form which race consciousness and race pride take among Negroes. They cannot return to a folk culture; they have no distinctive vernacular to revive; there is no ancestral land except America which can be idealized—for the Garvey "Back to Africa" movement probably did not mean any real understanding of, or desire to return to, Africa.[34] Consequently coloured people are forced to express themselves in the only culture they know—that of white America. This means that the Negro's efforts to improve himself and his race necessitate his becoming more like the white man, not in differentiating himself. By equalling the white man he demonstrates his ability and refutes the stigma of inferiority.

[33]Robert E. Park, "Education in Its Relation to the Conflict and Fusion of Cultures," *Publications of the American Sociological Society,* Vol. XIII, 1918, p. 46.

[34]E. Franklin Frazier writes, "Those who support this Movement pay for it because it gives them what they want—the identification with something that makes them feel like somebody among white people who have said they were nobody." "The Garvey Movement," *Opportunity,* November, 1921, p. 347.

But this is exactly what the white people who are prejudiced resent. They feel that the Negro should "remain a Negro." He should "stay in his place." Every effort of the latter to improve himself beyond a certain point is likely to be considered by this group of whites—and they are not all in the South—as an attempt to secure "social equality," if not to marry the white man's daughter. White Americans have a rather fixed conception of what the Negro is and should be, and any deviation from this surprises and confuses them, if it does not arouse their hostility.

The effect of the white man's "stereotype" of the Negro has been something like a wall imprisoning the activities of the educated coloured person. For example, the latter if a singer is expected to be able to sing only spirituals. So ingrained is this attitude that, when a Negro musician shows himself a master of a German or French classic, white individuals can be found who will insist that "He is much better in the Negro folk-songs!" The Negro novelist or poet until recently has had difficulty in finding a white audience for anything not written in the dialect; the Negro actor has been confined almost exclusively to the rôle of the black-faced comedian.

The white man's conception of the Negro has lagged behind the latter's cultural advance. The Negro who is affected by this attitude is in a marginal situation. He is not accommodated to the conventional white stereotype of the Negro; his conception of himself is in conflict with the white man's conception of him. Thence arises a sense of frustration, of injustice, and a consciousness of prejudice.

It is not merely a question of the white man's prejudice, but also of inconsistency in the white man's attitudes. The issue of slavery was instrumental in bringing about the Civil War, out of which the Negro emerged a free man and a citizen. His legal equality was written into the Federal Constitution, but this did not alter deep-seated sentiments in the South. In spite of the Federal Constitution, these sentiments have been expressed by discrimination in local legislation and custom. Even in the North support for racial equality has become largely formal or sentimental. The coloured person who thinks about his racial status cannot but be impressed by this inconsistency in the theory and practice of American democracy. This is particularly true of those who are more ambitious and educated.

The misconception which most white people have of the Negro can be explained in part by the nature of their mutual relations. White people do not generally have contacts with educated coloured persons; indeed, they scarcely know that educated Negroes exist. Consequently they form their notions of the Negro from traditions and current anecdotes, and in certain sections by contacts with servants and other subordinates, or even by casual observation of unskilled labourers and ne'er-do-wells. Naturally they cannot know much of what goes on in the minds of Negroes. Undoubtedly they know less about Negroes than the latter know about them.[35] The coloured man or woman sees the white man in practically every aspect of life: in the intimacy of home and club life, in every occupation and rôle. The white man speaks his mind freely, without restraints; the coloured man listens and observes, but answers nothing. His reserve is his protection.

In spite of emancipation Negroes still feel it necessary to conceal their thoughts from white people. In speech and in manner they may convey the impression of concurrence and contentment when at heart they feel quite otherwise. In these recent days the psychologists have come to call this a "defense mechanism," and some are sure it is the only thing which enables the Negro to survive in his contact with the white man.

[35]For a discussion of this see Robert R. Moton, *What the Negro Thinks* (Garden City, New York, 1929), especially Chaps. I and II.

Negroes are sometimes warned, even now, that they dare not manifest any resentment toward mistreatment; that the safest policy to pursue is to acquiesce in the judgment of those white people who have manifested a friendly attitude toward them and appeal to their conscience for the redressing of wrongs and corrections of abuses. Small wonder that the Negro is so generally secretive.[36]

The white man knows even less about educated or upper-class Negroes. Due to segregation and discrimination, they live apart from him. "They own their own homes, so the white landlord does not see them; they carry insurance with a Negro insurance company, so no white collector comes to the door; their grocery man is a coloured man; they travel by auto rather than by street car or train; as a rule they live in the segregated districts; their physician, lawyer, dentist, and often their banker is a Negro."[37] Not knowing that such Negroes exist, the traditional conception of the Negro which the white man has acquired from the past and from Negro servants is not changed. To him, all Negroes are more or less alike. The term which he generally uses—"nigger"—expresses his conception, whether his attitude is friendly, indifferent or hostile.

It is the advanced and educated coloured people who are most acutely in the anomalous position of the marginal man. They live on the same level of culture as the corresponding white classes, but they are subject to the attitudes and treatment which the white man bestows upon less advanced Negroes. In their own race they occupy a high status; from the white point of view they are inferior. Legally they are American citizens; practically they are excluded from the white American world.

Among the educated class of Negroes, the mulattoes occupy a conspicuous position. They predominate in the higher circles of Negro society and contribute more than their proportionate

36 *Ibid.*, pp. 12–13.   37 *Ibid.*, pp. 17–18.

share to Negro leadership.[38] This fact has led some to assume that it is the influence of white blood which makes them superior, but others (or perhaps the same persons) are likely to believe that race-mixture is biologically degenerating and should be stopped at all costs. The same process of race mixture is claimed to produce two opposite effects. Is there not some other explanation for the achievement of the mulatto?

The history of the Negroes in the United States offers a clue to the greater achievements of the mulattoes. From the very beginning they secured a more favourable status in the eyes of the white man. They were made the favoured slaves, worked in the house of the master rather than as field hands, and benefited from their closer white contacts. The white master, if he were also the father, often felt a moral obligation toward his mulatto children—this obligation taking the form of providing education, bequeathing property, and frequently granting freedom.[39] The mulattoes thus achieved an early advantage or start over the unmixed Negroes, an advantage which has been maintained to the present day, although more and more black individuals are rising to Negro leadership.

As with the mixed blood generally, there has been a tendency for the mulatto to identify himself with the white race rather than with the black race. But the white man refuses to accept the mulatto and, indeed, refuses to give him a status superior to that of the black. From the white point of view, a drop of Negro blood makes a person a Negro, no matter how "white" he may appear. The very fact that the mulatto is closer to the white man in cultural attainments and physical traits renders it all the more difficult for him to accept this extreme colour

[38]E. B. Reuter, *The Mulatto in the United States*. Their influence upon Negro family life is brought out in the studies of E. F. Frazier. See especially *The Free Negro Family* (Nashville, Tennessee: 1932).

[39]While, according to the census, only 10.4 per cent of the total slave population in 1866 was listed as mulatto, 36.2 per cent of the Free Negroes was mulatto.

line. It has meant bitter frustration and mental conflict. The mulatto has found himself unable to enter the white group and unwilling to belong to the black group.

Continued pressure from the white world, however, compels the mulatto to cast his lot more and more with that of the black man. This has been facilitated by the progress of the darker Negro since Emancipation, and by the diffusion of white blood into the Negro population. The mulatto recognizes that he must gain his livelihood by serving in the Negro community. Meanwhile, his position of leadership gives him prestige, and the lack of a special group consciousness among darker Negroes prevents any line being drawn from that side. Consequently the group consciousness developing in the Negro race is embracing both mulatto and black man in a common sentiment and collective movement.

The difference in the psychology of the mulatto and that of the educated black man is decreasing. Race consciousness and common interests are bringing them together. There is a tendency for dark men to marry light women. Most significant, perhaps, is the fact that they both live in the same dual social situation. Thus, while the educated black man, unlike the mulatto, is not conscious of having white blood in his veins, he is acutely aware of the discrepancy between his cultural achievements and rights as an American citizen on the one hand, and the white group's attitude toward him on the other.

But if the mulatto and the black man feel a growing common interest and sentiment when facing the white world, all is not harmony within the Negro world. The general consciousness of colour, and the pressure and prestige of whiteness react back into Negro life and produce confusing cross-currents and eddies of sentiment. Colour differences within the Negro group give rise to social distances and discrimination. Membership in the more exclusive clubs and churches is sometimes tacitly if not openly restricted to the lighter shades of colour.[40] Even within the family circle and the children's play group such differences may be important sources of differential treatment. At times an individual who is darker feels discriminated against; just as the very light person may feel isolated. Standards of beauty are derived from the white world—as the extensive advertising of skin bleaches, hair straighteners, etc., in Negro publications testifies.[41] There is considerable "passing" into the white race, or into other races, by those who can do so.[42] Social relations, economic opportunities, and marriage preferences are affected by colour variations within the Negro group. For example, the largest Negro newspaper, *The Chicago Defender*, frequently prints letters or comments like the following:

Our social life is honeycombed with prejudice. I attended a social affair recently where only one brown-skinned woman was present, and she was the wife of the gentleman giving the affair. We are following the precedent set by white people in establishing a colour line. I know some churches that will not receive a black minister, and then I know some denominations that will not vote for a mulatto to be a bishop. We really don't know how to manage this question of colour. Comfort is found in the fact that it is not original with us—we are just imitating.[43]

The attitudes described above have many detailed aspects. Broadly speaking, however, they can be grouped into three overlapping classes which are bound up with the process of

[40]See Walter White, "The Paradox of Colour," in Alain Locke, *The New Negro* (New York, 1923), pp. 361 ff.
[41]Interestingly enough, the largest amount of such advertising occurs in the most race-conscious publications. See Guy B. Johnson, "Newspaper Advertisements and Negro Culture." *Journal of Social Forces*, III (1924–25), pp. 706 ff.
[42]See below, Chap. IX.
[43]The position of the black girl seems to be one of increasing difficulty. One writer states, "The black girl's case is tragedy, hopeless. Relegated to the rear economically, shunned socially, barred from propagating her kind, she passes." Gustavus A. Steward, "The Black Girl Passes," *Social Forces*, September, 1927, p. 103.

change from a traditional inferior status to one of equality and independence.

In the South there are many Negroes who are accommodated to their situation. They continue to live in the old plantation atmosphere characteristic of slavery. They often have more confidence in the white man, or at least in some white people, than they do in their own educated people. To them the white person represents a superior being. These custom-bound Negroes, together with those who are most emancipated, are least sensitive to the term "nigger." The former expect to be called by their first names.

. . . It is a reflex of the Negro's high estimate of the better class of white people that for a long time many of the race found it hard to believe that a Negro could be just as proficient as a white man in the same line, diplomas and licenses notwithstanding. And it is not unfair to the race to say that among many something of this feeling still survives, particularly among the older generation. . . . There are many aged Negroes who share the sentiment of "their white folks" that Negroes who refer to themselves as "Mr." and "Mrs.," who pronounce their words with cultivated accents and have servants in their homes —that these people are "putting on airs." But the advancing Negro, that is, the very large and increasing number of Negroes who think, is judging himself and wants to be judged by the common American standard.[44]

This accommodated Negro is sometimes the despair of the advancing and educated Negro. The latter is inclined to ascribe the behaviour of the former to an "inferiority complex." This is probably a mistaken analysis—a projection of his own viewpoint of the situation into the mind of the other. To have a sense of inferiority involves taking the attitude of one in a superior position. To do this one must have experienced this su-

[44]R. R. Moton, *What the Negro Thinks*, pp. 39 and 214-15.

perior position and come to judge it as superior. But this is what the accommodated Negro has not done: he lacks the wider social experience of his critic. He has the same attitude toward the white man that the accommodated lower classes in some European countries have toward their upper classes. The explanation is not to be found in "race" but in the social situation and social experience.

The Negro who is getting out of this situation and is in process of psychological emancipation reverses these attitudes. Anything which reminds him of the old order is resented. He is acutely sensitive to the term "nigger." He will not sing the old folk songs nor live under the old conditions. He moves to the city or to the North. This attitude was interestingly shown in letters written to Negro newspapers at the showing of the plantation film entitled "Hallelujah."

... I never witnessed such a meaningless, aimless and thoughtless picture before. It was a revelation of the depths of human suffering that brought to a focus the unpleasant memories of reconstruction days, when the Race was dying upon the altar of sacrifice.

We are not interested in a picture that portrays the depths from which we came, but more interested in a revelation of the heights to which we have ascended. The indecent and suggestive scenes in this debacle of human emotion seek to discredit the true worth and intelligence of the Race and hold in ridicule religion and our ministerial group. The Negro youth of the country should not be permitted to gaze upon such a display of indiscreet and iniquitous situations, which contaminate his mind and bring about an inferiority complex.

When we begin to protest against the capitalization of our shortcomings by others; when a race pride has been fully awakened, and the true worth and intelligence of the Race will be made manifest, we shall not indorse nor rejoice in the universal ridicule of our group. "Hallelujah."[45]

[45]"What the People Say," *Chicago Defender*, Feb. 15, 1930, p. 14.

Finally there are the responses of a third group—responses which are characterized in general by more realistic, objective views of the situation, although they differ much among themselves. These individuals have a larger outlook on the race situation; they have compared it with similar situations at other times and in other places. They have thus achieved a perspective in point of view which often expresses itself in remarkable tolerance, although this tolerance just as rarely signifies acquiescence in things as they are. The contrast between the "flight from reality" attitude and the more objective viewpoint can be given many illustrations. Two examples are presented below. A letter written by a Negro youth protesting against the term "Negro"[46] illustrates again the oversensitive attitude; the reply by Doctor Du Bois, editor of *The Crisis,* exemplifies the realistic and objective mind of the intellectual.

Dear Sir:

I am only a high-school student in my Sophomore year, and have not the understanding of you college-educated men. It seems to me that since *The Crisis* is the official Organ of the National Association for the Advancement of Coloured People which stands for equality for all Americans, why would it designate, and segregate us as "Negroes," and not as "Americans."

The most piercing thing that hurts me in this February *Crisis,* which forced me to write, was the notice that called the natives of Africa "Negroes," instead of calling them "Africans," or "natives."

The word "Negro," or "nigger," is a white man's word to make us feel inferior. I hope to be a worker for my race, that is why I wrote this letter. I hope that by the time I become a man, that this word, "Negro," will be abolished.

[46]*The Chicago Defender,* the most successful Negro newspaper, avoids the use of the term Negro and writes instead "Race citizens," "Race actors," "Race drama," "members of our group," "non-whites," etc.

Part of the reply of Doctor Du Bois follows:

Suppose now that we could change the name. Suppose we arose tomorrow morning and lo! instead of being "Negroes," all the world called us "cheiropolidi"—do you really think this would make a vast and momentous difference to you and me? Would the Negro problem be suddenly and eternally settled? Would you be any less ashamed of being descended from a black man, or would your schoolmates feel any less superior to you? The feeling of inferiority is in you, not in any names. The name merely evokes what is already there. Exorcise the hateful complex and no names can ever make you hang your head. . . .

Historically, of course, your dislike of the word Negro is easily explained: "Negroes" among your grandfathers meant black folks; "Coloured" people were mulattoes. The mulattoes hated and despised the blacks and were insulted if called "Negroes." But we are not insulted—not you and I. We are quite as proud of our black ancestors as of our white. And perhaps a little prouder. What hurts us is the mere memory that any man of Negro descent was ever so cowardly as to despise any part of his own blood.[47]

Some of the letters in regard to the film "Hallelujah" also illustrate this more realistic attitude. These individuals looked at the film as a work of art rather than from the point of view of what it reveals about Negroes:

. . . "Hallelujah" is the greatest piece of work in its full and fit to reality as I have ever seen of the black race. I have seen in life the very same almost identical things in life's travels. I have played the very same rôle in my natural life as "Hotshot" in that picture. That picture was so natural until it was on my mind and my dreams all night. And besides we must give all concerned credit as real artists in that line. Of course, we are somewhat ashamed of such today, but with fifty or more

[47]*The Crisis,* March, 1929, p. 96.

years from now that will be a great picture for all people of America to look at. King Vidor is a great artist. His knowledge of what to leave out of which would have been a reality proves him a man of deep thought. For instance, had there been a few "crackers" standing around winking and laughing, also trying to dance, it would have been more truth, but that would have ruined the picture in America—and he knew well it would.[48]

Among the emancipated group there are Negroes who are able to laugh at the supersensitive foibles of some members of their own race. They also appreciate the irony and humour in the white man's inconsistencies and neurotic fears of the Negro. They are the Menckens and Will Rogerses of the coloured people and exhibit the same attitude of healthy self-criticism. One example among many is chosen from the impish and biting "Shafts and Darts" of George S. Schuyler:

Another generalization current among white people is to the effect that Negroes are ashamed of the pigment of their skin, and the texture of their hair, and are strenuously, yea, painfully, toiling to reach the "right" shade. Could anything be farther from the truth? This statement just shows how far the "Nordic" propaganda is being carried.

While it *is* true that the leading lady or the leading man and the chorus girls of all our successful musical comedies are as near the "right" colour as possible (who has ever seen a jet-black leading lady?), that the face-bleach advertisements in the average Negro newspaper (including Garvey's rag) make an intelligent person ashamed to open one in a street car, that more and more dusky damsels are getting their epidermis calcimined, that the picture of a black beauty (and there are oodles of them!) is never seen in the Negro newspapers along with the "high" yellows, "teasing" browns, and *voluntary* Negroes, and that the standards of feminine pulchritude of the white and black inhabitants of the U. S. of Moronia are almost identical —still there are exceptions.

[48]"What the People Say," *Chicago Defender*, Feb. 8, 1930, p. 14.

Occasionally one *does* see a Negro lass whose hair has not been straightened, who has not been whitewashed, and who uses powder the colour of her complexion. Once in a while one even sees a black girl the leader in society. Wonders will never cease![49]

The earlier hope of assimilation and amalgamation into the white group is evidently being replaced by a sentiment that the Negro has a contribution of his own to make. This is a natural development from the new race consciousness and race pride which are the most significant characteristics of recent Negro psychology. The Negro will be something of a "nation within a nation," as Booker T. Washington expressed it. This reaction is probably a result of physical differences from the whites, differences which the latter have erected into an impassable colour line. Immigrants, including even the Jews, can be more easily amalgamated because they lack distinctive racial marks.

The new race consciousness of the Negro may take a militant and aggressive form—symbolized by the National Association for the Advancement of Coloured People; or it may be more conciliatory, but at bottom equally determined, as in the Hampton-Tuskegee movement.[50] Seen in the larger context of race relations these two apparently conflicting philosophies are in fact complementary. They are but the left and right wings of the same collective race-movement.

[49]*The Messenger*, November, 1923, p. 862.
[50]In recent years other tendencies also have become evident. Communism has made a few converts, especially among the unemployed. More significant if less sensational, however, are the realistic politics which have emerged in Northern cities among Negroes who have migrated from the South during the past two decades. See Harold F. Gosnell, *Negro Politicians* (Chicago, 1935).

CHAPTER V

The Life-Cycle of the Marginal Man

INTRODUCTION

THE DISCUSSION up to this point has been devoted mainly to the analysis of specific types of situations in which the marginal man can be observed: those of the mixed blood, the Europeanized African, the Occidentalized Oriental, the denationalized European, the emancipated, "assimilated" Jew, the immigrant in process of assimilation, the second generation in an immigrant group, and the Negro in the United States. The emphasis has been placed upon the social effects of certain general processes, such as migration and race mixture, and culture diffusion and culture conflict, as they appear in particular cases. Some parallels and contrasts have been drawn in the course of the discussion. In this and the five subsequent chapters the interest will be chiefly in the personality of the marginal man: how this reflects the evolving situation (1) in terms of a general pattern of development; (2) in typical psychological traits; and (3) in rôles, or forms of adjustment and maladjustment.

When various concrete situations are compared, it is evident that specific racial and cultural differences can be eliminated in the analysis. Today the marginal personality is found among all races and in all cultures, whether Oriental or Occidental, advanced or primitive, among "pure bloods" as well as "mixed bloods": he is a world-wide type. What is it, then, that constitutes the essence of the situation? Briefly, it is a contrast, tension or conflict of social groups divergent in race or possessing distinct cultures in which members of one group are seeking to adjust themselves to the group believed to possess greater prestige and power. The groups are in a relationship of inequality, whether or not this is openly asserted. The individuals of the subordinate or minority group whose social contacts have led them to become partially assimilated and psychologically identified with the dominant group without being fully accepted, are in the marginal situation. They are on the margin of each society, partly in and partly out. They experience mentally the contrasts, tensions, or conflicts of the two races or cultures and tend to become a characteristic type of personality. This is particularly the case when the clash of societies is fundamental and inclusive; when it derives from historic differences of race and nationality.

THE TYPICAL LIFE-CYCLE

What is the typical life-history or cycle of the marginal man? In attempting an answer to this question it must be obvious that there is no stereotyped uniformity in the personal lives of such individuals any more than among human beings generally. The same individual differences of heredity, training, and opportunity exist here as elsewhere. Furthermore, in no two areas is the racial or nationality problem quite the same. Thus it may be affirmed that no two marginal persons have quite the same experience.

Having made these qualifications we may nevertheless outline a pattern of individual development typical of the marginal man. A comparative study of the available evidence suggests that the marginal person has at least three significant phases in his personal evolution: (1) a phase when he is not aware that the racial or nationality conflict embraces his own career;

(2) a period when he consciously experiences this conflict; and (3) the more permanent adjustments, or lack of adjustments, which he makes or attempts to make to his situation. In a rough manner these three stages frequently correspond to the protected environment of childhood, the widening of social contacts and ensuing conflicts of adolescence, and the necessary accommodations of maturity; but they also vary significantly with the character of the individual experience and the specific social environment.

The first period is one in which the individual has as yet no inner conflict of the kind we are interested in. He is not sensitive about his race or nationality because he is not "race-conscious." Race-consciousness is one form of self-consciousness —a consciousness which arises in the person when he becomes aware that others regard him in a certain way because he belongs to a particular racial group. When, for instance, the Negro becomes aware that he is a Negro and that others are acting towards him in a certain way *because he is a Negro,* he is race-conscious. His own group and the other group both arise as objects in his imagination. In the marginal person such race-consciousness is a constantly recurring experience. It means not merely a consciousness of race as such but also an associated consciousness of uncertain, usually inferior status: the individual is under a certain stigma in the eyes of the dominant group.

This is the second stage in the development of the marginal man, the phase in which he becomes marginal. It constitutes a "crisis"—a situation in which his usual habits and attitudes break down to some extent. There is an important change in his conception of himself, although the total transformation may come only after a prolonged and painful process, especially if the crisis has been severe. The individual must then "find himself" again. He must reconstruct his conception of himself

as well as his place or rôle in society. The two are interrelated;
they are two aspects of the personal-social process.

The third stage consists of the ways in which the individual
responds to his situation; the adjustments he makes or attempts
to make. He may reach a successful adjustment which permits
him to be at ease again: he then evolves out of the marginal
class. Again, he may fluctuate from one position to another—
at one time reaching a satisfactory adjustment, then being
thrown back again into a condition of conflict. Or he may assume a rôle which, while it organizes his life, does not completely free his consciousness from his situation: he remains a
partially adjusted marginal man.[1] Or, lastly, the difficulties
may be so overwhelming, relative to the individual's resources,
that he is unable to adjust himself and so becomes disorganized.

To make this abstract analysis clearer and more vivid, the
following autobiographical narrative is introduced. The original account has been abridged at those points which do not add
to the understanding of the process. While the story reveals a
person of somewhat more than average ability and expressive-
ness it is quite typical of the process of development, or life-
cycle.

First the subject describes his earliest years. This is the period of unconscious assimilation when the individual is not
aware of racial difficulties.

The first six years of my grammar school I spent in a small
village school. There were something like 400 students attend-

[1] A somewhat different but related analysis of creative personalities and
creative minorities has been recently made by Arnold J. Toynbee in that
monumental work of scholarship, *A Study of History* (London, 1934). He
reduces the creative process to one of "Withdrawal-and-Return" wherein
the individual, after participating in the practical affairs of life, withdraws
temporarily. This withdrawal constitutes a spiritual crisis and creative experience. Eventually the "transfigured" personality returns to the social
scene in a new rôle. Many of the individual cases discussed by Toynbee
come under the concept of culture conflict as used in this study. See especially Vol. III, pp. 217 ff. (See also Chap. XI below.)

ing the school, of which 394 were Gentiles. Four of us, and two brothers from the other Jewish family comprised the entire Jewish representation. While among the little children in the grade schools, I do not recall being discriminated against, but on the contrary due to my skill at reading and spelling bees, I attracted the friendship of my two choicest friends, one a Yankee, the other Swedish. My life, as a child, among the Gentiles was rather peaceful in so far as it was free from persecution. Queer as it may have seemed to me then, the only fights which I would enter with genuine anger and hatred were those in which I opposed the Jewish boy of the other family. He seemed to me then obnoxious. I was always an average participant in games, and never had cause to feel that I was an outcast. . . .

Then comes the first experience of racial discrimination, although at that time its significance for his future career was not understood.

I did not become "race conscious" until my sixth grade, when I was 11 or 12 years old. My brother and I were walking down the main street of the village one Sunday, and we noticed a large band of Polish boys behind us. They did not attend our school, but their own school which was attached to their church. They came only to town on Sunday. As we were thus walking, I suddenly heard cries of "Jew! SHEENEY! Christ-killer! Zhid!" (Polish for Jew). Then I felt the sharp wind of a passing stone. We did not turn back but ran for shelter. It seemed as if we received this treatment only from the hand of the Poles. I soon learned to hate these rowdies with their white hair, and white wash ties and ignorant grins. . . .

With adolescence and the necessity for planning a career, he came to understand in a personal way the implications of the Jewish-Gentile conflict.

I did not feel a race problem, nor was I attracted to its work until we came to the city. I finished the last two years of grammar school among Friedmans, Goldbergs, Cohns, etc. The

Friedmans, etc., also followed me to high school where we were always a majority. I attended day high school for a year, and then was compelled to go to work. It was then that I met with subtle discrimination. They did not cry "Jew, Sheeney" but very suavely intimated that I was inexperienced, or others put the salary so ridiculously low that it lost all its flavour. Still others were bold enough to say, "We don't hire Jews!" Once I found employment at one of the largest banks in the city owned and operated for the most part by Jews. When I came there the chief-clerk told me that of 400 employees, only three were Jews; that up to last year there had existed a policy of employment restricting Jews! "But," I stammered, "Jews run this place, don't they?" The chief-clerk, a Gentile, said no more. After I had worked there for three weeks several of the tellers and clerks upon becoming familiar with me took sport in kidding me and making fun of the fact that I was a Jew, and that I would own the bank with my aggressive ideas (which I never disclosed to them at least). I had hardly ever experienced this before, and I resented it. I was sensitive and hurt. I argued bitterly. . . .

Ordinarily boys worked for six months or so at one station, and then were promoted to some higher position. I was neither offered, nor did I make any advances for promotion. I rose to captain of the office-boys, and I became the sole office-boy of one of the highest officers of the bank; the man whose name the bank bore, a Jew. For two years I worked for him, and I felt a certain security in him. The fact that he was a millionaire, probably a multi-millionaire, and known throughout the country for his philanthropies and power, and I a humble and poverty-stricken student, meant little or nothing to me. I did feel the remoteness, but I said happily to myself, "Weren't we both Jews after all?" I would dream of his suddenly turning toward me, and taking me in hand personally, sweeping me into success in one grand move, passing up all these insignificant "goyim" Gentiles until I finally landed in a desk at the railing on the main floor. After I worked for him for that length of time, I began to feel a bit doubtful as to whether he would after all serve as an influence in my long-awaited promotion. I purposely avoided promotions now, because I felt I wanted this prolonged stay to make itself worthwhile. Finally one day, after banking hours, and long after employees' hours, I found myself alone with the man whom I idealized. I determined to approach him upon the subject of my promotion. He listened attentively as I told him of the unreasonable length of time I purposely spent at this lowly position, so that when I would get promoted, I could get something better than merely the outdoor messenger department, which was next in the ordinary routine of promotion. "You know," he replied, "Jews are a funny people. Here all the young fellows have gone through the regular routine, and they're all patient about it, and not asking for any more"—and with a sudden turn in his chair, "Why, even I had to start from the bottom!" And thus he naïvely continued with bosh that I could only expect from a Polish rotarian. For several days I was disheartened, and I began to see the futility of working at a bank, so I left.

Consciousness of the "race" problem leads to reflection about the problem and to self-analysis. The individual realizes to some degree his own dual character, but tends to regard it in a restricted and personal manner.

There was little difference between the culture of my home and the community. Since I spent most of the time among my friends, I soon acquired what I called "the Gentile's sense of humour," his manner of discussing the Negro problem. The Gentile to me was so full of prejudice and discrimination.

I possess unmistakable physical characteristics of the Jew. I have the round Jewish nose that you often see depicted in the cartoons or comedies. Dark wavy hair (not curly), and comparatively short of stature. At twenty-one, now, I appear almost predisposed to be stout. Despite the fact that I was born in these United States, and in a good American state, such as Iowa, and also despite the fact that I never spoke Jewish to my folks, I was once said to have that guttural sound, "so characteristic of the Jews." This same individual learned to admire me after two years of friendship, and then said that by my Gentile environment, I had successfully rid myself of that "defect."

The critical phase of his psychic evolution impels him to seek the solidarity of his group. Here he finds a security, a self-expression, and a social recognition which he cannot find in the Gentile world.

When I felt the race problem most, I joined a group of Zionists. These nationalists sent up cries of perpetuating Jewish solidarity and culture. I was instilled with a dread and fear of intermarriage and assimilation. I was told to read Jewish nationalistic literature. Thus I read Lewisohn and Browne; Zangwill, Friedman, Ludwig, and many others. I heard eloquent "reformed" rabbis praising "the people of the book" and "God's chosen people," and I became inspired. Through my intense study of Jewish literature and fiction, I became a leader of my Zionist group, and then for a while felt the truth in the quotation, "The People of the Book." I was prepared to meet any Gentile who questioned the superior mentality of the Jews. I had plenty of stock arguments up my sleeve to convince them. I always felt happy, relieved and unrestrained among my people. I became a "better" Jew whenever I heard accounts of bloody pogroms and massacres. Zangwill's portrayal of the Kishinev massacre in his "Melting Pot" served as an inspiration for Jewish solidarity for several years.

But the wider and more tolerant horizons opened by college studies again creates a movement away from Zionism in the direction of assimilation. He favours internationalism and interracial marriage.

When I entered college and first heard of such words as "internationalism," "emancipated from all prejudices," "being objective"; when I studied psychology, ethics, philosophy and history from new viewpoints I felt differently. I read both intensively and extensively on all the academic subjects in which I was engaged. I forgot nationalism and petty religious differences when I studied physics and astronomy, and more so, when the thought came to me, in a course of evolution, that men are fundamentally alike, and that one's religion and nationalism were "acquired traits" and for the most part dispensable. I avoided my nationalistic friends. Then came more subjects, and more reading. I discussed and argued. I wrote and thought over philosophic speculations. I soon discovered that among those who had common interests with me were individuals with names such as: Breitenback, Smith, Jeffery, O'Brien, Johnson, and even Kowallski!

I have never felt a genuine aversion for the Negro. Sometimes as I look at a Negro in the class, I look at him with the same sorrowful expression that my mother many years ago looked at my father. So far as the League of Nations is concerned, I do not care to commit myself for, frankly, I know little of political science. Theoretically, I am in favour of Internationalism or Cosmopolitanism; anything that might break down these absurd standards of difference they call "my religion" and "my country."

If two individuals of different religions are above prejudice and discrimination, and are after a fashion intellectual, I see no objection to their marriage. While I am, I think, a radical from the point of view of economic discrimination (and this is not a racial problem), and in such questions as disturb the foundations of democracy, yet I am happy that I am on this side of the ocean. Democracy is undoubtedly perverted today, but at least the leaders of democracy don't take arms capriciously and decide to kill a couple hundred of Jews or so.

But his racial self-consciousness has not vanished. Even though he is a leader among Gentiles he experiences important social discrimination. So his future appears uncertain and his mind remains divided.

If I attempted to psychoanalyze myself, I suppose I could say that I am aggressive, however not ascendant. I am very restless and impatient, however not intolerant. My aggressiveness has led me into the highest student office of a Gentile school, aided by Gentile support. I am, I feel, too sensitive. My Jewish nose is not alone always with me physically, but as well mentally. In any public place, I foolishly sometimes avoid standing in a profile position. I have been considered egotistical because I expressed impatience before a group of former nationalist friends. My silence must have irritated them.

In concluding I might say that no matter how "Gentile" I have become (and since I now have renounced the concept of anthropomorphism which makes me irreligious); and while I observe no tradition that is distinctly Jewish, yet some of my endeared Gentile friends have retreated themselves in the seclusion of a coterie, disguised in Greek letters, and wave at me from the inside looking out. Jewish students have approached me, as a leader of activities, to aid them in organizing a fraternity. I discouraged the idea personally, and told them to follow their personal choice in the matter.

Oh, I guess what Lewisohn said was right; I suppose that when I'm a lawyer I'll be vice-president of the local B'nai Brith, secretary of the local congregation, Anshe Emes, Second vice-president of the Chicago Branch of the National Zionist Movement. My clientele will again be the Friedmans, Cohns, Goldbergs, Finkelsteins, etc. I wonder if I shall lose all my "highfalootin" and impractical ideas on theories of assimilation and intermarriage. They (Jewish patriots) tell me I will. I must. . . . Maybe.

This document illustrates the fluctuating type of response—one that is often exhibited by the Jew. The American environment is a baffling one for the Jew. He may establish contacts, especially in youth, which lead him strongly in the direction of assimilation. But he is also likely to encounter sharp anti-Semitism. Such experiences cause him to become inwardly apprehensive and uncertain, although outwardly he may give an impression of egotistical aggressiveness. His attitude shifts with his changing contacts and his growing maturity. The divergent currents of American life produce their counterpart in his psychic life. Thus, as in the above example, the individual secretly doubts himself even when he acts in terms of a theory of assimilation.

The pre-marginal phase of race unconsciousness is the period when members of the subordinate group are partly assimilated into the dominant culture. A certain degree of assimilation is a necessary prelude for the creation of the marginal personality. Ordinarily it takes place during the democracy of childhood when the barriers of the adult world have not yet been fully experienced. The play group and the public schoolroom are often the *milieu* where assimilation proceeds most naturally. Even in the Southern United States, where racial segregation is firmly institutionalized, white and coloured children may play together for years without any consciousness of race or colour lines.

The more completely the individual assimilates the culture of the dominant group the greater are his confusion and difficulty when he finds himself excluded. It is the growing awareness of the lines and barriers of the adult world which produces the typical characteristics of the marginal man. This may be the result of a single experience which climaxes a process of summation, or it may dawn in a more gradual and imperceptible manner not clearly recallable by the subject. The exact significance of the culture clash is not immediately comprehended, nor is the individual clear as to how he should respond to the situation. The variability in responses (the third phase of the lifecycle) becomes more understandable when it is considered in connection with the situation itself.

THE SITUATION AND THE LIFE-CYCLE

The connection between the particular type of marginal situation and the responses of the individual has been described in part in preceding chapters. In general these situations favour individual evolution in one of three major directions: (1) assimilation into the dominant group; (2) assimilation into the subordinate group; or (3) some form of accommodation, perhaps only temporary and incomplete, between the two groups.

Since the situation itself is dynamic, the individual may change his responses from one time to another.

When the racial and cultural barriers between the two groups are not felt to be impassable, assimilation into the dominant culture is the characteristic form of response. This is especially true of immigrant populations who do not differ widely in racial type or in culture. The very fact that they have migrated to a new country, and settled there, indicates that they have taken the initial step toward a cultural readjustment. An effort toward assimilation is expected of them as the price of living in the country; and it is likewise taken for granted in their children. In such conditions the conflicts of the marginal man represent the pains of transition from one culture to another.

It is quite different in the case of those indigenous societies which have been subjected to outside control or imperialism. The first wave of Western culture diffusion and dominance led to imitation and partial assimilation; but Westernization itself provided the stimulus, the concepts, and the methods for a movement of protest, of revolt. Westernization, then, gives way in part to a movement of cultural differentiation and political nationalism. As this movement develops, the marginal man, previously poised on the great divide of West and non-West, turns more and more against his earlier tendencies and becomes an ardent nationalist. Even the mixed blood sometimes finds this to be his salvation.

But there are other situations which are not so clear-cut as the two just described. The "assimilated" Jew awakens in a Hitlerized Germany to discover that he is not really a German; the American Negro is disillusioned to learn that Emancipation and the Constitutional Amendments have not made him a full-fledged American citizen; the Americanized son of the Oriental is baffled when he is still regarded as an Oriental; and from the side of the "dominant" group the apprehensive statesman at the helm believes that he cannot count upon the loyalty of the discontented national minorities within the ship of state. The marginal persons in such instances have a more complex situation to which to respond.

The responses of the American Negro depend in part upon his colour. The light person may "pass" for white, but the dark man must conform. Indeed parents may define the situation for the child in advance and so shape the child's responses into some rôle of racial adjustment or social reform. The following account written by a Negro girl of eighteen illustrates this process:

The community in which I lived when I was young was white. The little white children would come over to our house to play but mother would very seldom allow us to go to their houses to play. I didn't know why she wanted us to stay at home and play. I really didn't know any difference between white and coloured. I never thought once that these children were different from us. I don't think the white children knew any difference either.

When I was about seven years of age I realized the difference. Nobody told me, but I could see that the little children in our community were different in colour and physical make up. I realized that they went to a different school, and that their company or people who went to their houses were the same colour that the children were.

Ever since I have noticed more and more that I belonged to another race. Sometimes I wish that I belonged to some other race because it seems that the poor Negro has a difficult time. Mother has always said that she is glad that she is a Negro, she doesn't have any use for white people. I will or would be content in this race if I could do and have the same privileges that the white man has. Mother has always taught us to respect white, and in order to get along with them we must stay in our place by attending to our own business.

I have governed myself by my mother's instructions, and it seems that I get along with the white race fine. Since I have been able to read and discuss the Negro I see that it is far better to be white because the white man always comes first. I see that the southern Negro is no more than a "dog" in the sight of the white man. When we lived in a white community, just because we had a passable house, and carried ourselves as we should, people (white) would call us "niggers" and would always try to cause some disturbance but we would never pay any attention. Some Negroes in the city where I lived were so dirty, and carried themselves in such a way that whites could not respect them. The homes of some Negroes were so filthy that I always said I wish I could help the conditions. When I finished high school I said I would go to college and take a special course in sociology and probably would be able to remedy the conditions to some extent. I am now a Junior in college, and my greatest ambition is to get a good job doing social work, and to enter a graduate school.

Perhaps the dilemmas are most difficult to resolve in the case of the Jews. The intensity of their group spirit, the contrast of intellectual resiliency and fluidity with spiritual inflexibility, developed from the double necessity of adjustment to an alien environment while maintaining the Chosen People complex, make it hazardous to plot the life-pattern of the marginal Jew. As in the document cited earlier in this chapter, the marginal Jew oscillates forward and backward, out of his group and then back into his group. If the environing Gentiles are friendly he forgets his Jewishness; when they close ranks he knows again that he is a Jew. And the inability of the Jew to forget himself parallels and reciprocates the inability of the Gentile to regard him other than as a Jew.

For such reasons the marginal Jew tends to remain persistently in the psychological centre of the cultural conflict. Even when he throws his lot entirely with one group his attention turns back again and again to the other. The life of Heinrich Heine and the contemporary writings of Ludwig Lewisohn are but two vivid examples of innumerable children and dreamers of the ghetto.

Perhaps it is significant that the Zionist movement emerged in its present form *pari passu* with emancipation from the ghetto. The destruction of the physical walls of the ghetto and the subsequent powerful impact of modern culture rendered some haven of refuge all the more necessary for many Jews. As in the experience of Theodore Herzl, the founder and leader of modern Jewish nationalism, full assimilation with the Gentile environment was impossible. A return to Judaism became psychologically necessary. Whether arrogant or not, the self-sufficient mentality of European nationalism made it inhospitable to the newcomer, and so stimulated a Jewish reaction. One sees this clearly portrayed in the experience of Maurice Samuel. He describes his youthful state of mind in these words:

From early childhood into first manhood my life was passed without interruption in the midst of a great western nation. English was the first language I learned to read and write, and it remains to this day—as it will probably remain forever—my most natural medium of expression; my first knowledge of history, my first appreciation of literature, were evoked by the records of England and the works of Englishmen; my first understanding of geography centred on the British Isles, and within that world my first self-consciousness evolved.

England was my nurse, my cradle, my home. I appropriated my surroundings as my natural right. English games, English moral slogans, English institutions—all were mine. . . . I thought the literature of England the greatest in the world, for I was young, and knew no other literature. But I also had an absolute appreciation of it, and through this medium, even more effectively than through England's history, I became English in my loves, my ideals. City-bred, and a complete stranger to anything but city life, I learned to "love" a thousand places I had not seen, calling them England's, my own. . . .

In my boyhood no one could have shaken my faith in myself as an Englishman, a child of the British people, part of its struggles, ambitions, and ideals. I knew, of course, that I had been born not in England, but in Roumania—but what of that? I knew that my parents were Jewish, and that, therefore, I, too, was a Jew. I went to synagogue and not to church. The ceremonies of the home, the touch of the Sabbath, the high holidays and fast-days, fortified the sense of particularity. But these particularities were drowned out by the more vivid inward and outward experiences of my daily life. Like my dissolving memories of the Roumanian village, like the Roumanian stories and the Roumanian tongue which still lingered in my home, they were a private matter of no large social importance. I can hardly reconstruct now the curious relationship between these two worlds, but as I see it in retrospect, Judaism was something additional and rather irrelevant. It did not crowd the English field, much less belong to it. Outside the home, the chader, the synagogue, I ignored it quite naturally, never suspecting that it was more than a quaint accident. In those days it was self-evident to me that nothing could be finer than being an Englishman—and nothing could be more natural for me. . . . Some day, I dreamed, I would become a leader among her leaders, a name among her names.[2]

At this stage Samuel had an English soul. But in the background of his mind lay the Jewish influence, ready to spring into consciousness. This occurred as he gradually realized that he was not quite a full-fledged Englishman, that he did not really belong to England's past. To a person of imagination and delicate sensibilities such a realization may be a spiritual shock, and in a country of old traditions, the barriers, though not obtrusive, may be sufficient to inhibit personal identification with the nation.

As I grew out of boyhood I mingled with men older than myself, men born to England, as their fathers had been. In them I began to perceive a love of England which differed from

[2] *I, the Jew* (New York, 1927). Adapted from pp. 3–8.

mine, and because of them I began to perceive it also in the things I read. It was (I could not help feeling it) another love, not more intense than mine, not more abundant, but more implicit in circumstances beyond their control—a love which could endure side by side with hatred and rebellion. I became conscious now of the strange power of time, and felt that their love was not of today alone and did not reside in the individual. Those men loved England not as the land they found it; they loved it (the word "love" is subtly inaccurate)—they clove to England, flesh of their flesh, bone of their bone—they loved it as it had been in the past and would be in time to come. For them love of country was a loyalty which could not spring from spiritual kinship alone, but from the consciousness of blood relationship.

In these new circles the blind adoration of my boyhood faltered while it offered itself, touched for the first time by a suspicion of inadequacy. There were men who pointed to the records of their family, and with fierce and silent pride took their part in England as a personal inheritance. Others, who could trace their descent no further back than two or three generations, still knew that in a past of lost identities, their kin had been a part of the thing they loved. Their love of England was none the less the love of an ideal in that it was not abstract, but it gave a decisive edge to their emotions. They spoke of "my England" as a man speaks of his own family, with an intimacy to which no stranger could presume.

The civilization of England was the civilization of their race. Their pride in it was the pride of race.

From this essential participation in England I felt myself tacitly excluded. It was not an act of deliberate extrusion. I only knew, when these men talked of "their" England—the best men, men I admired, men whose motives were lofty, whose minds were uncorrupted by vulgar prejudices—that their relationship to the subject was one I could not share. I met very little anti-Semitism in those days; and if I met it, I considered it something too trivial to merit serious attention. For these men were not anti-Semites. They had no need to be.

Indeed, they greeted my participation in England's civilization with a natural kindness. They were willing to admit me, but their graciousness was of no avail, for they could not undo the past, and they could not help taking a son's pride in a father's greatness. And I could not share their forefathers with them.

On both sides there was a certain embarrassment. I must confess I felt a certain humiliation because somebody had to "admit" me to the life which I had thought naturally mine. This reason alone might have prevented me from accepting the invitation, for in so serious a matter, how could I let myself be considered an object of charity? They, on the other hand, would have felt that any effort on my part to press the advantage of their kindness too closely would have been indelicate and offensive. There are certain things in life which cannot be given and taken. Cemeteries and a past history are among these.[3]

Samuel then describes his subsequent development: his revolt against this barrier formed by the past; his anguish: "I had been excluded from the ultimate spiritual benefit of being an Englishman because, born of Jewish parents, I was assumed to have inherited a mysterious quality which marked me off from the rest of mankind. My first sufferings had been intense. I had been made to feel a stranger, with no ultimate share in the life around me."[4] He inquires into biology, psychology, and all that any science can tell him about race and nationality, seeking for a solution to his perplexity, a formula which will permit him to find inner peace. Science cannot answer his riddle; socialism and economic radicalism cannot fill the void. At first his liberal and international tendencies make him ashamed to turn to Jewish nationalism. But cosmopolitanism is a "world without moods"; Esperanto "a perfect illustration of the vague and benevolent dreams of the schoolmaster idealist." The racial basis of the Jewish people may be an illusion—but the world requires races: "we must have them in order that life may utter itself culturally." And so he returns to the culture of his an-

[3]*Ibid.,* pp. 9–12.   [4]*Ibid.,* p. 23.

cestors and becomes an ardent Jew and a Zionist. Here he finds
the home and the security which were taken away from him
by his dawning race-consciousness.

The third phase may represent a prolongation of the tensions
and conflicts of the second. Adjustment proves impossible with
either society. The individual has identified himself too far
with each culture, and the groups themselves persist in a state
of tension. The position of the Jew, especially in Central European countries, often gives rise to this chronic maladjustment. It becomes a theme of biography and a source of literature. It is portrayed with melancholy eloquence in the significantly titled autobiography of Jakob Wassermann, *My Life as
German and Jew.*[5]

Born and reared in one of the oldest Jewish communities in
Germany, he thoroughly absorbed German culture, living and
associating with Christians. His self-identification with Germany was furthered by his blonde and non-Jewish appearance,
so that as a youth he did not interpret the anti-Semitism he encountered as being directed against himself personally but
against the Jewish community.[6] But gradually the problem of
being a Jew as well as a German became more and more consciously central in his life, motivating and colouring his creative
work. Unlike Samuel, he could not embrace Zionism, for he felt
too thoroughly German in spirit. Yet he was haunted by the
German attitude which regarded him and his writings as alien
—as un-German. "I found myself rejected and isolated in a
triply difficult position: as a man of letters, as a German without social standing, as a Jew detached from my group."[7] Nevertheless, even to his old age, he maintains his conception of
himself as both a German and a Jew, and declares in ringing
words: "I refuse to deny myself, I refuse to betray myself."[8]

[5]New York, 1933.   [6]*Ibid.,* p.11.
[7]*Ibid.,* p. 125.   [8]*Ibid.,* p. 263.

CHAPTER VI

Personality Traits

INTRODUCTION

THE PERSONALITY TRAITS of the marginal man reflect the general situation he is in, his experience with that situation, the phase of his life-cycle, and perhaps certain inherited or previously acquired personality traits. Since the social situation varies from one extreme racial and cultural conflict—as with some mixed bloods, the Negro in America, or the Jew in Central Europe—to one of mild and almost imperceptible tension—as with English immigrants in the United States—one should expect the personality problems to vary correspondingly. With some individuals the characteristic inner conflict is a minor problem; in such cases one cannot speak of a "personality type." It is only in those instances where the conflict is intense and of considerable duration that the personality is oriented around the conflict. The individual seems almost to be "obsessed" with his problem; his moods are reshaped. Then, in spite of differences in race and culture, the type is clearly delineated.

Again, individuals within a given situation have diverse experiences. Some live their lives within the boundaries of their own group; others enter into the activity of the dominant culture only occasionally or merely in the form of business or economic contacts. Theirs is primarily a symbiotic relationship. It is the individual who participates *extensively and intimately* in the culture of the dominant group who, when he is rejected, becomes the extreme type of marginal person. The extent of his assimilation measures the depth of his psychic identification, and this in turn measures the severity of the mental shock when he experiences the conflict of cultures as it bears upon his own social acceptability.

The Crisis Experience

The individual is not a marginal person until he experiences the group conflict as a personal problem. At first he absorbs the culture of the dominant group without any clear consciousness that he does not belong to it. In fact, frequently the opposite is true: he dislikes the contacts he has with the subordinate group; it does not attract or interest him. What Wassermann wrote of himself could be duplicated: "As for the Jewish community, I felt no inner relationship whatsoever with it. Religion was a study, and not a pleasant one. A lesson taught soullessly by a soulless old man. Even today I sometimes see his evil, conceited old face in my dreams. Curiously enough I have seldom heard of a kindly or lovable Jewish religious teacher."[1] This premarginal stage seems to be one of a vague and obscurely defined response to the culture conflict by an effort at assimilation. The youthful individual in particular is simply striving to advance himself away from what he does not like to that which attracts him. In any event, without at least partial assimilation into both cultures the individual would not later experience the conflict of cultures.

Experiencing the conflict of cultures constitutes the turning point in the career of the individual. This is the period when the characteristic personality traits first appear. The experience itself is a shock. The individual finds his social world disorganized. Personal relations and cultural forms which he had pre-

[1] *My Life as German and Jew*, p. 12. Edward A. Steiner uses almost identical language. See his *Against the Current* (New York, 1910), pp. 186–87.

viously taken for granted suddenly become problematic. He does not know quite how to act. There is a feeling of confusion, of loss of direction, of being overwhelmed.

The experience of Ludwig Lewisohn, who has written brilliantly concerning the problem of the Jews in the Western World, is now almost classic. Born in Germany and brought to the United States as a young boy he rapidly assimilated American culture and identified himself completely with American life. His literary talents induced him to set his heart on becoming a professor of English literature. At that time he did not realize the widespread nature of the prejudice against Jews. The difficulties he encountered seemed to him to be local and transitory. He did graduate work in a university and then looked for a teaching position. After receiving a letter from his teacher telling him "how terribly hard it is for a man of Jewish birth to get a good position" teaching in an American university Lewisohn finally—as a kind of climax to a summation of events—realized the bearing of the Jewish-Gentile cleavage upon his personal life:

I sat in my boarding-house room playing with this letter. I seemed to have no feeling at all for the moment. By the light of a sunbeam that fell in I saw that the picture of my parents on the mantelpiece was very dusty. I got up and wiped the dust off carefully. Gradually an eerie, lost feeling came over me. I took my hat and walked out and up Amsterdam Avenue, farther and farther to High Bridge and stood on the bridge and watched the swift, tiny tandems on the Speedway below and the skiffs gliding up and down the Harlem River. A numbness held my soul and mutely I watched life, like a dream pageant, float by me. . . . I ate nothing till evening when I went into a bakery and, catching sight of myself in a mirror, noted with dull objectivity my dark hair, my melancholy eyes, my unmistakably Semitic nose. . . . An outcast. . . . A sentence arose in my mind which I have remembered and used ever since. So long as there is discrimination there is exile. And for the first time in my life my heart turned with grief and remorse to the thought of my brethren in exile all over the world. . . .[2]

This passage is of great interest. As he gets the larger social pattern into his mind he turns to his "brethren in exile all over the world. . . ." This is the moment when Lewisohn gives up assimilation and again becomes a Jew. He at last accepts the definition of the situation. This awakening or reawakening Jewish consciousness even turns to his physical characteristics— "my dark hair, my melancholy eyes, my unmistakably Semitic nose," for these are a kind of objective confirmation of his spiritual change and his ancestral heritage. He feels his isola- tion—"an outcast"—and states the cause and the effect in one ever-remembered sentence: "So long as there is discrimination, there is exile."

Nevertheless, Lewisohn could not, in a moment, become a satisfied Jew. For he had thoroughly assimilated American culture, and even become a Christian and married a Gentile. This made his situation all the more difficult, for, as he notes, his problem was more than one of earning a living:

I didn't know how to go on living a reasonable and reason- ably harmonious inner life. I could take no refuge in the spirit and traditions of my own people. I knew little of them. My psychical life was Aryan through and through. Slowly, in the course of the years, I have discovered traits in me which I sometimes call Jewish. But that interpretation is open to grave doubt. I can, in reality, find no difference between my own inner life of thought and impulse and that of my very close friends whether American or German. So that the picture of a young man disappointed because he can't get the kind of a job he wants, doesn't exhaust, barely indeed touched the dilemma. I didn't know what to do with my life or with myself.[3]

It must not be thought that this is true only of Lewisohn or

[2]*Up Stream,* pp. 122–23.   [3]*Ibid.,* p. 125.

of the Jews. It is implicit in the situation—no matter what the colour of the skin or the form of the culture. W. E. B. Du Bois in his eloquent volume on *The Souls of Black Folk* has set down with characteristic brilliance his own experiences. It deserves to be reproduced in full so that the comparison with Lewisohn can be made:

Between me and the other world there is ever an unasked question: unasked by some through feelings of delicacy; by others through the difficulty of rightly framing it. All, nevertheless, flutter round it. They approach me in a half-hesitant sort of way, eye me curiously or compassionately, and then, instead of saying directly, How does it feel to be a problem? they say, I know an excellent coloured man in my town; or, I fought at Mechanicville; or, do these Southern outrages make your blood boil? At these I smile, or am interested, or reduce the boiling to a simmer, as the occasion may require. To the real question, How does it feel to be a problem? I answer seldom a word.

And yet, being a problem is a strange experience—peculiar even for one who has never been anything else, save perhaps in babyhood and in Europe. It is in the early days of rollicking boyhood that the revelation first bursts upon one, all in a day, as it were. I remember well when the shadow swept across me. I was a little thing, away up in the hills of New England, where the dark Housatonic winds between Housac and Taghkanic to the sea. In a wee wooden school-house, something put it into the boys' and girls' heads to buy gorgeous visiting-cards—ten cents a package—and exchange. The exchange was merry, till one girl, a tall newcomer, refused my card—refused it preemptorily, with a glance. Then it dawned upon me with a certain suddenness that I was different from the others; or like, mayhap, in heart and life and longing, but shut out from their world by a vast veil. I had thereafter no desire to tear down that veil, to creep through; I held all beyond it in common contempt, and lived above it in a region of blue sky and great wandering shadows. The sky was bluest when I could beat my mates at examination time, or beat them at a foot-race, or even beat their stringy heads. Alas, with the years all this fine contempt began to fade; for the worlds I longed for, and all their dazzling opportunities, were theirs, not mine. But they should not keep these prizes, I said; some, all, I would wrest from them. Just how I would do it, I could never decide; by reading law, by healing the sick, by telling the wonderful tales that swam in my head—some way. With other black boys, the strife was not so fiercely sunny: their youth shrank into tasteless sycophancy, or into silent hatred of the pale world about them and mocking distrust of everything white; or wasted itself in a bitter cry, Why did God make me an outcast and a stranger in mine own house? The shades of the prison-house closed round about us all: walls strait and stubborn to the whitest, but relentlessly narrow, tall, and unscalable to sons of night who must plod darkly on in resignation, or beat unavailing palms against the stone, or steadily, half hopelessly, watch the streak of blue above.[4]

As these quotations from Lewisohn and Du Bois illustrate, the crisis is not merely a simple experience of discrimination. Many persons are the objects of some form of discrimination at some time or other in their lives. But with them it is an incidental, perhaps unpleasant happening. In the experience of the marginal man it is crucial, for it involves his whole life-organization and future career. It defines his place in the world in a way which he had not anticipated. It delimits his present and future in terms of his career, his ideals and aspirations, and his inmost conception of himself. And it is a shock because his previous contacts have led him to identify himself with the cultural world which now refuses to accept him.

TYPICAL PERSONALITY TRAITS

As a consequence of the crisis experience the individual finds himself estranged from both cultures. Having participated in each he is now able to look at himself from two viewpoints:

[4]Pp. 1–3.

the marginal Jew sees himself from the Jewish standpoint and from the Gentile standpoint; the marginal Negro from that of the white man as well as the black man. Since these two standpoints are in conflict—the contempt or prejudice of the one conflicting with the self-respect and demand for loyalty of the other—the individual experiences this conflict. He has something of a dual personality, a "double consciousness," to use the words of Du Bois:

... the Negro is a sort of seventh son, born with a veil, and gifted with second-sight in this American world—a world which yields him no true self-consciousness, but only lets him see himself through the revelation of the other world. It is a peculiar sensation, this double-consciousness, this sense of always looking at one's self through the eyes of others, of measuring one's soul by the tape of a world that looks on in amused contempt and pity. One ever feels this two-ness—an American, a Negro; two souls, two thoughts, two unreconciled strivings; two warring ideals in one dark body, whose dogged strength alone keeps it from being torn asunder.[5]

This "double consciousness" can be made clearer in terms of Cooley's analysis of the reflected or looking-glass self.[6] We develop an idea of ourselves through imagining how we appear to other persons, and imagining their judgment of that appearance. Thence arises a self-feeling ranging from pride to mortification. In the case of the marginal man it is as if he were placed simultaneously between two looking-glasses, each presenting a sharply different image of himself. The clash in the

[5]*Ibid.*, p. 3. Max Schmidt in his *Primitive Races of Mankind: A Study in Ethnology* (Boston, 1926), pp. 189–90, makes a similar observation about natives of Brazil who have lived among Europeans for a time, and developed two personality patterns. He quotes Goethe's famous lines in regard to "two souls in one breast." The first two lines are of interest in this connection, although Goethe had a different situation in mind when he wrote them: "Two souls, alas! reside within my breast, And each withdraws from, and repels, its brother." (Translation of Bayard Taylor.)
[6]See Charles H. Cooley, *Human Nature and the Social Order* (New York, Revised Edition, 1922), p. 184.

images gives rise to a mental conflict as well as to a dual self-consciousness and identification.

Lewisohn, Du Bois, Samuel, Wassermann, and all those who assimilate the culture in which they live, have unwittingly identified themselves with it. When they become conscious of the cultural cleavage which involves their own personal destiny, this identification is disturbed and thrown into consciousness. But the process of dissociating oneself from something which has formed the matrix of one's deepest personal characteristics can only be painful and incomplete. The making of a new racial or national identification is forced by the violent emotional reaction against the old. The old identification, however, though shaken, continues to exist and trouble the mind. It will not be stilled or easily thrust aside. On the other hand, a new racial identification can not be formed by the mere willing of it. It must grow, if at all, with time and experience. In the interval of transition the individual suffers from a divided loyalty—an ambivalent attitude.

This ambivalence of attitude and sentiment is at the core of those things which characterize the marginal man. He is torn between two courses of action and is unable calmly to take the one and leave the other. The unattainable white world or Gentile world, to restrict ourselves for the moment, continues to haunt his imagination and stir his emotions. At one moment it may be idealized and longed for; at another moment despised and hated. The other world to which he has been assigned has the same contradictory character: at times it appears as a beloved place of refuge, solace and recognition; again it may seem like a prison—something cursed and hateful, or even shameful.

Lewisohn writes of a conversation which he had in Chicago with two Jewish friends. One of them, after a discussion concerning the "everlasting Jewish question," summed up his feelings with the statement "We are not wanted anywhere." The other, following an interval of brooding, cried out, "I hate the Jews! I hate myself!" Lewisohn remarks that "From these two sayings it is possible to gain a profound insight into the position of every minority group within any civilization and, above all, of that permanent and classical minority group which is post-exilic Jewry."[7]

It is this divided loyalty and ambivalent attitude which explains the fluctuating and contradictory opinions and actions of the marginal person. At one moment he may affirm one point of view; at another he as positively voices an opposite opinion. Some individuals are able to control these divergent tendencies, although realizing their existence. Some express one tendency in one situation and the opposite in another situation; the suppression of one is compensated for by an over-expression of the other.

The ambivalence of attitude appears in different ways. A very light mulatto who can pass states: "I have several times passed for white at theatres, but never thought anything about it for I have never wished that I belonged to another race." In response to the question, "Do you like to be mistaken for white?" she answers affirmatively. But in a later part of her life story writes, "The southern people are not well educated, that is all I can say about them, for that is the cause of them being so mean to the Negro. I am glad they do not want the Negro to sit beside them on the street cars and go to the same shows. I have never been one to want to go where I was not 'wanted.'"

Possibly this ambivalence, together with nervous strain, is at the root of most if not all of the behaviour which has fre-

[7]*Israel* (New York, 1925), p. 20.

quently been viewed by the biologically minded in terms of "racial disharmony," "the clash of blood," "unstable genetic constitution," etc., when considering mixed-blood persons. The apparently irrational, moody, "temperamental" conduct of racial hybrids is often paralleled among racially pure cultural hybrids, but the lack of obvious biological difference has made such explanations less applicable in their case. The prevalence of neurasthenia and hysteria among supposedly racially pure Jews is significant in this connection.[8]

The marginal situation produces excessive self-consciousness and race-consciousness. The individual is conscious of his anomalous position between the two cultures and his attention is repeatedly focussed upon each group attitude and his relationship to it. This continual calling in question of his racial status naturally turns his attention upon himself to an excessive degree. He becomes a problem to himself and supersensitive about his racial connections. He may wish that he belonged to some other race; and may, by a kind of psychological introjection, despise himself as the dominant race despises him.

"Inferiority complexes" are a common affliction. Alfred Adler, who makes this concept the center of his system, traces it back to a social maladjustment of the individual arising from some physical or organic deficiency. The difficulty need not be physical, however; it may lie in a "mistaken attitude toward a physical situation."[9] The consequence of the feeling of inferiority is a constant striving to find a situation in which the individual can excel. "We should not strive to be superior and to succeed if we did not feel a certain lack in our present condition."[10] A "superiority complex" may then develop as a compensation for the "inferiority complex." The individual, ac-

---

[8]For a further discussion of the maladjustment of the marginal man see Chap. X.
[9]*The Science of Living* (Garden City, New York, 1932), p. 72.
[10]*Ibid.*, p. 79.

cording to Adler, may or may not be aware of these complexes. The origin of the inferiority feeling or complex is to be found in childhood, especially in the helplessness of the infant.

With the marginal man, the inferiority feeling arises out of the group situation where he is stigmatized as an inferior or made to feel unacceptable. In the case of mixed bloods and those of a different race from the dominant group, the physical element stressed by Adler is apparent. But it is a "deficiency" primarily in the eyes of the dominant race; the group definition precedes the individual's definition of himself. The individual may or may not consciously accept this definition; it influences him none the less.

In the following account the sense of inferiority was more than usually prominent, verging upon an obsession:

I have always been more or less possessed of what writers call an inferiority complex. It has affected my every waking moment so that my life has seemed meaningless and without purpose. On one occasion I sought out a psycho-analyst but his high fees ($10 a visit) kept me from going further in that field.

I have wondered a great deal about this feeling of inferiority. Is it due to laziness, to what Louis Wirth calls the ghetto spirit or to actual inferiority, i.e., inability to cope with the environment?

This so-called inferiority complex has made me an egotistical, self-centred, jealous individual. It has made me incapable of adjusting myself to home life, to a bonhomie with my fellow-workers, to an interest in any one but myself. In short it has made me an anti-social being. It has given me personality traits which are all on the debit side of the ledger—lack of self-confidence, restlessness; moody, contrary and radical and always worried.

My childhood was a drab colourless affair; I remember nothing in it that brings back beautiful memories. I was brought up in a foreign-born neighbourhood (Polish) and I was taunted many times with the words "sheeney," "kike" and the like until it made my blood boil. It gave me a feeling of helplessness against the brute strength of these tormentors.

I have always kept to myself for the most part and haven't formed more than two intimate acquaintances in all my experience.

I am very indefinite in my likes and dislikes so that my opinion in most matters is worthless.

These reactions stamp me as a neurotic individual; Jews, I am told, are predisposed that way, but nevertheless I have become pessimistic as a result of this and life has become a soured and uninteresting experience.[11]

In this case the individual concerned was not quite clear as to the source of his feelings. Although he mentions the possible influence of the "ghetto spirit" he does not connect his present feelings with the many taunts which he suffered as a child, and which made his "blood boil" and gave him a "feeling of helplessness." It is probable that these childhood experiences built up emotional patterns which continue to operate. In reply to further questions he adds, "I felt superior as a child but I was always beset with a fear mechanism of some sort—a fear of the future, persisting to the present." Concerning his attitude toward the Jewish group he writes: "I identify myself with the Jewish group only when I hear of Jewish persecution. Otherwise I feel that the Jews have made a mistake in retaining their ethnic group origin." The last statement indicates that no effort has been made to overcome the inferiority feeling by identification with some form of Jewish nationalism.

The hypersensitiveness of the marginal man has been repeatedly noted. This trait is related to the exaggerated self-consciousness developed by continually looking at himself through the eyes of others. It may result in a tendency to find malice and discrimination where none was intended. By brood-

[11]Life history document.

ing over his situation and by repeatedly rehearsing past experiences in his imagination a distorted view of the world is built up. Having this conception of the world in his mind he is more likely to provoke antagonism and prejudice against himself. His own attitude evokes the responses which he dislikes. The consequence is the creation of a vicious circle. Lewisohn has suggested something of this when he writes: "A pushing or insinuating fellow might, assuredly, have made his way. But my sensitiveness was so alert that I, no doubt, at times created division by suspecting it and at once shrinking away."[12]

Or it may lead to a withdrawal which prevents the individual from having experiences which might change his attitude and give him more self-confidence. "Racial prejudice has made me too conscious to try to associate particularly with other than Jews but the fault lies in my own efforts and reactions. I have never tried to obtain a position or a purpose which has had a chance to be thwarted by racial differences as yet."[13] Allied to this is the American Negro's "defense mechanism"—that shell of reserve or of smiles which covers feelings unsuspected by the superficial observer. It may be pertinent to recall the poem of Paul Laurence Dunbar, "We Wear the Mask":

WE WEAR THE MASK

We wear the mask that grins and lies,
It hides our cheeks and shades our eyes—
This debt we pay to human guile;
With torn and bleeding hearts we smile,
And mouth with myriad subtleties.
Why should the world be over-wise,
In counting all our tears and sighs?
Nay, let them only see us, while
We wear the mask.

[12]*Up Stream*, p. 89.   [13]Life history document.

We smile, but, O great Christ, our cries
To thee from tortured souls arise.
We sing, but oh, the clay is vile
Beneath our feet, and long the mile;
But let the world dream otherwise,
We wear the mask!

Out of the inferiority complex emerge various compensatory
reactions. These differ greatly with the particular individual.
Excessive egocentrism is present in but relatively few cases—
and even in these it may antedate the crisis experience.[14] The
tendency to "rationalize" is evident with some. The person of
weaker character finds his race or nationality a convenient
scapegoat: failure through personal defect is attributed to the
discrimination of race prejudice. Correct diagnosis, however,
is difficult, since prejudice is frequent enough to make the individual's plaint a fair one.

The less sensitive or more aggressive person, he who "over-
compensates," or he who is driven by an inner compulsion to
express himself, may push on in spite of difficulties. This
sometimes enables him to establish friendly contacts or achieve
a success which gives him a place in the dominant culture. It is
also true that aggressiveness accentuates the dominant group's
resentment. It is proverbial that the Gentile considers the Jew
too "pushing," "grabbing," or "aggressive." Similar remarks
are made about Negroes in northern cities. To those on top the
rising and ambitious individuals are viewed with disfavour, if
not fear. They are getting "out of their place" and are regarded as "upstarts." When the ambitious person is aiming
at purely material and personal success his opportunism is also

[14]This cannot easily be checked since the marginal personality is generally
a creation of youth and early maturity. It is also necessary to distinguish
(excessive) egocentrism from (excessive) self-consciousness; the latter is a
more typical trait of the marginal man. Probably the egocentric personality
is a product of early family experience.

stigmatized by an epithet from his own group.[15] Fundamentally, the striving upward of the under group is a healthy reaction which leads to increased self-respect and eventually forces recognition and respect from the over group. Individuals who make their mark in the world become models and sources of inspiration. "The book which I enjoy reading is *Up from Slavery* by Booker Washington. I do want to be like him and do something for my race" is the way one Negro girl in the United States closes her life story. Discrimination stimulates some and depresses others: "Through the white man's meanness toward us it has stimulated a desire in me to always be something elevating. . . . I do wish some day I could become a Congress woman." Day-dreaming is another form of compensation. "As a result of my increased knowledge of our 'persecution' I became a day-dreamer. I used to sit around and dream of being some powerful man, influential in politics and world affairs—in fact so great as to make the people feel ashamed of themselves for persecuting the Jews."[16]

One of the most interesting analyses of the conflicts of the marginal man is to be found in Lewis Browne's biography, *That Man Heine.* Heinrich Heine was a man who did not "belong" either to Jews or to Gentiles, and his inner conflicts closely reflected the shifting situation in which he found himself. His pessimism, sentimentalism, dreaming and wit have been described by Browne as evidences of "spiritual distress":

The evidences of Heine's spiritual distress before 1831 are patent in all his work. First there is his corroding pessimism, his continual dwelling on death and the grave. Next there is his frequent indulgence in maudlin sentimentality—an almost unfailing symptom of spiritual instability. Sentimentality is the

[15]Two somewhat different types, the "allrightnick" among Jews in New York, and the "caffone" among Italians in America, are described by Robert E. Park and Herbert A. Miller in *Old World Traits Transplanted* (Chicago, 1925), pp. 101–4.
[16]From autobiographical documents.

device resorted to by one who has no really valid principles to which to cling, and who therefore must give a fictitious validity to whatever thin and flimsy beliefs he can lay hold of. It is the imputation of false values to things: the attribution of gravity and meaning to notions which in actuality do not and cannot possess such qualities. Sentimentalism is in the emotional morass what rationalism is in the intellectual; a desperate attempt to save oneself by believing that the reeds in one's clutch are really stout ropes. . . .

The third indication of Heine's spiritual conflict before 1831 is his weakness for dreaming. Had he possessed a healthy mind he would not have felt the need to flee at every crisis to his eerie fantasy-world. He would have been able to meet the harshest exigencies without a tremor, and would at least have *tried* to vanquish them in the realm of reality. But, as it was, Heine turned tail at the least sign of trouble, and he did not dare halt and show fight until he was safe in the realm of his imagination. He lacked the courage which can come only of spiritual conviction. His arms were weak because his mind was divided; his hands were nerveless because his soul was in turmoil.

But the most striking indication of all is Heine's wit. Sigmund Freud in his *Wit and its Relation to the Unconscious,* points out the parallel that exists between the technique of wit and the technique of dreams. He makes frequent mention of Heine in the volume, and offers him as an outstanding example of an individual who used wit as a mechanism to relieve an internal spiritual conflict. Heine's willingness to mock his tenderest emotion reveals an acute consciousness of how open to mockery his emotions really were. More than that, it reveals a panicky fear that others might also be conscious of it, and might be laughing not only at those emotions but also at him who cherished them. That was why Heine so frequently concluded his most ecstatic poems with a line of devastating cynicism. He feared his reader might be suspicious of the sighs and tears whereof he so glibly sang, and therefore he hastily leaped up and laughed at them even before the reader could do so.[17]

Because of his in-between situation, the marginal man may

[17]*That Man Heine* (New York, 1927), pp. 251–52.

become an acute and able critic of the dominant group and its culture. This is because he combines the knowledge and insight of the insider with the critical attitude of the outsider. His analysis is not necessarily objective—there is too much emotional tension underneath to make such an attitude easy of achievement. But he is skillful in noting the contradictions and the "hypocrisies" in the dominant culture. The gap between its moral pretensions and its actual achievements jumps to his eye. While the American pacifist and internationalist, for instance, talks solemnly about the beneficence of peace and the necessity for seeing the point of view of other nations, or berates the Nazis for persecuting the Jews, the marginal Negro cries out: "What about the lynching and raping of the Negro in the South?" Fighting to make the world safe for democracy while letting democracy in the South remain a fiction strikes him as the height of hypocrisy. The sentiments if not the rôles of the radical and the revolutionary are therefore natural ones to take.

If it is true that "the origin of thinking is some perplexity, confusion, or doubt,"[18] then the marginal man is likely to do more reflecting than the ordinary person. There is some evidence that this is true. Autobiographical materials, unpublished and published, indicate that following the crisis experience the marginal person is impelled to think about himself and his position. There is also evidence of a more objective nature. The mixed blood, in spite of the anomalies and difficulties of his position, is generally superior in achievement at least to the "inferior" parent race. The Jew likewise, in open competition, generally reaches a higher average level of business, professional and intellectual success than the neighbouring Gentile.

But much of this increased mental activity is imitative and conformist, not creative, in nature. The individual at first seeks primarily to fit himself into the forms sanctioned by the domi-

[18]John Dewey, *How We Think* (New York, 1910), p. 12.

nant culture. This sometimes produces social conformity at the expense of inner harmony. The specific nature of the marginal situation becomes significant here: does it promote creative mental expression or does it impose a stereotyped conformity?

It is interesting to note that certain mixed-blood situations apparently produce fewer creative persons than others: those like India, South Africa and Jamaica, where the mixed bloods are a lower middle class and have an outcast or buffer-conformist rôle. In the United States, however, the mulatto identifies himself with the Negro race and finds expression in a dynamic race movement. In Brazil the mixed blood feels he is the emerging racial type—the "new Brazilian"—and this, too, promotes mental freedom. Each of these two very different situations seems to produce creative types of personality.

Again, if the "Americanization" of immigrants and their children only meant a kind of mimesis on the 100 per cent plan the results would probably be the exclusive production of Main Street "Babbitts." Fortunately there are other and healthier currents in American life which are kindling new forms of thought and sentiment—indeed, transforming somewhat the older êthos. In the case of the Jews in Europe there are a tradition and group consciousness, including the powerful sentiment of a "Chosen People," to support them against the pressures of the hostile Gentile world: so the marginal Jew is frequently a creative mind. It appears, therefore, that the stimulus of the marginal position develops varying degrees of mental conformity or originality according to the opportunities for expression and collective movements which exist in any given situation.

THE INFLUENCE OF THE SITUATION

The discussion of the preceding section refers to the individual who is experiencing the inner conflicts in their clearest and sharpest form. This may represent simply a period of transition, or it may be a more permanent condition. As we have noted in earlier chapters, the individual in certain situations solves or reduces his problem by assimilation into the dominant group or through identifying himself with the subordinate group. In the former case, if he is fully accepted, his personal problem ends, or merely echoes recurrently as a memory. This seems to be a more likely solution for the immigrant and his children, especially when no racial (physical) barrier is present. It is less true of "passing" and the pseudo-assimilation of subject nationalities.

When identification with the subordinate group takes place, the inner conflict in some instances is merely pushed below the threshold of consciousness; in others it is sublimated in some intermediary rôle. In the case of nationalism, however, the inner conflict is resolved or redefined in the group conflict, the hostile tendencies toward the dominant group overriding the friendly sentiments, and sometimes overcompensating in the form of bitter hatred. Just as the denationalized convert (see Chapter III) is *plus royaliste que le roi,* so the reconverted Westernized Orientals sometimes become the most zealous leaders of nationalist and anti-foreign movements.

Within an area like the United States the reactions of such varied groups as the Negro, the Jew and other European immigrants differ considerably in certain traits. The Negro does not expect to be merged immediately with the white race and so thinks more and more in terms of a distinctive mission for his race; the second-generation Jew is divided in feelings; whereas other second-generation Europeans seldom have such sentiments. Thus in answer to the question, "Do you think your race or nationality has a unique task or mission to perform in the world? . . . Do you feel this strongly? . . . Very

strongly? . . . the percentage distribution of replies in a sampl
study of college students was as follows:

GROUP	"NO"	"YES"	STRONGLY	VERY STRONGLY	TOTAL NUMBER OF CASE
Second-generation Europeans (excluding Jews)...	79	7	8	6	61
Second-generation Jews..........	47	16	30	7	68
Negroes	9	8	33	50	149

The divided feelings of the Jew render him all the more con
scious of his group, as one would logically expect. Statistica
evidence for this was also found in the students' answers to th
question, "Are you very conscious of, or preoccupied with
your race or nationality?"

GROUP	PER CENT ANSWERING				TOTAL NUMBER OF CASE
	"NO"	"SLIGHT-LY"	"MODER-ATELY"	"VERY MUCH"	
Second generation (excluding Jews)	63	15	17	5	65
Negroes	26	22	34	18	134
Second-generation Jews	6	20	39	35	71

Thus the particular type of social situation of the margina
man affects his response to it (the third phase of the life-cycle)
and so modifies his psychological traits. This leads us to th
final aspect of the marginal personality: the rôles of adjust
ment or maladjustment which he assumes.

CHAPTER VII

The Nationalist Rôle

THE PROBLEM OF ADJUSTMENT

How SHALL the marginal man meet his problem? No simple or universal answer to this question is possible, for if there were a serious marginal problem would not exist. In any case, it is desirable first of all to take note of what responses are actually made.

Being a marginal man always involves something of a problem, although it may elicit more amusement than despair, and stimulate rather than depress the individual. At its minimum it denotes a subtle, perhaps indefinable, sense of estrangement and *malaise,* an inner isolation related to his social life. The traits of personality discussed in the preceding chapter reflect and describe this unsettled condition. The maladjustment may be purely inner. It may be so well controlled or concealed that others do not realize what is going on. If they sense something unusual, they are unaware of the cause. At the other extreme are those conflicts which are severe enough to demoralize the individual, throwing him into continual restlessness, and initiating a process of disorganization which ends in dissipation, crime, suicide or psychosis. To some individuals the situation is a challenge bringing about greater mental activity as a compensation for a questionable status. Here as elsewhere, inherited traits, together with early training and experience, affect the reactions of the individual; but since individual differences exist everywhere and tend to cancel each other, the type

160 THE MARGINAL MAN

of social situation becomes primary in determining the characteristic rôles. Furthermore, the situational approach is basic because activity that constitutes "adjustment" in one situation may be a sign of "maladjustment" in another situation.

THE NATIONALIST RÔLE

The crisis experience defines a group division which tends to force the individual to identify himself with one of the two or more interacting groups. One form of adjustment, or at least of partial adjustment, for the marginal man is found through identification with the subordinate or "oppressed" group, and perhaps the assumption of a rôle of leadership in that group. Such leadership frequently takes the form of nationalism, or of a "racial" movement. The Garvey "Back to Africa" movement, the nationalisms of Europe and Asia, Jewish Zionism, and the New Negro renaissance in the United States, are examples of such responses. When the tendency toward identification with the dominant culture or group is rebuffed, such a reaction seems to be a natural one.[1] By leading the minority group the individual acquires status and self-respect. He secures a rôle through which he can organize and integrate his attitudes and aspirations. As his group advances in organization its power increases and it gains greater dignity and *esprit de corps*. This is reflected in his own personality.

Nationalism, from this point of view, is a second stage following an initial identification with the over group. Several of the biographical and autobiographical documents already quoted illustrate as well as confirm this hypothesis.[2] From such cases it appears that the more complete the identification with

[1]This is analogous to the "transfer of the allegiance of the intellectuals" in the revolutionary process. See Lyford P. Edwards, *The Natural History of Revolution* (Chicago, 1927), especially Chap. IX. There is also a tendency for the opposite to occur, for "rebels" to become "renegades." See Max Nomad, *Rebels and Renegades* (New York, 1932).
[2]See especially Chapters V and VI above.

the dominant culture the greater the succeeding disillusionment and emotional reaction when the individual is denied the status to which he aspires. The mechanism seems to be the same as that which sometimes causes quarrels between close friends to turn the friendship into the most bitter of hatreds. The individual's pride and self-esteem suffer from the humiliation involved. He has shared too much with the other—he has given too much of himself—and the emotional rebound is proportionately the greater.

Among Westernized Peoples: India

Doctor B. Schrieke has made an interesting analysis along these lines concerning the influence of Western civilization upon native cultures and the way in which it leads to the development of nationalism. The difficulties and discriminations encountered by the natives result in the development of an inferiority complex.

The inferiority complex, which is of such preponderating importance to so-called nationalism, expresses itself, as mentioned above, in two directions. The first is the desire for *assimilation with the European group of the population.* (The Government endeavours to meet that desire by prescribing that equal remuneration is to be paid for equal qualifications.) Where, under the present colonial relations, the West determines social standards, education bears a Western character. The unavoidable result is that the education of the natives in this manner is inharmonious. The desire for assimilation arouses the desire for equal education with that of the Europeans, if necessary, by neglecting the teaching of the native languages, etc., since the study of the latter is regarded as an impediment to obtaining as great a quantity of Western knowledge as possible. In aiming at assimilation the individual's own culture is purposely neglected and there is even a feeling of enmity against those elements in his own cultural inheritance which appear to stand in the way of this object—an object which, under the present political constellation, is regarded as of primary importance.

The second tendency is that in which the realization of inferiority is compensated by a self-exaltation, by a higher and
often exaggerated self-appreciation. We might indicate this
tendency by the name of cultural nationalism. Here again
resentment is directed against everything which seems to
stand in the way of the individual's own cultural values. Criticism is exercised against any form of education which estranges
the children of the people from their own culture. A nationalist
education is demanded, but it is not always sufficiently realized
that the present society is of a dual character and that, if the
educational system is to be of practical value, it must take the
character of the community into consideration.[3]

The shift from conscious assimilation to conscious nationalism is clearly illustrated in the recent history of India. In the
following discussion only an outline of the main events can be
presented, but it may be sufficient to reveal the process of transformation.[4]

Once the initial suspicion toward a foreign people had declined, many Indians showed themselves eager to assimilate
English culture. Their attitude was one of naïve admiration
and imitation. Hindus and some Indian Mohammedans were
among the most zealous supporters of English education and
the reform of Indian customs and institutions in conformity
with Western ideas. "Westernism became the fashion of the
day—and Westernism demanded of its votaries that they should
cry down the civilization of their own country. The more ardent
their admiration for everything Western, the more vehement
became their denunciation of everything Eastern."[5] An illus-

[3]"Native Society in the Transformation Period" in *The Effect of Western Influence on Native Civilizations in the Malay Archipelago*, pp. 244–45.
(See the section on the Indo-Europeans of Java, Chap. II above, and also
Chap. III.)
[4]See also the appropriate section in Chap. III above.
[5]Statement of Lord Ronaldshay quoted in Prithwis Chandra Ray, *Life
and Times of C. R. Das* (London, 1927), p. 9. Such an uprooting also involved some personal disorganization. See Hans Kohn, *A History of Nationalism in the East* (New York, 1927), p. 118.

tration of their mental attitude is found in a typical letter written by an aristocratic Indian Mohammedan reformer, Sir Syed Ahmed Khan, on the occasion of a visit to England in 1869:

. . . although I do not absolve the English in India of discourtesy, and of looking upon the natives of that country as animals and beneath contempt, I think they do so from not understanding us; and I am afraid I must confess that they are not far wrong in their opinion of us. Without flattering the English, I can truly say that the natives of India, high and low, merchants and petty shopkeepers, educated and illiterate, when contrasted with the English in education, manners, and uprightness, are as like them as a dirty animal is to an able and handsome man. The English have reason for believing us in India to be imbecile brutes. . . . What I have seen and seen daily, is utterly beyond the imagination of the native of India. . . . All good things, spiritual and worldly, which should be found in man, have been bestowed by the Almighty on Europe, and especially on England.[6]

The British, on their part, tried to live up to the obligations called for by their position in India. During the first half of the nineteenth century there was much less feeling of colour or racial antagonism. The distance from Britain led many to spend their lives in India, sometimes marrying native women.[7] English scholars and Christian missionaries rediscovered and translated some of the finest works of Indian literature, and contributed greatly in making vernacular dialects into literary languages. It was an Englishman, Allan Octavian Hume, who created the Indian National Congress. Since the number of Englishmen in India was small, and since they were a fairly

[6] G. F. I. Graham, *The Life and Work of Sir Syed Ahmed Khan* (London, 1929), p. 125. Quoted from Hans Kohn, *op. cit.*, p. 112. Because of such tendencies, enthusiastic Englishmen like Macaulay looked forward to the complete anglicizing of educated Indians. Sir Valentine Chirol, *India* (New York, 1926), p. 75.
[7] See Chap. II above.

select group, the Indians of the interior especially had a more favourable opinion of them than is true today. The small number of Western educated Indians found ready employment with the Government.[8]

Then the situation began to change. The increase in the number of Western-educated Indians led to a demand for a larger share in administration than the British bureaucracy was willing to grant.[9] Indians visiting England were impressed by the contrast between the equal, cordial treatment they there received and the frigid aloofness of most Englishmen in India.[10] Grievances multiplied and found expression through the common medium of communication, English. Then, meeting in Bombay in 1885, came the first Indian National Congress, at this time completely loyal to the British connection. Religious movements sprang up based upon antagonism to foreign ideas and urging a return to Hinduism. Various incidents, legislative and otherwise, marked and accentuated the growing estrangement of the Western-educated Indians and the British official classes. Crop failures and the bubonic plague shook the confidence of the masses in the omnipotence of British rule. Antagonism to British capitalists mounted. The prestige of the British as representatives of the white race was pierced and undermined by the difficulties in the Boer War, the destruction of the Italian army in Abyssinia, the defeat of Russia by Japan, and finally by events of the World War.[11]

The connection between the Japanese victory over Russia and the growth of Indian nationalism can be illustrated by the

[8]For fuller details see Chirol, *op. cit.*, pp. 73 ff. Also Kohn, *op. cit.*

[9]Even the Liberal Viceroy, Lord Ripon, was unable to overcome the resistance of this race-prejudiced bureaucracy. Cf. Chirol, *ibid.*, pp. 85–86.

[10]There is a good statement of British-Indian social relations, or their lack, in J. H. Oldham, *Christianity and the Race Problem* (London, 1930), pp. 161 ff. Arthur Osburn in *Must England Lose India?* (New York, 1930) has made a devastating analysis of English "race" prejudice toward Indians.

[11]In this paragraph I have followed the account in Chirol, *op. cit.*, Chaps. V and VI.

following "conversion" of a young Hindu student, cited by C. F. Andrews:

... He had been educated at a mission school where he came under strong Christian influence, and he was passionately devoted to modern Western science. But until he reached the age of twenty he led a selfish and worldly life. His thoughts and ambitions centred in his family and his caste. He had hardly ever looked beyond that narrow circle and regarded India as an integral unit. Then came the Russo-Japanese War, and made him reflect. His outlook became broader. Day after day news of fresh victories arrived from the Far East. Finally he read of the total destruction of the Russian fleet in the Straits of Tsushima. That night he could not sleep. He had a vision of his country standing before him in visible form. She appeared like a sad, despairing mother yearning for his love. Her face was beautiful but indescribably sad. The vision was so real to him that months later he could shut his eyes and recall it to mind as vividly as when it first appeared. His experience was akin to what is called conversion in the phraseology of religion. With overwhelming power he received the call to sacrifice himself for his mother country. He could think of nothing else. Day and night the vision was before his eyes. He resolved to test himself, and the nature of the test was significant. He as a Hindu began to seek the friendship of Mohammedans and to inspire them with his new ideal. For he grasped at once the essential fact that a united India required the union of the two principal sections of the population. Again and again he was repulsed, but he persisted and gained his point. Then new difficulties arose. With all the authority with which an Eastern father is clothed, his father insisted on his marrying and establishing a home. A suitable bride was found for him, and an agreeable position assured, with a generous dowry. But he resisted and chose to be banished from his father's house and to accept poverty rather than to be false to the call he had received. Subsequently he joined the Arya Samaj and took part in famine relief work. Later still he worked in plague-stricken camps.[12]

[12]Cited in Kohn, *op. cit.*, pp. 377–78. Compare this with the experience of Doctor Kudirka, cited below.

In short, from an attitude of simple and frank admiration, the Westernized Indians passed through a phase of growing criticism, finally, after the World War, reaching a mood of flaming antagonism and rebelliousness to things British and Western. As the mood of conscious identification with English culture declined, the sentiment of attachment to Indian culture developed. This bridged the gulf between the educated classes and the masses. As a result, a movement of romantic nationalism involving cultural as well as political self-determination arose—a mass movement personified and led by Mahatma Gandhi, and distinctive in its doctrine of passive resistance. The leaders of this nationalistic movement, including such men as Gandhi[13] and C. R. Das, have come from the Western-educated, politically minded classes discussed above; while the seething, nationalistic movement, spreading rapidly in the population mass of nearly 350,000,000, is clearly the reflex product of Western culture diffusion. To view it merely as an instance of the natural claim of peoples to self-government is to miss its deeper psychological and cultural meaning.

The experience of India illustrates the typical setting for the nationalist rôle: regions which have been subjected to outside control, yet not effectively settled by the invading population. These are chiefly the Westernized areas of the globe where large indigenous populations continue to be the main body of inhabitants. The marginal individuals in such regions, although for a time attracted by the culture of the Occident, eventually find that there are unbridgeable distances to span, so

[13]Cf. *Mahatma Gandhi: His Own Story*. Edited by C. F. Andrews (New York, 1930). Here Gandhi tells his experiences with English culture and the conflicts he felt relating to such matters as diet, clothing, etiquette, religion and marriage. He writes, for instance, that because of child marriages "Indian youths in England felt ashamed to confess that they were married. I too caught the contagion, and did not hesitate to pass myself off as a bachelor, though I was married and the father of a son." P. 87.

For a biography of Das see P. C. Ray, *Life and Times of C. R. Das* (London, 1927).

they turn about and become leaders of their peoples. Some nationalist leaders like Gandhi react sentimentally against all things Western, even to urging the hand-spinning of cloth, but they inevitably make use of many Western devices, especially political, in seeking their ends. Others like Sun Yat-sen frankly adopt Western ideas, or take a step in advance as in the case of Lenin and the Soviets. As such movements sweep on they also draw more and more of the mixed bloods within their orbits. Thus in the Philippines the mixed bloods have been leaders of the independence movement.

AMONG NATIONAL MINORITIES: CENTRAL EUROPE

Nationalist sentiments likewise emerge among minorities who are subject to discrimination, especially in civil and political affairs. Legal discrimination implies a degree of public segregation which offends the self-respect of the more advanced members of the minority. Assimilation is thereby prevented or made undignified. Consequently an individual who at one stage of his life is denationalized may later return enthusiastically to his original nationality. This return is more apt to occur when the underlying social situation changes in such a way as to give moral if not material support to the individual's new attitude. The reconversion to the native people may be all the more intensely dramatic because of the previous years of strain and suppression of natural sentiments, particularly in the case of persons of deeper attachments. The following is an illuminating example:

Doctor Kudirka had been profoundly influenced by Polish nationalism at the College of Mariapolis. . . . He permitted himself to be still further Polonized while he was studying at the University of Warsaw. It was the fate of all the Lithuanians of that period, and he made no exception. But suddenly he changed and, from being an incipient Pole, he became an ardent

Lithuanian patriot. This is the way he describes his conversion: "At the time I was completing my studies at college, I was convinced that an intellectual person could not be a Lithuanian. I felt this way all the more as every one despised the Lithuanians.

"I preferred to tell any one who asked me my nationality that I was a Lithuanian-Pole because, as a matter of fact, Lithuania and Poland had been historically united. I considered myself then as Polish by adoption. This seemed a partial compensation for the mistake of being Lithuanian. What a hypocritical interpretation of the facts! Nevertheless, it was sufficient for me as it was for others like me, all the more as nothing had occurred to compel me to really think about the matter.

"It was with such a conception of my nationality that I entered the University of Warsaw, where there were very few Lithuanians, and even those who were there were not known among themselves. My feelings for Lithuania, in short, grew less and less.

"During my vacation I returned to Lithuania. A priest related to me one day that a Lithuanian journal was soon to appear. He showed me verses he had written in Lithuanian, and a letter of Bessanavicius concerning the publication of the journal. I read the letter. Something touched my heart, but the sentiment passed. Child's play, I thought to myself, in Polish. From that moment thoughts in regard to Lithuania visited my mind more frequently, but my heart remained cold and indifferent to everything which touched Lithuania and the Lithuanians.

"Six months elapsed; I received the first number of *Austra;* I looked at the first page, and there I saw Bessanavicius. 'Apostle,' I thought at once, but this time in Lithuanian. Suddenly I began to turn the pages of the journal, and then I do not remember anything more distinctly. I remember only that I arose and bowed my head, not daring to raise my eyes. . . . It seemed that I heard the voice of Lithuania accusing me and pardoning me at the same time: 'Misguided man, where are you at this present moment?'

"Immediately I felt my heart tighten; I sank into my chair and began weeping like a child. I regretted the time that I had lost when I had done nothing for Lithuania, time that I could never recover. I blushed for shame that I had persevered so long in my misguided course. . . . Then my heart filled with new pride and new energy. It seemed as if I had suddenly expanded and the world had grown smaller. I felt as powerful as a giant; I felt that I had recovered my Lithuanian nationality."

It is thus that Kudirka relates his conversion to Lithuanianism, which he characterizes as a second birth, and considers the most important moment of his life.[14]

The experience of Kudirka suggests the influence of linguistic and cultural revivals in fostering nationalism. In most cases political nationalism follows a phase of cultural nationalism, although the factors in each are often inextricably interrelated.[15] Cultural revivals foster the written use of the mother-tongue, stimulate national pride, and build up morale. There is a strong disposition to examine the nation's origins and history, and to glorify its achievements. Each nationality eventually conceives itself as having a historically indispensable rôle: "The Magyars emphasized the struggle against the Turks, defending Christianity, as their national mission; the Poles felt themselves as exponents of Western culture against the barbarism of Russian Tsarism; the Croats regarded themselves as pioneers of Roman Catholicism against Byzantism; the Roumanians claimed the honour of being the continuers of the Roman Dacia; the Czechs kindled their national enthusiasm by the memory of Huss, as the beginner of continental reformation."[16]

With the close of the World War four European empires had broken to pieces. Turkey nearly vanished from the map of Europe; Austria-Hungary as such ceased to exist; Russia lost

[14]Jean Pelissier, *Les Principaux Artisans de la Renaissance Nationale Lithuanienne.* In Robert E. Park, *The Immigrant Press and Its Control* (New York, 1922), pp. 44–45.

[15]For a good case study see *Nationalism in·Modern Finland* by John H. Wuorinen (New York, 1931). For the best general discussion consult C. J. H. Hayes, *Essays in Nationalism* (1928); and *The Historical Evolution of Modern Nationalism* (1931).

[16]Oscar Jaszi, *The Dissolution of the Habsburg Monarchy* (Chicago, 1929), p. 259.

a number of nationalities on her western borders; Germany contracted on all sides, especially in the east. Peoples who had formerly been oppressed were now independent and, in fact, in a position to oppress their former masters. Today it is the minorities of German, Austrian and Hungarian nationality who are the chief cause of sleepless nights for the diplomatic guardians of peace. Although the minorities are much fewer in number than in 1914, they are more articulate and aggressive in spirit. International treaties designed to guarantee them cultural and political liberty—the minorities treaties—have not as yet greatly altered deep-seated antagonisms on both sides.[17] Mere rearrangements of political boundaries can help but little; indeed attempts to change them by coercion may produce another general war. The only road ahead is for these nations slowly to learn that differences of nationality, like religion, can be tolerated since they do not necessarily hinder either political integration or economic cooperation. Little Switzerland with her contented Germans, French and Italians stands as a shining example for her neighbours to emulate. Progress would seem to lie in secularizing politics, or in "de-politicizing nationality."[18]

Where there is no territorial basis to support nationalistic sentiments, the psychological tendencies are particularly complex and conflicting, increasing the internal divisions within the minority and reducing the effectiveness of group action. For instance, the dispersed character of the Jewish population, and the varieties of situation in which each fragment finds itself, divide that group into wings and sections varying from the most zealous of Zionists to those who long for assimilation.

[17]Apparently Latvia, Estonia, Czecho-Slovakia and Finland have succeeded best in their minorities policies. Arnold J. Zurcher, *The Experiment with Democracy in Central Europe* (New York, 1933), p. 251. For the viewpoint of Czecho-Slovakia's eminent President, Doctor Thomas G. Masaryk, see his *The Making of a State* (New York, 1927), especially pages 431 ff.

[18]Alfred E. Zimmern, *The Prospects of Democracy* (London, 1929), p. 108.

Nevertheless, the ancient history of the Jews, their common religious background, and the existence of widespread anti-Semitism help to keep alive an intense group consciousness which is potentially nationalistic.

AMONG RACIAL MINORITIES: THE UNITED STATES

Nationalistic sentiments are particularly difficult to organize in minority groups like the American Negro. Where Negroes are most highly concentrated—in the "Black Belt" counties of the South—they are least race-conscious or nationalistic. Since the American Negro has lost almost all of his African cultural heritage, a cultural revival of the traditional kind is impossible. Only one factor provides a lever of differentiation: that of physical race. And the extensive race mixture of the past prevents even that from having its full force. Besides, to discriminate upon the sole ground of physical difference is morally fragile, and the consequent resentment all the more acute. This may be illustrated by the following account of a young Negro woman reared in an institution:

I was born in New York. My father died two months before I was born. At a very early age I was placed in a Catholic home. I was neither spoiled nor ignored. There was no discrimination made between races. There were about fifty babies to be raised by those loving sisters. I must say though I was favoured by several of the sisters, and the father always called me Bright Eyes. I first remembered that I was a human being by being told by one of the sisters that we kids must not let the puppy lick our faces. It was then I realized that there was some difference, but what I could never tell. I must say that I was very happy during my childhood days. There was no hard work to be done. I would eat, sleep, play and pray. Prayer was the most essential thing in my young life. After prayer came study. The schoolroom was very distasteful in my early life. I soon grew out of that.

In my small group of fifty kids there were all races except

the Jew. I was loved by all. I took the foremost part in games and school activities. I also can remember that it was I who won several prizes for our school. I could outrun or outswim any of the kids. In my class in classical dancing I would do more studying than in any other class until I reached the sixth grade. Then I took a liking for mathematics and music. I spent many an hour studying the two subjects.

It was at the age of nine years that I first knew that I was a negro—not that I was told, but I was reading in my book about negroes and I asked one of the sisters what was a negro. The word negro was never used by the father nor the sisters. We were all children in their care. Some of us were there because of death, others by divorce and different reasons. Two years later a Southern white child was placed in our home by her divorced parents. This girl would call all the dark-skinned children "niggers." She was placed on bread and water several times for this act. She soon was broken of it. I never had any feelings when she said negro. Negro to me was only a word used by angry children.

I finished grammar school in this home. Then I was taken out of this school and sent to a Southern College for Negroes. This is where my sorrows began. I longed and cried for those days of peace and happiness. The outside world was very displeasing to me. I was at ———— two weeks when I learned all these things about race separation. I almost swear that I wish that I had remained in the convent the rest of my life. I wrote and begged my mother to send me back to ———— Academy where I would not have to come in contact with the people of the world. Her answer was that I must remain so that I could be liberal and broad and feel the winds of the world. I thought I would die at times when certain speakers would come and tell how different negroes were from whites. At one of these chapel services I got up and walked out. The next day the Dean of Women sent for me. She asked me several things about my early home training and I explained to her that I was raised by white sisters and things were very different in my life. She sent me to my room and asked me never to do that again. As long as I was at ———— I learned to hate certain classes of white people. I mean hate in its truest sense. I was taught never to hate but at times I forgot this element in my training and was very nasty to several of my southern teachers. The story soon travelled to them about me and my funny actions.

Race problems have caused my poor head and heart to hurt. When I first thought of my race I wished and prayed that the negroes would get together and kill all of the protestant white people. Then I would read all the books I could get on negro life, such as follows:

Fire and Flint, Flight, Leopard Spot, There Is Confusion, Hazel, Quest of the Silver Fleece, Uncle Tom's Cabin, Veiled Aristocrats.

The more I read the more I brooded over just what was fit for the negro to do. Then I turned and went back to studying my music trying to forget the problem of the negroes. I left ———— during the strike. I was very glad there was a strike at ————. Too long had the white man held the whip over the negro's head. The negro must rise up and fight for his own. Pleading, begging and arguing will not solve the problem, only war can and must. I have studied that when two major cultures come in contact with each other the result is war, or there would rise up a third culture.

I think that the negro and immigrants do not present to the American a problem in objective culture but in attitude of living. As long as the negro and the immigrant are treated with prejudice the subject of Americanizing these factors is bunk. If America is such a melting pot why can't she consider the negro as one of her finest products. The negro is not a by-product but a true product produced and raised on American soil.[19]

The intensity of this girl's emotional disturbance is evidently a result of her complete identification with the white race and the fact that she knew nothing of the Negro-white situation in the South. The militant mood is not typical of most American Negroes, although critical experiences of "bumping into the colour line" are common enough. The more usual process of developing the nationalistic attitude among Southern Negroes

[19]Life history document.

is through a growth of pride in the achievements of certain
Negro leaders and of learning of the Negro's rights and disabilities through personal experiences, education, the reading of
newspapers, etc.[20] This nationalism does not seek an independent political organization, but simply the rights of American citizens.

The aggressive and militant nationalist or radical has an important part in the interracial or international situation. He
acts as a leader in organizing the subordinate group, and often
helps to revive the traditional culture and to modernize it—for
the dominant group must be met with its own ideas and tech-
niques before it will give way. For this reason further acculturation in utilitarian spheres accompanies the cultural renaissance. As an agitator, the nationalist acts as a ferment, constantly keeping old issues alive and pointing out new ones. He
prevents accommodation on any particular level from becoming
too fixed and crystallized, thereby helping to raise the ultimate
status of his group. His "extreme" and "destructive" views
promote concessions to the moderates, who appear mild in
comparison. By losing himself in a cause larger than himself
the marginal nationalist overrides, if he does not solve, his own
personal conflicts.

[20]For a good illustration see Albon L. Holsey, "Learning How To Be
Black," *The American Mercury*, 16 (1929), pp. 421 ff. Compare this, or
the experience of Robert R. Moton in *Finding a Way Out*, with W. E. B.
DuBois, a Northern-born Negro leader, in *The Souls of Black Folk*
(quoted above, Chaps. II and VI).

CHAPTER VIII

The Intermediary Rôle

CERTAIN CONDITIONS favour the development of intermediary rôles. This is true in the earlier phases of Westernization; it is quite frequent in the case of some minority groups; and in a less defined manner it is characteristic of immigrants in process of assimilation.

In the early contacts of the Western and non-Western worlds, those individuals who are Westernized in advance of their compatriots find a useful rôle as intermediaries between the two societies. Mixed bloods are logically suited for this part since in physical and social make-up they are attached to each of the parent races. They are generally bilingual in speech, and so prove to be valuable interpreters. In public administration and business relations they are often indispensable. At this stage, it should be remembered, the Western invaders are small in numbers, and if relatively weak in strength may feel it necessary to practice a conciliatory policy. This is especially true when the economic relations are primarily those of trade and commerce. Westernized individuals who are not of mixed blood have a like position. Even if personally disposed toward anti-Western views, they will not at this stage secure support from their own people. The masses are not adequately organized; they may be under the spell of the power and prestige of the invaders; they may believe the trading and cultural relationship to be a profitable one—or, perhaps, as with many Orientals, even a necessary evil.

Intermediaries have been particularly prominent in the Westernization of Japan. In the course of two generations Japan has sprung from an obscure and divided feudal condition to the rank of a great world power. What this remarkable transformation meant in the life of one distinguished personality has been told with delightful frankness and charm in *The Autobiography of Fukuzawa Yukichi*.[1]

Fukuzawa was not a passive onlooker in the swift mutations of Japanese society, but apparently its most daring and able leader in the direction of Westernization. As a teacher his wide learning embraced such varied fields as world history and geography; the elements of physics, chemistry, and astronomy; double-entry bookkeeping methods, the art of public speaking, and also military science. He was much in advance of his contemporaries in outlook and so was able to work effectively to shape Japan into a modern nation. Since this objective was particularly unpopular in the early period following the visit of Commodore Perry (1853), Fukuzawa like others found himself under the suspicion and hatred of fanatical patriots who violently opposed all foreign influences. At one period he despaired of the future of his divided and confused people, and confessed that he seriously considered having his sons enter the Christian priesthood so that they might escape the insults of foreign domination. "I seemed alone in my anxiety and I knew I did not have the power to save my country" (p. 220). But Fukuzawa lived long enough (1901) to see his country reach the position of leader among the Oriental states.

Another intimate picture of Japan in transition has been painted by a foreigner, Erwin Baelz.[2] He not only married a Japanese but also identified himself with Japanese interests. In this way he became an interpreter between Japan and Europe, particularly Germany. In Japan he pleaded the cause of Ger-

[1]Translated by Eiichi Kiyooka. Published by the Hokuseido Press, Tokyo, in 1934.
[2]*Awakening Japan: The Diary of a German Doctor: Erwin Baelz*. Edited by his son, Toku Baelz. (New York: The Viking Press, 1932.)

many; in Germany, that of Japan. This rôle had its difficulties, and they have been admirably stated in the Preface by his son Toku Baelz: "Every one who stands between two contrasted civilizations, not as a benevolent neutral, not as a blind admirer of both, but as a mediator, will find that his rôle has its tragical aspect. Their contrasts arouse tensions within himself, and he has perforce to adopt an attitude defensive on both sides. . . . Baelz was inclined to be rueful because his 'intellectual parallaxes had been shifted' by prolonged residence under alien skies. But in fact his position in this respect gave him wide outlooks upon two antipodal civilizations, and thus enabled him to see both in accurate perspective. . . . The aforesaid polar tensions secured their discharge in . . . critical utterances" (p. xvii).

The intermediary rôle is also frequently assumed in the case of minority groups living within a larger culture. When such minorities exist as a consequence of migration they are not in a position to proceed logically in the political nationalist's demand for independent self-government. Yet they may claim political equality and the right to a certain religious and cultural toleration. In such situations the marginal man is more likely to evolve into some intermediary rôle which leads to an accommodation and *rapprochement* between the clashing cultures: he often becomes an interpreter, conciliator, reformer, teacher.

Intermediary rôles are conspicuous in the history of the Jews, and are not necessarily inconsistent with Zionistic sentiments. The Jews' position of social isolation in the Christian world really made them strangers. The sociologist Georg Simmel, himself a Jew, has made an acute analysis of the rôle and psychology of the stranger. The stranger, he writes, first appears as a trader, one who is not fixed in space, yet settles for a time in the community—a "potential wanderer." He unites in his person the qualities of "nearness and remoteness, concern and indifference." This in turn gives him an attitude of objectivity, a freedom from local prejudices and values, and so renders his social relations more abstract and generalized; and the objectivity in combination with nearness (sympathy) facilitates the relationship of the *confidant*.[3]

This conception of the stranger pictures him as one who is not intimately and personally concerned with the social life about him. His relative detachment frees him from the self-consciousness, the concern for status, and the divided loyalties of the marginal man. When the stranger seeks to identify himself integrally with the group into which he has moved, but is held at arm's length, he has evolved into the marginal position. Then his "nearness and remoteness" do not include the same kind of objectivity, detachment and indifference, for too great a portion of his personality has become affected by the situation.

If the intermediary rôle of the stranger is typically that of the trader—a business relationship—the intermediary rôle of the marginal man involves a cultural relationship. This may take a creative form. His insight into the two cultures peculiarly qualifies him for this; and to the degree that it is successful he contributes to his own inner adjustment. As a constructive rather than a subversive force he gains the approval of the liberally minded men of the dominant group, and this also strengthens his consciousness of adjustment.

The modern world with its large-scale communication and movement has brought many individuals into wider cultural participation. Trade and commerce, the travels of the student and sometimes of the tourist, are making more individuals multi-cultural. Each acquisition of a foreign language opens the door to a new way of life. The individual who penetrates

[3]Georg Simmel, *Soziologie* (Leipzig: Duncker und Humbolt, 1908). See R. E. Park and E. W. Burgess, *Introduction to the Science of Sociology* (Chicago, 1921), pp. 322-27.

deeply enough into a foreign culture becomes a richer personality. He readily shifts from one language to another; from one set of habits, attitudes and values to another. Thus he is in a position to look at problems from more than one viewpoint, and to see the essential ethnocentrism of each. This is undoubtedly what is involved in the creation of the "international mind," if defined in its profounder meaning.

This capacity to take the rôle of another culture—to see life and its problems from another fundamentally different standpoint—should not be confused with the *déraciné* cosmopolitan. The latter has broken away from his traditional moorings and is culturally adrift. He lives on the surface of life, becomes blasé and easily bored, and restlessly moves about looking for new thrills. He is an unstable personality; whereas the internationalist, as defined above, has consciously grasped the distinctive meaning and values of each of the rounded cultures in which he moves.

The true internationalist has not become a "citizen of the world" through renouncing his own nationality and the values which it carries. Quite the contrary. He is able to understand the values in other national cultures because he understands and is basically in harmony with those of his own. Self-understanding promotes the understanding of others. "One thing, however, is clear, that we cannot attain international-mindedness until we have attained a higher degree of national-mindedness than we possess at present."[4] The humanistic scholar is frequently the best illustration of the internationalist.

The internationalist is anathema to the touchy nationalist. The latter fears the foreigner in the same breath that he vaunts his own country. To him the internationalist appears as a traitor, as a vacuous idealist, or as a fawning social climber. *The*

[4]George H. Mead, "National-Mindedness and International-Mindedness," *The International Journal of Ethics,* XXXIX, 4, (July, 1929), p. 406.

Chicago Tribune in a characteristic editorial giving advice to a
newly appointed secretary of state concludes in these words:

> The temptations of the secretary of state to run his office at
> the direction of Europe have been great and they will be tre-
> mendous in the next four years, but if he responds in this job
> as he did as secretary of war the nation will not quarrel with
> him. Other important international affairs will be settled with
> honour to the United States if Mr. Stimson remembers his war
> department training. There will be questions arising from the
> German reparations settlement and the proposed international
> superbank, as well as our participation in the preparatory dis-
> armament conference.
>
> If Mr. Stimson is more impressed by the ideals of the soldier
> than by the flattery of Europe and of those Americans eager to
> sacrifice their self-respect to be patronized by Europe, we are
> confident that his administration will be memorable.[5]

Sometimes the nationalist sentiment among minorities gives
rise to the socialist reformer or to the revolutionary. Henry de
Man has traced this transformation in the careers of socialist
intellectuals who have sprung from oppressed European nationalities.[6] He describes his own experience as the reaction of a
cultivated member of the Flemish minority in Belgium against
the Flemish bourgeoisie who despised Flemish and aped French
culture:

> Thus in childhood I learned to despise the French-speaking
> bourgeoisie of my country, the persons who awkwardly imi-
> tated Paris; and, although in other respects the feeling which
> prevailed in my home was antiproletarian, I came to feel that
> the common people were more closely akin to me than the
> French-speaking bourgeoisie, and stood higher than these in a
> cultural respect. Thus the transition from a national cultural
> to a social cultural community sense was an easy one.[7]

[5]*Chicago Tribune,* March 27, 1929.
[6]*The Psychology of Socialism* (New York). Translated from the Second
German Edition (1927) by Eden and Cedar Paul. See especially pp. 179–81.
[7]P. 181. De Man analyzes the origins of European socialism in terms of
a "social inferiority complex" giving rise to a compensatory movement.

However, like many other socialists of middle or upper class origin, he found it difficult to renounce the tastes and habits formed in his early environment and to feel genuinely at home in the proletarian world—although this was attempted:

Unconsciously I tried to reduce the distance separating me from the workers in the matter of dress, gestures, and speech; though seldom, and only for brief periods, was I able to realize my ideal, which was to live like a working man, by the performance of a task as exhausting and dirty as possible, thus transforming myself into an authentic proletarian. Not until a good many years had passed did I begin to realize that a man may, after all, be a good socialist without renouncing the advantages given to him by his education.[8]

In a situation like that of the Negro in the United States the intermediary rôle has special difficulties and satisfactions. It made Booker T. Washington the foremost Negro of his day, although he had to move diplomatically between his Scylla and Charybdis: on the one hand he had to reassure the white Southerner that the Negro was not pretending to "social equality"; on the other he had to contend with a critical left-wing group of Negroes who insisted upon making no compromise with white prejudice. His famous Atlanta speech formula that "In all things that are purely social we can be as separate as the fingers, yet one as the hand in all things essential to mutual progress" was typical of his whole life-policy of conciliation and creative accommodation. His astuteness in harmonizing conflicting points of view can be illustrated by the following statement concerning the Negro's political rights:

I am often asked to express myself more freely than I do upon the political condition and the political future of my race.

[8]*Ibid.*, pp. 230–31. On p. 231 he describes "the inferiority complex from which I suffered as a non-proletarian in a proletarian movement" as "the product of autosuggestion."

These recollections of my experience in Atlanta give me the opportunity to do so briefly. My own belief is, although I have never before said so in so many words, that the time will come when the Negro in the South will be accorded all the political rights which his ability, character, and material possessions entitle him to. I think, though, that opportunity to freely exercise such political rights will not come in any large degree through outside or artificial forcing, but will be accorded to the Negro by the Southern white people themselves, and that they will protect him in the exercise of these rights. Just as soon as the South gets over the old feeling that it is being forced by the "foreigners," or "aliens," to do something which it does not want to do, I believe that the change in the direction that I have indicated is going to begin. In fact there are indications that it is already beginning in a slight degree.[9]

Any activity the purpose of which is to promote interracial understanding and cooperation may be considered as having an intermediary character. It may be of an educational nature like that of Booker T. Washington, Robert R. Moton, and J. E. K. Aggrey; it may go in the direction of social work and reform, or the "uplift" of backward members of the group; it may express itself through the writing of a poem or of a history. Among immigrants it also takes the form of specific acts of individual assistance, the indirect result of which is to promote broader cultural assimilation.

The intermediary transforms the relations of the races or nationalities from within outwards. His is an unconscious "boring from within" by which the underlying conditions are slowly changed so that new attitudes and accommodations become inevitable. His work belongs in the category of the slow, silent changes of history, not the spectacular and cataclysmic mutations. He may appear timid, compromising, or opportunistic to impatient temperaments; yet his persistent and steady

[9]*Up from Slavery*, pp. 234-35.

pressure is an essential part in the progress of the subordinate group. His method has the further virtue of softening or undermining resistance, instead of hardening it. Thus the rôle of the moderate complements and reciprocally facilitates the rôle of the radical.

CHAPTER IX

Assimilation and Passing

PARTIAL OR COMPLETE incorporation into the dominant culture is a third possible goal of endeavor for the marginal man. This may take the form of assimilation, as with the immigrant and his children; it may take the form of "passing" as a member of the dominant group where such assimilation is impossible. In order to pass the individual must possess the general physical and social traits of the dominant group. The Jew who is not accepted on terms of equality can pass provided his language, name, and other social characteristics do not betray him; but the person of mixed blood must be able to conform physically as well as culturally.

Where assimilation is possible, the marginal stage is relatively short, although it may be acute. This is noticeable in the experience of many immigrants. While the usual immigrant does not fully acquire the culture of his new homeland, he generally succeeds in making a working adjustment to it. His relationship is symbiotic or economic rather than social. In those cases where he does not live in the immigrant community but mingles with Americans he is likely to become more completely assimilated. The extent to which he becomes assimilated depends upon such factors as age, degree of cultural difference, the frequency and quality of the prejudice he encounters, and the opportunities for participation that he enjoys. In so far as he succeeds in becoming assimilated, his marginal experience proves to be a period of transition from the old culture to the new.[1]

[1]The problem of the marginal immigrant was discussed in Chapter IV.

The Function of "Racial Marks"

Assimilation is not always possible. The attitude of the dominant group may be such that, no matter how completely individuals of subordinate groups take over its culture patterns, they are still made to feel that they do not really belong. In the Western world such exclusion is frequently true for the Jews and for the coloured races, such as Negroes and Orientals. In the United States members of such groups may be quite fully Americanized and yet be referred to as "Jews," "Negroes," "Chinese," etc. The native American unconsciously excludes them when he speaks of "Americans."

"Racial marks"—the distinguishing physical or social traits of a group—become significant in the adjustment of excluded or "unassimilable" groups. The colour and other physical characteristics of Negroes and Orientals clearly place them in a separate category. This is not equally true of the Jews. They are so mixed in race that identification by physical traits alone is difficult if not impossible. Sometimes the Jewish cast of countenance acquired through prolonged living in the ghetto seems to be a means of identification.[2] When physical traits fail to be distinctive, the spoken language, the clothing, the name, the religion, or even the manners and gestures may be indicative of racial or national origin.

Such marks of identification range from the most obvious to the most obscure. Their significance varies according to the place they have on this scale. When they are obvious, as in the case of colour, few mistakes in recognition occur. The individual's "racial" identity is recognized at once and he is therefore treated in a relatively uniform manner. Such uniformity

---

[2] In spite of this, Jews have been forced to wear badges so as to prevent their being mistaken for Christians. For a discussion of this whole question see Maurice Fishberg, *The Jews: A Study of Race and Environment* (New York, 1911), Chapter V.

in treatment is probably a factor in promoting personal adjustment. One Negro writes: "My nationality is so outstanding
that I cannot be taken for any other race, and I do not try to
pass for anything else than my own race. I have no hard feelings when my race is being discussed."[3]

When the differences are more obscure the individual cannot at once be racially categorized. There are opportunities for
mistakes of identification to occur and for intimate contacts to
develop. These mistakes and their later discovery often prove
to be disturbing. Friendships begin and then are suddenly ter-
minated or gradually cooled when the individual's racial or national identity is discovered. The result of a few such experiences is to render the subject acutely conscious of himself and
his race. He becomes uncertain about the proper conduct to
pursue, and is likely to develop either a protective reserve or
an aggressive initiative. Shall he conceal his race or nationality
origin and so avoid unpleasant experiences? or shall he aggres-
sively declare it at once so that no misconceptions can arise?
Either course involves difficulties—but so does that of allowing
relations to develop spontaneously and naturally.

The following case is that of a "Negro" girl who is white in
appearance but has passed only twice. It illustrates the peculiar
difficulties of such an individual both as regards the white race
and the Negro race. Not conforming to the expected appearance of a Negro she is the object of excessive attention and comment. In the company of darker Negroes she is singled out by
contrast. She believes that other Negroes are embarrassed in
her company and so she feels that she belongs to no race.

As a child and up till now, I have always been conscious that
I "look like white." I used to become very angry when remind-
ed of it, but have become used to it. When our playmates became angry with me or my brother, they invariably called us

[3]From a life history.

"sager," or "crackers," or "half-white." Even our first cousins, who are brownskin, used the terms. Our parents always told us to ignore such remarks, but I have cried myself to sleep many nights wishing that I was black. I have always been the object of curious stares from the other group and from strangers of my own group. I am extremely sensitive at such times.

As a child, I never went to town alone on a street car because I hated to be stared at because I was sitting with "coloured" people. Until recently I have walked to and from town because I was afraid there would be no one on the car who knew me and they would think I was out of my place. An experience I once had was partially responsible for such an attitude. One day on the street car (I was sitting in the back of course) the conductor came to me and told me to move up front where I belonged. I stammered that I knew where I belonged. I became very angry. A woman who knew me told him that I was coloured. Needless to say I was very much mortified.

Although I realize that I can cast my lot with either group, I prefer my own people. . . .

I often feel that I belong to no race. I sometimes feel that even members of my own race would rather not be in my company because I "look like white." I recall vividly a remark made by a friend once when my presence in the group caused stares and whispered comments from white people. It was "I bet they think you're white and that we belong to a low class of Negroes who associate with whites." I was horribly hurt—I'll never forget that remark. I have been to Chicago and New York and have noticed to my relief that my presence with my own group does not cause as much curiosity as it does in the South. I plan to make my home somewhere in the North before long. I feel that I can be more at ease.

I frequently engage in daydreams. In my daydreams, I plan to go to some foreign country where it won't make any difference whether I am white or black. I often think that I'd like to live in France.[4]

Recently, about three months ago, influenced by a friend, I went to a white beauty parlor to have my hair marcelled. I

[4]France is almost a Mecca for the marginal Negro.

gave my given and my middle name, but omitted my last name.
The proprietress and girls exclaimed over the colour of my hair
(as I said, it is auburn), saying that they would give anything
to possess it. I knew they would be horrified if they knew I was
coloured. The second time I went back, while having my hair
marcelled, one of the girls came in the booth and told the girl
that there was a coloured woman outside and asked jokingly
if she came to have her hair marcelled. They laughed and began a discussion of coloured people saying that they would refuse absolutely to do any work for any coloured people and
they would not stand for the freedom which the Negro has in
the North. I felt like crying out that she was doing work for
a "nigger" then, but I couldn't afford to open my mouth. Incidentally, the "coloured woman" had come to bring some white
children. I discovered to my consternation that she was a neighbour of mine. I hated it, but I had to walk by her without speaking. I've never been back since. I couldn't after I heard that
conversation. This is the only time in my life that I have ever
deliberately "passed." My friends often tell me that I ought
to go to white shows but I don't care to do so. Last summer
I worked at a summer resort near New York with some of my
school mates. They tried to persuade me to apply for a position in New York as white, but I preferred being with them.[5]

Racial marks also complicate the association of the sexes.
If one member of a pair is light enough to pass for white the
relationship may be regarded as an instance of racial amalgamation. This sometimes gives rise to hostility from the Negro
side as well as from the white, particularly as Negroes grow
in race consciousness and race pride. Passing is out of the
question in such cases, except as a temporary action of one of
the partners. Such relations present some of the problems of
interracial marriage where this is tabooed by the *mores*. The
following excerpts illustrate the predicament:

My eyes are light blue, my hair is light brown, my features

[5]Life history document.

are undeniably Nordic, my skin is white; yet in my veins run a few drops of Negro blood. Therefore, in America I am a Negro.

My wife and daughter and I live on the outskirts of Negro Harlem, in New York City. My wife is of olive-brown skin, with lustrous black hair. Others than myself have called her beautiful. When first I saw her I thought instantly of a mantilla-clad Castilian in some lovely old Spanish town. Frequently we travel downtown to dine in one of the better-class restaurants. We have yet to enter a restaurant without the almost imperceptible, yet none the less visible, hesitancy in seating us on the part of the waiter, the turning of heads, and subdued buzzing comments of the other diners—inaudible, yet unmistakable, discussion of the racial identity of my wife and me. No disturbance has ever occurred—nothing so crude as that—but just as galling is the consciousness of being conspicuous. The struggle to keep one's composure, the fighting back of the blood that seems to flood one's face, the seemingly endless march to one's table—all are a part of this monstrous system that marks a man's worth by the colour of his skin.

... Or perhaps we walk down Seventh Avenue between 130th and 145th Streets, the promenade of Negro New York. Here the staring is sometimes insolent and hostile, sometimes softly enquiring. Written on the faces of many is the conviction that my wife and I flaunt ourselves shamelessly, she a coloured woman, I her white lover. The growing bitterness of Negroes against that sort of thing reacts on us, though they know not how.[6]

Thus the mere likelihood of being mistaken for a member of the dominant race, or of a race less subject to prejudice, tends to create personality problems. In a study of 192 American Negro college students it was found that 45 were sufficiently different in physical appearance to be mistaken for some other race—usually white but occasionally Indian or Mexican. These

[6]"White, but Black: A Document on the Race Problem," *Century*, 109, N.S. (1924–25), Anonymous, pp. 492–93.

45 persons had greater psychological difficulties with which to contend.[7]

PASSING AMONG AMERICAN NEGROES

There is a considerable amount of passing among American Negroes of mixed blood.[8] It seems to be sufficient to affect the census statistics of population, notably in the proportion of male mulattoes to female mulattoes. Thus, while in 1920 there were 1020 black males for each 1000 black females, the return showed only 854 mulatto males for each 1000 mulatto females. The differences were even more marked in certain age groups, as the census for 1910 indicated. Among mulattoes under 15 years of age the sex-ratios were nearly equal, but in the age-group 15–19 years there were only 831 males for each 1000 females. In the age-group 20–44 years the contrast was most impressive, there being only 799 males for each 1000 females. There were fewer male mulattoes in urban communities than in rural communities: 810 males per 1000 females in the former compared with 931 per 1000 in the latter. These figures concur with expectation: males have more incentive and opportunity to pass than females—they break family ties more easily

[7]In terms of an "index of racial maladjustment" the 192 Negroes averaged 8.64 while the 45 light Negroes averaged 11.84, a difference which could have occurred by chance only once out of 1700 times. Twenty-five individuals whose race was mistaken "occasionally" averaged 9.96; 14 who were "often mistaken" averaged 13.64; while 6 who were "very often mistaken" averaged 15.50. The figures for the sub-groups are suggestive but are not statistically conclusive in view of the small numbers.

[8]One writer states that "There are few Negroes in the United States who do not know some other Negro who has 'crossed over' or is 'passing' for white. In some instances, the passing is an economic and daytime occupation, a mask which he doffs at night when he returns to the Negro district to laugh, to play, or to sleep. But there is an increasing number of these whitewashed Ethiopians who have forever deserted the Lares and Penates of the Negro race. They disappear, are suddenly missed from their usual haunts—and the Negro explains the disappearance by the single word "Passing." Elmer A. Carter, "Crossing Over," *Opportunity*, Vol. 4, No. 48, December, 1926, p. 377.

and travel farther. During the productive years, 15 to 45, economic competition and spatial mobility both favour passing; while the impersonal and anonymous character of city-life facilitates escape from racial and social ties which are hampering.[9]

Such figures give us clues concerning passing by male mulattoes; they tell us nothing about passing by females. It is known that the latter also occurs, only to a lesser degree. For every female who passes we must, by the logic of the sex-ratio, increase the above figures by another male. Again we do not know whether the deficiency of males in the mulatto population is due to permanent or only temporary passing. It is likely that many who pass merely for the day's work live in Negro communities and so are enumerated as mulattoes. To that extent also the total number of individuals who pass is underestimated.

The deficiency in mulatto males accords with another inter-

[9]The census explained the excess of mulatto females as follows: "Since the blacks are far more numerous than the mulattoes, the enumerators were likely to return as blacks those Negroes whom they did not see in person, and since the Negro women at home were more apt to be seen by the enumerators than the men, the erroneous return of mulattoes as blacks probably occurred more frequently in regard to men than in regard to women." *Fourteenth Census of the United States,* 1920, Vol. II, p. 104. While some truth probably inheres in this interpretation, it cannot explain the whole difference, since the excess of female mulattoes is not counterbalanced by a corresponding excess of male blacks. In 1910 the excess of female mulattoes was 123,588 while the excess of male blacks was only 67,587. In 1920 the excess of female mulattoes was 130,710 while the excess of male blacks was 86,451. This excess of male blacks does not seem to be abnormal. In fact it is slightly less than that of the native white population of native parentage.

Other evidence has also been suggested. The native-born whites of native parentage who were 10-14 years old in 1900 had increased in numbers when enumerated in 1910 as 20-24 years old. Hornell Hart has suggested that this may be due to the passing of light mulattoes. (See *Opportunity,* October, 1925, p. 291.) The difficulty is that the actual increase occurred among the white females, not among the white males, where one would expect it. The males diminished by about 32,000; the females increased by about 54,000. The latter can hardly be due to mulatto females crossing over, for the Negro females of these age-groups also increased.

esting fact : the tendency of dark men to marry lighter women.[10] This tendency is in part attributable to a preference for lightness of skin, although other influences naturally play a part in the individual's marital choice. But do not women also prefer mates who are lighter in colour? Probably most of them do—although the belief that darker men are more anxious to please and provide for a wife who is lighter-complexioned may have some effect upon the choices of women. Allowing for such attitudes, there is also a more elementary explanation for the tendency of wives to be lighter in colour : if male mulattoes pass more frequently than females, as appears to be true, then the females, if they are to marry at all, must select husbands from the available supply—in other words, they must frequently marry a man darker than themselves. This tendency is probably favoured by the greater ease with which dark males can rise, economically and socially, in comparison with dark females.

The attitude of Negroes toward the passing of other Negroes does not seem to be uniform. Probably most of them do not object. As Baker states, they may enjoy the fact of knowing that the white man is not able to close all the gaps in the colour line :

Once, in a gathering of mulattoes I heard the discussion turn to the stories of those who had "gone over to white"—friends or acquaintances of those who were present. Few such cases are known to white people, but the Negroes know many of them. It developed from this conversation (and afterward I

[10]M. Herskovits found evidence for this. See his book *The American Negro: A Study in Race Crossing* (New York, 1928). Our questionnaire study also indicated a definite tendency for the wife to be lighter than the husband, the wife being lighter in 61 per cent of the marriages. When the husband was lighter, there was a tendency for the wife to be more educated, *i.e.*, in 63 per cent of the cases. The number of cases on this point was rather small, however, there being 10 cases where the husband was lighter and also more educated than his wife; 17 cases where the wife was darker and more educated. "Educated" here refers to schooling.

got the same impression many times) that there is a sort of conspiracy of silence to protect the Negro who "crosses the line" and takes his place as a white man. Such cases even awaken glee among them, as though the Negro, thus, in some way, was getting even with the dominant white man.[11]

The growth of race consciousness and pride creates a sentiment unfavourable to passing, the act being regarded as that of a renegade. One student wrote the following, "I am proud that any trait I possess is characteristic of Negroes, and that I can't pass as a member of another race. For I do detest any one so weak that he will pass to keep from enduring the hardships and privations of his own race." Sometimes, of course, such sentiments express personal envy rather than race pride. Greater hostility is evoked on occasions when individuals seek to have their status as whites confirmed by court action. In an editorial entitled "We Lost One," *The Chicago Defender* voiced the following among other sentiments, "Mr. —— quit because he couldn't stay. The power was not in him. A man is as are his affections. . . . The law has helped Mr. ——, but he will be remembered not only as the man without a race but as a white man who had to have a lawsuit to prove himself to be one."

THE MENTAL CONFLICTS OF PASSING

Many individuals who can pass do not do so. Their position seems to indicate that there are difficulties whichever side of the colour-line is chosen. Others who pass for a time later return to the fold. Passing may be a technique of practical significance, as in the case of one who investigates Southern lynchings.[12] To some it involves personal and social disorganization.

It is a doubtful form of adjustment. Whereas assimilation is largely an unconscious process in which social backgrounds

[11]Ray Stannard Baker, *Following the Colour Line,* pp. 162–63.
[12]Walter White, "I Investigate Lynchings," *American Mercury,* January, 1929.

simply fade gradually away, passing is usually conscious and deliberate. It signifies that the group conflict is so severe that the individual is compelled to resort to subterfuge. Such a course of action may prove of advantage economically and socially, but it tends to create other problems, both social and moral. If it is temporary and occasional, such as attending a tabooed restaurant, theatre or hairdresser, it may be viewed merely as an amusing escapade. Even the securing of employment as a member of the dominant race will not always create a moral conflict, for the individual can justify his conduct as necessary because of the existing race prejudice. Nevertheless, it often does involve some moral struggle, as in the following:

Here, in Chicago, I really began to see what a nationality means to a person—I couldn't get a job in an office, nor anywhere as far as that goes, because I truthfully said I was Jewish. This fact gave me quite a problem and worried me for some time. Gee! who would think that just because I was Jewish—regardless of qualification—I was automatically excluded from society. Of course I could have gotten a job as a department store clerk or something like that, but for one who had ideals this would have been quite a setback. I plugged away in hopes of finding a job without having to lie—and then I visited the Y. M. C. A. Employment Bureau. "Oh, how I love this bureau!" I was politely informed that I was Jewish and would have some time finding a position because of this.— Alas! what to do—I left the building in a quandary.

I had been working all my life—and now nationality stood between me and starvation. I resolved to change my nationality and go to work—I went into another employment bureau, changed my name, nationality, etc., and got a job—right away, mind you! It was easy for me to get along as a Gentile as I had mostly Gentile habits—not having lived amongst members of my own race for any great length of time, and fortunately I looked like a German and that helped— You can bet. But I ran into some difficulties; some Gentile people can't stand an ambitious and hard worker and get jealous, so what did they do but try to attack the industrious worker on a social and religious issue. So the question was put to me: "Dave, aren't you Jewish?" Those words at times made me inwardly mad but outwardly I displayed no change. To save my face I was obliged to deny this with my mouth, but in heart I felt quite proud of my nationality—for it seems to me the great difference between a Jew and a Gentile and the reason for the more or less success of the Jew is because he judges a man by his qualifications—not his religious beliefs; heavens, aren't we all human —don't we all acknowledge a common and one God; don't we live in the same world—what difference should it make whether I'm Jew, Irish, Italian; Catholic, Jewish, Protestant, as long as I have my qualifications for the position I seek to fill.[13]

Another aspect of the moral problem involved in partial passing is the necessity for continual secrecy. A light Negro who passes in order to secure better work but who lives with his family is under constant apprehension that some one will discover his dual racial rôle. As one individual remarked, "The thing finally became unbearable. No decent man could stand it. I preferred to be a Negro and hold up my head rather than to be a sneak."[14]

In the following example an acute moral conflict developed out of a passing which began as a mistaken identity. The importance of this experience hinges upon the fact that it arose out of social assimilation, not mere economic expediency, and that there was also a change of religion. A Jewish college student found himself drawn into the comradeship of Gentiles who accepted him as one of themselves.

Somehow I could not bring myself to reveal the truth about

[13]From a life history.
[14]Cited by Ray Stannard Baker, *Following the Colour Line* (New York, 1908), p. 161. The problem of passing is a frequent theme of Negro literature. Probably no writer has equalled the depiction of James Weldon Johnson in *The Autobiography of an Ex-Colored Man*. (Garden City, N. Y., 1912, 1927). The relations of passing and recreation are discussed by W. H. Jones in *Recreation and Amusement Among Negroes in Washington, D. C.*

my own identity. I felt they would learn sooner or later. I was
too happy over being admitted into their small circle of com-
panionship to persuade myself deliberately to ruin, as I felt I
would by telling them, this short-lived satisfaction.

I remember the day the boys learned that I was a Jew. I
detected it in the atmosphere. Their attitudes, their greetings
to me, their bearing in my presence seemed to undergo a per-
ceptible change. I was still accepted as a member of the group
but I felt I was on the fringe, although I can't really recall the
times I was "counted out." Occasionally remarks were made
which were rather pointed. Toward the close of the year one
of the group was pledged to a fraternity, the other two were
introduced to the same fraternity by the first student—the matter was not even broached to me.

He did not feel sympathetic to Jewish association, and so
found an excuse for not accepting an invitation to join a leading Jewish fraternity. He made further Gentile friends, including his roommate. "Increasingly, however, I found myself
becoming more sensitive to my racial heritage and to the
'stigma' (as I then considered it) of 'Jew.' . . . I felt that it was
limiting in the number of contacts I could make and in the
extent to which I could enter the inner circle of a group. A
factor that tended to increase the conflict was that the great
majority of my Gentile acquaintances accepted me off-hand as
one of them, never suspecting my racial identity until it was
revealed to them." He gave up Jewish religious practices.
These were associated with an unhappy home life, especially
with his father: ". . . religion remained to me the thing I saw
in him—the faithful performance of certain ritualistic practices,
the attendance of synagogue on the three annual festival occasions and blind loyalty to the Jewish group." By contrast, Gentile family life and Christianity appealed to him more and more
as he came to experience them. At length he determined to conceal his Jewish background. He joined a Christian denomina-

tion where "I felt strangely at peace with myself and the world," and decided to train for the Christian ministry. He entered the seminary and continued to pass as of Gentile origin. But the conflict concerning this grew deeper and deeper. The longer the time of passing the more involved he became in his new life. He balanced in his mind the two possible courses of action: whether to continue to conceal his identity or to reveal it. He finally determined, after intense struggle, on the latter course, and thereby succeeded in integrating his life:

The girl, who later became my wife, is responsible for the sharing of my "secret" with others. The method she used was simply a frank insistence that I take into my confidence at least one professor and one student. Almost every one of my daily devotions brought into relief the conflict that was ever present in my consciousness. I had rationalized well—I was in the innermost group of the school life, an integral part of its life and activities; I had become the intimate companion of at least three men; I had been elected the President of my Senior class; what mattered it to any one what I was born—the only thing that really mattered was what I was then; if I should tell I would be ashamed that I had not spoken sooner to those whose life secrets I had shared; if it were known I might ruin my chances for securing a position; if it were known the world which I had found so friendly and in which I had been so happy might turn on me—I had heard the boys speak slightingly of other Jews; so on and on I went in this vicious circle. Before I finally capitulated a whole night's struggle was necessary. The following morning I laid the whole matter before the professor whose warmth and cordiality had already kindled confidence and love for him within me. He, very sympathetically and, I realize now, intelligently, helped to cut this mental "boil" from my mind. That same day I spoke to one of my closest friends whom I had already asked to act as the best man at my wedding. His reactions were so warm and reassuring that I began gradually to see the folly and falseness of the whole hypersensitive fear structure I had built up. At about the same time my mother received a letter from me giving her the truth about my work.

However, I still had not reached the position which would allow me to speak freely of myself. It required the experience of the pastorate to bring me to that place. Six months after I graduated from Seminary I wrote to all my intimate friends making the revelation which should have normally been made in my intimate relations with them. Almost every one who was told responded so warmly as to dislodge completely any suspecting and sensitive thoughts that may have lingered. About two years ago, as a test to myself that I had completely overcome, I preached a sermon on "The Christian and the Jew" to a university congregation mentioning incidentally that the first half of my life had been spent in a Jewish home. I speak freely on the subject now whenever I feel the occasion is appropriate —I am not in the least concerned about the reactions such a statement produces. The few unfavourable impressions that have resulted have not affected my attitude or conduct. In fact I count it as part of my responsibility wherever possible to dispel the prejudice that is still abundantly evident. Within the last few years I have formed several fast Jewish friendships (one Jewish rabbi among them) who have helped to build up my interest in the problem of the Jew and given me a new appreciation of liberal Judaism.[15]

Passing is found in every race situation where the subordinate race is held in disesteem. It is noted by students of mixed bloods in such varied regions as India, South Africa, the West Indies, and in South America. Among Jews[16] it has long been a problem, in the past leading Gentiles to protect themselves by making regulations which provided for the wearing of a distinctive badge. It is found in the relations of classes and castes. For instance, among the despised class or caste of the Japanese, the *Eta,* individuals find it essential to conceal their group

[15]From a life history.
[16]For a discussion of the problem among Jews in the United States see George E. Sokolsky, *We Jews* (Garden City, N. Y., 1935).

identity in order to avoid discrimination.[17] Among immigrant groups it is a frequent phenomenon, taking curious forms in local environments. Thus, besides the tendency to Americanize names—which often simply indicates a process of natural assimilation rather than passing—one finds that in Jewish districts in Chicago there are individuals of Italian origin who have passed as Jews. Among Germans, a Polish girl may prefer to be German. A Swedish young man on an Irish baseball team passes as Irish. A white child among coloured children wishes she were dark so that she would not be excluded. During the World War many Germans found it more comfortable to be Scandinavians or Dutch. The principle seems to be that of the minority wishing to share the advantages of membership in the majority, or to escape its discriminations and antagonisms.

RELIGIOUS BAPTISM AND ASSIMILATION

An intermediate form of adjustment between passing and assimilation is baptism. This has been prominent among the Jews.[18] By embracing the faith of the dominant people of his environment the Jew removes the disabilities under which he labours. In pre-war Russia baptism afforded him a complete change of status from that of ghettoes in the Pale of Settlement to free participation in Russian life; in pre-war Germany[19] it signified the removal of social prejudices which hindered his occupational advancement, especially in the army and university; in pre-war Austria it removed legal obstacles to intermarriage. While baptism takes place everywhere it occurs least where the Jew is accepted as a full equal, and most often where he has been emancipated from the ghetto and yet finds

[17]See Shigeaki Ninomiya, "The Japanese *Eta*," in *The Transactions of the Asiatic Society of Japan,* December, 1933, Chap. VII.
[18]See also the section on the Jews in Chap. IV.
[19]Under the present Nazi rule, of course, the position of the Jew is much worse; in Communistic Russia it is much improved.

himself limited by less open social prejudices. When repression is severe the revival of Jewish consciousness and the increase of social isolation reduce the amount of baptism.[20]

Baptism can be viewed as a late stage in the process of assimilation, but it also indicates the existence of considerable social pressure and religious prejudice, and therefore is psychologically akin to passing. One important difference is present: the baptized is often known to be such and his acceptance is seldom without an element of *arrière-pensée* which renders his "assimilation" somewhat specious. Adjustment is more genuine in the case of his descendants, or with those individuals who sincerely undergo a change of religion and who are less under the influence of social ambition.

[20]See Maurice Fishberg, *The Jews*, Chap. XXI.

CHAPTER X

Maladjustment and Adjustment

A CERTAIN DEGREE of personal maladjustment is inherent in the marginal situation, but it varies both in terms of individuals and situations. At a minimum it consists of an inner strain and *malaise,* a feeling of isolation or of not quite belonging. This may be subtle and evanescent in quality—coming and going with particular experiences and shifting moods. From an external point of view, the individual appears to be socially adjusted: he has a family and friends, perhaps a good position and a measure of success. But his mind is not quite in harmony with his social world. He need not be unhappy; in fact, he may laugh at his position; but laughter may be compensatory and not satisfactorily disclose his real state of mind. The problems can be "forgotten" or "outgrown" by some. This will depend upon the individual's success or accomplishments relative to his expectations and philosophy of values. Perhaps it is the socially sensitive but introverted person who has idealistically identified himself with a culture or scheme of life which subsequently proves unrealizable, who finds it hardest to contract his spiritual life into a narrower framework. He cannot rid himself of his earlier sentiments and aspirations; and even when he adopts the rôle of intermediary, or becomes a flaming nationalist, the mental tension persists as an underlying motive colouring his moods and driving his thoughts. Such personalities, when superior in intelligence and will, may become outstanding leaders.

At the other extreme, the mental conflict becomes a disorganizing force. Inability to diagnose the source of the con-

flict, the conviction of facing an unscalable wall, and persona
failures, overwhelm the individual. Mental conflict leads to dis
couragement and perhaps despair. With the adult this mean
a breakdown in individual "life-organization"[1]—that structure
of attitudes and values in which the individual has his being
and through which he realizes his purposes. In its extreme form
this eventuates in mental disorganization and in suicide. The
following account illustrates the experience of some persons o
mixed racial ancestry who find themselves socially ostracized

There was a boy whom I knew in Canton. He was sever
years younger than I, a school friend of my brother's and a son
of a British Vice Consul. His father later married a European
This boy stood at the head of his class easily. He excelled in
athletics, and he was very likeable and full of confidence. I
knew him because he used to come home with my brother for
vacations.

Upon his graduation his father placed him in a docking com
pany in Canton. He was very happy there and was very quickly
promoted. Then some English boys arrived. These English
boys were asked to dinner by the head of the firm; he was not
He could find no society. He wouldn't mix with the merchant
and sailor class of whites, who were a tough and vulgar crowd.
He thought his education entitled him to a different position.
Finally he took up gambling and began to smoke.

Before this happened, however, he married off his sister, who
had been in an Italian convent. He had always felt responsible
for her.

The head of the school sent me to see him when I was in
Canton. I said, "You shouldn't do this, you are hurting the
name of the whole Eurasian colony; you should make a fight."

"Clive," he said, "that isn't fair; you have your father's
house to go to. You are accepted everywhere on his account.
I can find no society at all. What have I to fight for?" He took
raw opium and killed himself.[2]

[1] W. I. Thomas and F. Znaniecki, *The Polish Peasant in Europe and Amer-ica* (New York, 1927), Vol. II, p. 1843.
[2] Survey Major Document 31. Quoted in C. C. Wu, *Chinatowns*, pp. 338–39. (Unpublished Ph.D. thesis, University of Chicago, 1928.)

MALADJUSTMENT AND ADJUSTMENT 203

Among immigrant populations, the rate of suicide reflects the disorganization typical of such cultural transplantation. In the United States the suicide rates of certain cities are higher for the immigrant than for the native-born. Among the foreign-born of Chicago in 1930, for example, the rate was 38.8 per 100,000 population, while for the native-born it was 12.4.[3] In the United States generally the rate for each immigrant group is two or three times higher than for the same nationality in Europe.[4] The suicide rates of Orientals in the United States are likewise higher than for the corresponding Asiatic countries. Among Orientals in Hawaii, however, suicides were less frequent than among Orientals in California—an evidence of the difference in ease of adjustment.[5]

Apart from the specific problem of suicide, the general disorganization of the immigrant has been the subject of much recent investigation.[6] The cultural traditions of the old world are broken through migration and can only be partially re-created in the new situation. Again, the individual loses his former rôle and status and must at first descend in occupation and social position. Social pressure which kept him "straight" in the old world no longer functions so effectively. Customs in the new world are misunderstood and he interprets differences as indicative of license, or gets into trouble through sheer ignorance.

At home the immigrant was almost completely controlled by the community; in America this lifelong control is relaxed. Here the community of his people is at best far from complete, and, moreover, it is located within the American community,

[3]M. A. Elliott and F. E. Merrill, *Social Disorganization* (New York, 1934), p. 401.
[4]Ruth S. Cavan, *Suicide* (Chicago, 1928), p. 33.   [5]*Ibid.*, p. 36.
[6]See particularly W. I. Thomas and F. Znaniecki, *The Polish Peasant in Europe and America*, Part III, Vol. II, of the two-volume edition; R. E. Park and H. A. Miller, *Old World Traits Transplanted*, Chap. IV; William I. Thomas, *The Unadjusted Girl* (Boston, 1923).

which lives by different and more individualistic standards, and shows, as we have seen, a contempt for all the characteristics of newcomers. All the old habits of the immigrant consequently tend to break down. The new situation has the nature of a crisis, and in a crisis the individual tends either to reorganize his life positively, adopt new habits and standards to meet the new situation, or to repudiate the old habits and their restraint without reorganizing his life—which is demoralization.[7]

Culture conflict in the immigrant family between the Americanized children and the unassimilated parents has been found to be an important factor in delinquency, crime, and other forms of personal disorganization.[8] The immigrant usually brings a mature character which helps him to make a fair adjustment if he lives in an immigrant community. However, old-world rules of conduct are ill-adapted for truly American conditions, and are frequently despised by the immigrant's own children. The second generation is therefore unable to receive the usual benefits of guidance and control from the older generation, and does not sufficiently assimilate American standards, nor possess the maturity wisely to control its own conduct. It is not to be wondered at, then, that statistical evidence should show a higher rate of crime among the second generation than is true of the immigrants.[9]

The "second generation" of immigrants generally come into contact with the courts as delinquents more frequently than the first generation. The Census report of 1910 which shows the opposite can be disregarded because of the lack of homogeneity in the groups concerned. Laughlin's study of prisoners in 1921–22 resulted in the criminality rates as follows: native white,

[7]R. E. Park and H. A. Miller, *Old World Traits Transplanted*, p. 61.
[8]See Louis Wirth, "Culture Conflict and Delinquency," *Social Forces*, June, 1931, pp. 484 ff.
[9]The rates vary for different groups and according to the situation. Thus the Chinese and Japanese in Hawaii as yet have had very little delinquency or crime.

both parents native-born, 81.84; native-born, both parents for-eign-born, 91.14; native-born, one parent native-born and one foreign-born, 115.58. In 1920 in Massachusetts per 100,000 population fifteen years of age and over the following numbers were committed to penal or reformatory institutions for adults: 120 native-born of native parents, 226 native-born of foreign or mixed parents, and 143 foreign-born. This is in general the rating of the three groups, native-born whites of native parents having the smallest number of commitments, foreign-born whites rank second, and native-born of foreign or mixed par-ents (the second generation) rank highest.[10]

Among the Jews, the prevalence of derangements of the nerv-ous system is conspicuous. The orthodox Jew lives a well-or-ganized group life centring around the Jewish religious and social code and under the leadership of the rabbi, who is a learned man as well as the guide of the community. But the position and rôle of the Jews in Europe have subjected them to intense nervous strain. The environment of hostility and perse-cution, the concentration upon commerce, banking, speculating and other "precarious" occupations, and their social isolation in the cities, are the outstanding factors. With the decline of orthodoxy and the ghetto, the character of disorganization also changes: suicide, no longer viewed as a sin, increases; but the decrease of persecution among Western Jews results in less hysteria and neurasthenia.[11]

From this brief survey of pathological aspects it is evident, perhaps, that the situational approach offers a lead to under-standing both the extent and kind of disorganization entailed by racial and cultural conflict. As tension subsides through working adjustments and gradual assimilation, personal disor-ganization also declines. This is the general direction which race

[10]E. H. Sutherland, *Criminology* (Philadelphia, 1924), pp. 100-1. The de-linquency of the second generation does not necessarily include a mental con-flict; it may be purely a matter of gang behaviour.

[11]For a detailed discussion see Maurice Fishberg, *op. cit.*, Chap. XV.

relations tend to take: from an initial phase when contacts are being established, on through successive phases of competition and conflict, each ending in shorter or longer periods of accommodation, there is an accompanying process of cultural interpenetration and biological amalgamation which slowly reduces distances and differences so that a larger common understanding replaces the conflicts. As this occurs, adjustment rather than maladjustment becomes the rule.

ADJUSTMENT

What is the "best" adjustment for the marginal person? Is it to aim for assimilation, to turn to nationalism, or to strive for some intermediary rôle? No categorical answer can be given. The nature of the situation as well as the traits of the individual must be considered.

Situations which permit social acceptance upon a self-respecting basis are the simplest. Here the natural tendency toward assimilation automatically produces a certain degree of adjustment. Indeed, the danger often arises from too rapid assimilation. In the United States many immigrants, and particularly the children of immigrants, have been only too willing to discard their traditional values. Like innumerable well-meaning native exponents of Americanization, they have confused good citizenship with 100 per cent cultural conformity. Perhaps the finest citizens of foreign origin are those who have been able to preserve the best in their ancestral heritages while reaching out for the best that America could offer. They have been able to create a balance between continuity and change, and so have maintained reasonably stable characters.

Where a self-respecting acceptance is difficult or impossible of attainment, the goal of adjustment must be different. A nationalistic attitude is normal in those regions where the dominant group is only an invading minority: one cannot expect the East to continue to bow to the West. But here likewise it will be necessary to make a creative adjustment. The East cannot merely reject the West, any more than it can become an imitation of the West; but it *can* make an adjustment to certain Western ideas and methods. In the process of so doing the Western world on its side will develop a new attitude of respect and appreciation for non-Western cultures and non-Western races. It will then become possible for the peoples of the West and the East to cooperate as equals in promoting certain common objectives such as peace and economic welfare. If, for example, the place of India within the British Commonwealth of Nations can be successfully worked out, the world will have a practical illustration of such cooperation. Furthermore, if the League of Nations can be fashioned into an effective instrument of international cooperation, the whole problem of nationalism and race relations will be greatly simplified.

The most difficult situations are those where neither assimilation nor nationalism is feasible. But even in such cases the *principles* of adjustment seem to be clear: equality of public rights and loyalty to the state combined with cultural freedom, if genuinely carried out, will make possible political unity and economic cooperation while leaving each group free to follow its distinctive cultural life. More than one nation has already proved the practicability of reconciling a large degree of cultural diversity with strong political unity. Switzerland is the best small-scale example of such a reconciliation; the British Empire or Commonwealth of Nations—despite some serious deviations and waverings—is the best large-scale illustration.

In the last analysis the world adjustment of races and nationalities is a matter of slow evolution. It will be conditioned by progress in the diffusion of culture, by the stabilization of populations, by mastery over economic forces, and by the growth of democratic-humanitarian sentiments. Such changes may shift the focus of group conflicts in new directions so that racial and national sentiments will automatically weaken. Class or economic conflicts may increase and deflect attention in their direction, thereby rearranging the main in-group and out-group pattern of loyalty.

So far we have considered the problem in terms of the external situation. Now we turn very briefly to the individual himself.

From the individual's standpoint the problem of adjustment is one of psychological integration. Whether he takes an attitude for assimilation, for nationalism, or for an intermediary rôle, he must in each case face his own inner conflicts. And he must do so in a confused and unfriendly world.

Psychological integration is promoted by a realistic interpretation of the social situation and by understanding its influence upon the personality. Such clarification does not always adjust the problem, but it is a necessary first step. Further integration is achieved by adjustment in other important segments of life such as marriage and family relations, occupation, and religion. If the individual can identify himself with a movement or task which enlists his energies and interests, the racial and national difficulty can be made secondary. Creative minds may find an outlet through using the conflict as a theme of artistic expression[12] or scientific investigation. It is possible for some individuals to move to localities where racial problems are less acute. Friendships also have their part in adjustment, for congenial personal association provides a protective barrier against the

12This is noticeable in the writings of Ludwig Lewisohn. For an interesting analysis of the interrelations between Lewisohn's personality and his writings see Ernest Sutherland Bates, "Lewisohn into Crump," *The American Mercury*, April, 1934, pp. 441–50. Upon returning to the United States after ten years in Europe, Lewisohn expresses a more appreciative opinion of American culture. See *Harpers*, October, 1934, "An American Comes Home."

assaults of the outside world as well as a release for pent-up emotions.

What seems generally essential, if the individual possesses insight and wishes to maintain his self-respect, is that he shall not evade the issues, deceive himself, or act a rôle which does not have the fullest possible support of his deeper thoughts and sentiments. If he is of mixed blood[13]—why deny it? If racially he belongs to one group but culturally to another, the dilemma cannot simply be side-stepped. If his nationality is despised he will not solve his difficulty by denationalization and escape into some spurious form of cosmopolitanism, for the development of an "international mind" presupposes the existence of an integrated national mind. And if, on the other hand, he takes refuge in bitter, fanatical nationalism he may not achieve a genuine harmony of inner attitude and sentiment but merely release his hatreds on the out-group and his loves on the in-group.

To confront the issues with courage will not necessarily solve the whole conflict, for the action of one person cannot eliminate, although it may significantly modify, the objective social situation: thus Jakob Wassermann, though firmly insisting upon his dual status of German and Jew, did not perceptibly change the German-Jewish cleavage. But those who maintain their personal integrity—the "I am myself" attitude—do reaffirm the rights of personality in the face of external pressures, and so become pioneers and creative agents in that new social order which seems to evolve as narrower group loyalties gradually give way to larger human values.

[13]In George E. Sokolsky's "My Mixed Marriage," *The Atlantic Monthly,* August, 1933, the interested reader will find a frank discussion of the problems of mixed marriages and also some pertinent suggestions about rearing mixed-blood children.

CHAPTER XI

The Sociological Significance of the Marginal Man

THE CONCEPT

THE PERSONALITY PROBLEM which forms the theme of this study has often been noted and discussed in its separate and concrete aspects. The anomalous position and mental tensions of the racial hybrid have attracted much attention. The character of the Jew has interested Jews as well as Gentiles. Immigrants, as also the children of immigrants, have naturally received much consideration from those who are concerned about assimilation. And the conflicts of the *êthos* of East and West have caused more than one Kipling to burst into poetry and prophecy.

Out of common-sense observation and everyday relations come identifying names and epithets. Even words of respectability acquire questionable connotations because they are tinctured with attitudes of prejudice and associated with lowliness of status. As a consequence the term "Eurasian" is changed to "Anglo-Indian"; the Negro prefers to be called "African" or "Coloured"; and sometimes the immigrant hesitates about referring to himself as such. In particular situations special terms have arisen which point directly to the dual or marginal character: "Europeanized African," "Anglicised Indian," "half-caste," "métis," "déraciné," "parvenu," "allrightnick," "denationalized," *"haolefied,"* "hyphenated citizen," etc. Occasionally a writer makes a comparison between two of them.

By bringing such scattered terms under one embracing concept—the marginal man—comparison and analysis are furthered. Elements common to all may be abstracted, and the major outlines of the situation and personality defined. The essential and the universal become separable from the accidental and unique; the deviations or sub-types more accurately understood in terms of the special conditions. Thus a scientific conception can be developed. Dewey's statement with reference to the rôle of scientific conceptions is pertinent: "Scientific conceptions are not a revelation of prior and independent reality. They are a system of hypotheses worked out under conditions of definite test, by means of which our intellectual and practical traffic with nature is rendered freer, more secure and more significant."[1]

THE BIOLOGICAL FACTOR

The assumption of this study has been that the marginal personality is a function of social conditions. An appeal to facts seems to support this assumption. Thus the marginal type appears in every major race, among unmixed groups as well as among racial hybrids, and in almost every culture. The common factor is not biological but a certain social situation. The chief way in which physical race enters is as a mark of identification. This facilitates the focussing of race prejudice, reduces social contact, and so impedes the natural process of assimilation. The clearest, or most obvious, marginal types are often those who culturally belong to the dominant group but who racially are members of the subordinate group.

[1]John Dewey, *The Quest for Certainty* (New York, 1929), p. 165. An effort has been made to keep the concept empirically valid, and not to construct an "ideal type" as in Max Weber's sociology. See Theodore Abel, *Systematic Sociology in Germany* (New York, 1929), Chap. IV.

Even within a specific type of problem, such as that of the mixed bloods, the marginal personality varies with the nature of the situation. This fact, taken together with the general resemblance of the racial hybrid to the cultural hybrid, suggests if it does not fully establish that race mixture as such does not produce unstable genetic constitutions or disharmonic personalities. Fuller proof for this must await further research in genetics as well as detailed studies of mixed bloods in different social environments.

The question is sometimes asked whether the marginal man does not reflect individual variations in inherited temperament and sensitivity. Do not those who are sensitive by nature become the most sensitive marginal men? There is probably some truth in this assertion, but it can easily be over-emphasized. Interviews and the life histories of many cases show that sensitivity develops largely with the crisis phase. Furthermore, it fluctuates with the situation in which the individual is living; rising and declining in terms of his experience. Finally, the variations between different groups can hardly be accounted for in terms of individual predisposition. Other factors seem to be more important in the individual's traits—especially the degree to which he has psychologically identified himself with the dominant culture and then been repulsed.

THE MARGINAL CULTURE AREA

Social anthropologists have sometimes referred to distant and border cultures, such as those of primitive Australia and Patagonia, as "marginal cultures."[2] It is evident that such cultures have little in common with the subject of this study; indeed, if isolated, they tend toward cultural stability, if not stagnation, rather than culture conflict.

[2]Clark Wissler, *Man and Culture* (New York, 1923), pp. 38, 147.

The concept of "marginal area" refers to a region where two cultures overlap, and where the occupying group combines the traits of both cultures. This, as Goldenweiser states, is a purely objective concept: "Psychologically, the marginal area is but a type of cultural area, for its cultural content is as much of a unit and has the same value to its human carriers as the content of a full-fledged culture area."[3] Such marginal areas may or may not involve culture conflict. When they do, we may also expect to find marginal men.

The expansion of Western civilization over the globe has brought about marginal areas of conflict and produced persons living within both cultures. Such culture conflict is particularly evident in the urban centers. These are the points of maximum cultural interpenetration. From such centers the new influences radiate out along the paths of communication and transportation.

The rural indigenous population, as well as foreign immigrants, stream into the cities, and are sorted into areas inhabited by their own kind. Thus the modern large city is a mosaic of minor culture units which shift their residence as the city grows and gradually lose their identities in the process of assimilation. These centers are the real melting-pots of culture. Consequently, the place of residence within the city becomes a significant index of cultural status.[4] Competition and mobility, however, are so active that the conception of the marginal area as employed by the anthropologist does not fully indicate the dynamic complexity of the cultural process.

[3]A. Goldenweiser, "Cultural Anthropology" in H. E. Barnes (Editor), *History and Prospects of the Social Sciences* (New York, 1925), p. 245.
[4]For a number of special studies of this type see R. E. Park and E. W. Burgess, *The City* (Chicago, 1925); E. W. Burgess, *The Urban Community* (Chicago, 1926); F. Thrasher, *The Gang* (Chicago, 1927); E. W. Mowrer, *Family Disorganization* (Chicago, 1927); L. Wirth, *The Ghetto* (Chicago, 1928); H. Zorbaugh, *The Gold Coast and the Slum* (Chicago, 1929); Robert Redfield, *Tepoztlan* (Chicago, 1930); and E. F. Frazier, *The Negro Family in Chicago* (Chicago, 1932).

Culture Content and Culture Conflict

The core of traits which characterize the marginal personality springs from the conflict of cultures, and not from the specific content of any culture. Each society has a distinctive culture which creates its own type of personality: English, Italian, Japanese, Hawaiian. For the purposes of this study, such nationality differences—like the differences arising from individual heredity and differential experience within a culture—are excluded from consideration. It is the conflict of groups possessing different cultures which is the determining influence in creating the marginal man, and the typical traits are social-psychological, rather than cultural, in nature.

Membership within a social group is more vital to the individual than sharing any particular culture; the first is a prerequisite to the second. Accordingly, when his social status is endangered, the psychological consequences are fundamental. It is because the marginal individual has an uncertain status in two or more groups that he becomes a distinct type of personality irrespective of the particular content of the cultures.

Culture conflict is simply a form of group conflict where the source of the conflict lies in the cultural difference. This difference is interpreted in moral terms. Two systems of *mores* are struggling, each commanding the loyalty of its members. Fundamentally, it is a struggle for existence: which group shall control the situation? Each group—particularly the one in control—seeks to protect itself by keeping the other in its place. This is a matter of maintaining social distance; when the position of the controlling group is threatened by the advance of the subordinate group it responds with fear and antipathy—*i.e.,* race prejudice.[5]

[5]Robert E. Park, "The Bases of Race Prejudice," *Annals of the American Academy of Political and Social Science*, November, 1928, pp. 11–20.

Race prejudice is a collective attitude directed to the other racial group as a whole. Individual members of the latter are treated in terms of the attitude toward the group—not in accordance with their own personality traits. The educated Negro is placed in the same class as the uneducated Negro; the assimilated Jew or Oriental is regarded like the unassimilated Jew or Oriental. A few members of the dominant group who know the assimilated individual intimately may treat him in terms of his individual traits. Thus culture conflict and differential assimilation are the basic factors in creating the marginal man.

THE MARGINAL MAN AND THE SOCIAL THEORY OF PERSONALITY

The scientific study of personality is still in its early stages. Approaches in terms of physiology, individual psychology, psychiatry and psychoanalysis, with all their schools and personal interpretations, have as yet reached no common standpoint. In this conflict of interpretations and methods, sociological students have insisted upon the necessity of viewing personality as shaped by, as well as shaping, a social process. One may go back to the psychologist William James and his analysis of the self, particularly the "social self." The individual, writes James, "has as many different social selves as there are distinct *groups* of persons about whose opinion he cares. He generally shows a different side of himself to each of these different groups."[6] With the sociologist Charles H. Cooley the analysis of the self proceeds even more realistically and subtly than with James. There is always a "social reference" involved in the self, but in a "very large and interesting class of cases" it takes the form of a "reflected or looking-glass self" which consists of "the imagination of our appearance to the other person; the imagina-

[6]William James, *Psychology* (Briefer Course) (New York, 1920), Chap. XII, p. 179.

tion of his judgment of that appearance, and some sort of self-feeling, such as pride or mortification."[7]

The "social reference" of the self is the social group. Accordingly one may define personality as "the sum and organization of those traits which determine the rôle of the individual in the group."[8] The concept of rôle in the group provides a frame of reference within which various traits play their parts both as causes and consequences of the rôle. Thus intelligence may help to make an individual into a leader, and the rôle of leadership in turn produces certain personality traits, such as self-confidence. But, since the individual usually belongs to several groups in each of which he has a rôle, his personality has multiple facets. Thence arises the problem of harmonizing and integrating his various selves, so that a stable character and meaningful inner life can be achieved. To the degree that the individual lives in a society where change is rapid, and where different codes of conduct exist, his problem of achieving a harmonious personality and a stable character is correspondingly increased.

Here we must distinguish between social change which comes from the gradual introduction of new ideas from within and without a given society, and the type of social change which results from the sudden contact of two or more societies with different cultures. In the second the clash of codes and philosophies is profound. The effect upon the subordinate group which must do the major share of adjusting is particularly severe. For the individual, the contrast between his group rôles and imagined selves is often acute. This contrast is not merely a conflict of social groups within a culture system: it is

[7]Charles H. Cooley, *Human Nature and the Social Order* (New York, 1922, revised edition), p. 184.

[8]Robert E. Park and Ernest W. Burgess, *Introduction to the Science of Sociology* (Chicago, 1921), p. 70.

a conflict between two culture systems each having its subordinate groups. As a result the individual may have to readjust his life along several points: the language in which he communicates, the religion he believes in, the moral code he follows, the manner in which he earns his living, the government to which he owes allegiance, as well as in the subtler aspects of personality. The duality of cultures produces a duality of personality—a divided self.

It is the fact of cultural duality which is the determining influence in the life of the marginal man. His is not a clash between inborn temperament and social expectation, between congenial personality tendency and the patterns of a given culture.[9] His is not a problem of adjusting a single looking-glass self, but two or more such selves. And his adjustment pattern seldom secures complete cultural guidance and support, for his problem arises out of the shifting social order itself.

Today the social order is founded upon nationalities and races, real or fictitious. The political state is a reality to which all other loyalties must give way in times of test. In the past, religious loyalty has often been the supreme loyalty. Conflicts of religious identification have torn human souls asunder—vividly portrayed and dissected as they are in William James's *Varieties of Religious Experience*. Religious conflict in the deeper sense is a conflict of the inner moral or spiritual life; with God and the self, the ideal and the actual, as the objects of attention. Such conflicts also have their social reference, though less consciously so than with the marginal man whose concern is primarily with the objective social situation. The latter's divided self is not like those religious "sick souls who must be twice-born in order to be happy," nor has it a temperamental

[9]For an excellent statement of this problem see Ruth Benedict, *Patterns of Culture* (Boston, 1934), especially Chap. VIII.

basis.[10] The gradations of duality, therefore, are more nicely correlated with the social situation.

THE MARGINAL MAN AND THE CULTURAL PROCESS[11]

Culture is not only accumulated and transmitted from generation to generation: it is also diffused from group to group. Each process affects the other. Today no sooner does a new idea or method appear in one place than it reappears in another —either through simultaneous invention or through copying and diffusion. Diffusion in turn stimulates further discovery. Modern forms of communication and transportation have become the highways of culture change.

In the present, as well as in the past, migration performs a vital part in culture change. Through it the "cake of custom" is sufficiently disturbed and broken to release individuals for creative thought. Relatively isolated social groups do not suddenly change their mode of life except in direct or indirect response to changes in the physical environment. But where they live in close contact with other peoples they are also subject to human competition and conflict, and must—if they are to survive or remain independent—make constant readjustments. Population intrusion therefore sets in motion a process of culture change which breaks down old cultural forms, releases individuals from their domination, and so gives rise to periods of creative activity and advance. This is the theory developed by Frederick J. Teggart, who also calls attention to its implications in the study of great men:

[10]William James, *The Varieties of Religious Experience* (New York, 1902), p. 167. James was skeptical of the inborn temperamental basis. See p. 169.
[11]In this section I am particularly indebted to suggestions of Robert E. Park which have been formulated in his article entitled "Migration and the Marginal Man," *The American Journal of Sociology*, May, 1928. It is important, of course, to differentiate between culture change originating from the accumulation of individual inventions within a people, and culture change which springs from the collisions of peoples. Although these two processes interact, this section is concerned only with the second.

... Now, while, historically, advancement has been dependent upon the collision of groups, the resultant response has taken place in the minds of individuals, and so we are led to see that all transitional eras are alike in being periods of individual mental awakening, and of the release or emancipation of individual initiative in thought and action. This applies equally whether we consider the past or the present, and, consequently, since the antecedents of advance are realized only in exceptional cases, we are forced to rely, for the verification we are now discussing, upon the testimony of exceptional individuals. That the historical process of individualization of thought is also the form through which advancement proceeds today would be best shown by an extended examination of the biographies of notable men, but for the present we may accept the evidence adduced by psychologists and other investigators who have already called attention to the facts.[12]

The recently published study of Arnold J. Toynbee[13] may be considered as a partial answer to the last suggestion of Teggart. In the third volume of this study he makes brief analyses of the lives of such men of genius as Saint Paul, Gautama the Buddha, David, Cæsar, Muhammed, Peter the Great, Lenin, Confucius, Kant, etc., to discover the "interaction between individuals in growing civilizations." This he finds to consist of a "movement of withdrawal-and-return" in which the individual undergoes an "inward psychic experience."

In terms of his external relations with other individual human beings in the social life which is the common ground of his and their respective fields of action, we shall be describing the same movement if we call it a disengagement and temporary withdrawal of the creative personality from his social milieu, and his subsequent return to the same milieu transfigured: in a new capacity and with new powers. The disen-

---

[12]*Processes of History* (New Haven, 1918), pp. 155-56. See also his *Theory of History* (New Haven, 1925).

[13]*A Study of History* (London, 1934). Three parts, in three volumes, have appeared to date. The whole plan of the study includes thirteen parts.

gagement and withdrawal make it possible for the personality to realize individual potentialities which might have remained in abeyance if the individuals in whom they were immanent had not been released for a moment from his social toils and trammels.[14]

This analysis has much in common with the analysis of the marginal man presented above.[15] Here the "crisis experience" is the event which throws the individual back upon himself and produces a "disengagement and temporary withdrawal." Those individuals who have the potentialities to reconstruct their personalities and "return" as creative agents not only adjust themselves but also contribute to the solution of the conflict of races and cultures. Thus the career of Saint Paul,[16] for example, was a creative response to the impact of Greek culture upon Syriac society.

But the creative rôle of the individual varies with the situation. Typically, race relations develop in terms of a cycle[17] or sequence of processes. At first the relations of two or more races or nationalities who are living in a common territory under a single political and economic system assume a predominantly symbiotic or economic character. With the advance of time and acquaintance more intimate social relations develop. These include the mixing of blood and the transfer of culture. Out of this process emerge the marginal men, whether as racial hybrids or cultural hybrids. If sufficient time elapses a new racial stock and a new culture arise out of this contact and interaction, and the particular cycle of race relations comes to an end.

The Europeanization of the globe forms the setting for the latest act in the contacts of peoples. It has involved a twofold

[14]Vol. III, p. 248.   [15]Especially Chaps. V–X.
[16]See Toynbee, Vol. III, pp. 263–64.
[17]This is the "race relations cycle" defined by Robert E. Park. See *The Survey* (May, 1926), p. 192.

diffusion of European blood and of European culture. This diffusion has transformed the world from a collection of isolated or slowly interacting races, political units, and distinctive cultures into a condition where dynamic interchange and mutual economic if not political and cultural interdependence dominate each part. The first phase of this process has meant the extension of Western political and economic control—"imperialism"; a rapid mixture of races; the disorganization of non-Western cultures; and the gradual assimilation of European ideas. The second phase is now developing—a phase in which nationalist and racial movements are seeking to remove Western domination and to supplant it with reorganized, self-determined societies and governments. But, as the rise of Japan testifies, such movements succeed only to the degree that Western instruments of economic, political and military power can be employed.

The marginal man is the key-personality in the contacts of cultures. It is in his mind that the cultures come together, conflict, and eventually work out some kind of mutual adjustment and interpenetration. He is the crucible of cultural fusion. His life history recapitulates something of the processes described in the race-relations cycle: at first he is unaware of the cultural conflict going on; then through some crisis experience or series of experiences he becomes aware of it, and the external conflict finds an echo in his mind; and, finally, he tries and sometimes succeeds in making an adjustment to his situation.

Thus the practical efforts of the marginal person to solve his own problem lead him consciously or unconsciously to change the situation itself. His interest may shift from himself to the objective social conditions and launch him upon the career of nationalist, conciliator, interpreter, reformer or teacher. In these rôles he inevitably promotes acculturation, either upon a basis of larger political and cultural unity, or in terms of a modified political and cultural differentiation—a new state. Consequently, the life histories of marginal men offer the most significant material for the analysis of the cultural process as it springs from the contacts of social groups. And it is in the mind of the marginal man that the inner significance and the driving motives of such culture change are most luminously revealed.

Index